Words Like Daggers

Early Modern Cultural Studies

SERIES EDITORS

Carole Levin
Marguerite A. Tassi

Violent Female Speech in Early Modern England

KIRILKA STAVREVA

University of Nebraska Press • Lincoln and London

© 2015 by the Board of Regents of the University of Nebraska. Acknowledgment for the use of copyrighted material appears on page xi, which constitutes an extension of the copyright page. All rights reserved. Manufactured in the United States of America. ∞

Library of Congress Cataloging-in-Publication Data

Stavreva, Kirilka.
Words like daggers: violent female speech in early modern England / Kirilka Stavreva.

pages   cm.—(Early modern cultural studies)

Includes bibliographical references and index.

ISBN 978-0-8032-5488-6 (hardback)
ISBN 978-0-8032-9586-5 (paper)
ISBN 978-0-8032-8657-3 (epub)
ISBN 978-0-8032-8658-0 (mobi)
ISBN 978-0-8032-8659-7 (pdf).
1. English literature—Early modern, 1500–1700—History and criticism. 2. Women—England—Social conditions. 3. Language and languages in literature. 4. Women and literature—England—History. 5. Violence in literature. 6. Women in literature. I. Title.

PR428.W63S73 2015
820.9'9287—dc23
2014025633

Set in Garamond Pro by Renni Johnson.
Designed by A. Shahan.

A memorial to the sonorous shades of
Stavri Fotev Stavrev (1924–95),
Zafirka Georgieva Stavreva (1927–95), &
Kristalina Stavreva Statkova (1951–2010)

CONTENTS

List of Illustrations   viii

Acknowledgments   ix

Introduction: *Bitter Words and the Tuning of Gender*   xiii

1. Feminine Contentious Speech and the Religious Imagination   1
2. Gender and the Narratives of Scolding in the Church Courts   17
3. Unquiet Women on the Early Modern Stage   45
4. Witch-Speak in Late Elizabethan Docufiction   71
5. Courtly Witch-Speak on the Jacobean Stage   103
6. Gender and Politics in Early Quaker Women's Prophetic "Cries"   129

   Epilogue: *Margaret's Bitter Words and the Voice of (Divine) Justice, or, Compulsory Listening*   147

   Notes   157

   Bibliography   179

   Index   195

ILLUSTRATIONS

1. Mother Damnable of Kentish Town (undated)   xvi
2. Emblem of the unruly tongue, engraved by Crispin de Passe   6
3. Illustration from *The Apprehension and Confession of Three Notorious Witches* (1589)   91

ACKNOWLEDGMENTS

This book would have come to a screeching halt without the inspiration and support granted by so many communities and individuals. My greatest debt is to the scholars, editors, and writers who have shed critical light on the lives, speech, and writing of early modern women. Among these, Carole Levin's sparkling intellectual fervor, gentle friendship, and enthusiastic mentorship have proved, in Hamlet's words, elements of "wondrous potency" that steadied me throughout the research and writing process.

Words Like Daggers germinated from two sections of a chapter of my dissertation, and I am profoundly thankful to the community of the University of Iowa's English Department for scholarly, financial, and personal support during my graduate work. Huston Diehl (who did not live to see this project completed), Alan Nagel, Miriam Gilbert, and Alvin Snider helped me find an academic home in early modern studies; Garrett Stewart modeled the delight of creativity in close-grained analysis of sound and image; Eric Griffin, Kathryn Moncrief, Patrick Ryan, Kimball Smith, and the late Elizabeth Dietz, kindred spirits from "the tribe of Huston" all, made seminar work, archival research, conference presentations, and the critique of work-in-progress a joy; long since I received my Ph.D., the early modern reading group of the department, including, at several times, Doug Trevor, Gina Bloom, and Adam G. Hooks, continued to offer valuable insight on chapter drafts.

At Cornell College, Cindy Benton, Tina Fetner, Michelle Mouton, Catherine Stewart, and Jama Stillwell offered helpful comments, direction, and camaraderie as I was learning how to integrate writing into my life as faculty at a liberal arts college. Michelle helped focus my inquiry by asking the all-important question, "But what does speaking like this mean for gender?" Catherine Stewart and Sandra Dyas not only endured stoically my interminable musings on women with fiery tongues from bygone eras but asked probing—and witty—questions. Thanks for keeping me going and for keeping my sense of humor alive. Leslie K. Hankins's wisdom, creativity, and gumption continue to inspire. Christina Penn-Goetsch, an intrepid coteacher of our undergraduate seminar on Women, Power, and the Royal Court taught me a lot about poise, performance, and Renaissance architecture. My students in numerous Shakespeare classes and plays, as well as in courses on Renaissance women writers and non-Shakespearean Renaissance drama, were eager to discuss and reconstrue the voices of garrulous early women; their intellectual curiosity and adventurous spirit energized my writing. I cherish Dean Chris Carlson's sincere interest in the legal-historical aspects of my work, and Dean Brenda Tooley's expression of enthusiasm in conferring Cornell's first Faculty Research Award to a feminist historical project.

My research and writing owe much to plenary sessions, workshops, and hallway conversations at several Attending to Early Modern Women symposia; the ATW dialogic model of scholarship nourished the development of my ideas. Thanks especially to the conveners of the "Women and the Missionary Position?" workshop at the 2003 symposium, Sylvia Brown, Paulomi Chakraborty, Karine Hopper, Kelly Laycock, Aida Patient, and Kirsten Uszkalo, for the opportunity to voice my ideas about the wielding of verbal power by Quaker women traveling ministers. Early versions of several chapters were presented at meetings of the Shakespeare Association of America, the Renaissance Society of America, the Shakespeare at Kalamazoo Society (that most convivial of scholarly groups), as well as the Newberry Library seminar on medieval and early modern magic, the Symposium in Honor of Huston Diehl at the University of Iowa, and the Humanities and Arts Interest Group at Cornell College. I am grateful to the organizers and responders to my work at these venues, and especially to Linda Austern, Michael Bailey, Mary Lou Emery, Nancy Hayes, Laury Magnus, Adelaide Morris, Kavita Mudan Finn, Erica T. Lin, Anna Riehl Bertolet, Joe Stephenson, Mihoko Suzuki, John Watkins, Michael Witmore, and Carla Zecher.

Archival research for this project was graciously assisted by the staff of the Newberry, Huntington, British, and Guildhall libraries, the Oxfordshire History Centre, the Library of the Religious Society of Friends in Britain, the Quaker and Special Collections of the Haverford College Library, and the University of Iowa Libraries. Gill Gage at the Newberry Library, Heather Rowland at the Library of the Religious Society of Friends, and Alison Smith at the Oxfordshire History Centre were guiding lights in my research.

Several funding sources made writing this book possible. I am grateful to Cornell College for supporting my project with several faculty development and travel grants, a Ryan-Sklenicka Faculty Research Award, and a Campbell McConnell sabbatical award and leave. The Quaker Collection at the Haverford College Library kindly arranged for on-campus accommodations for the duration of my research there. The Newberry Library—whose vibrant intellectual community has sustained me for years of research and writing—awarded me, in conjunction with the British Academy, a Fellowship for Study in Great Britain and thus enabled my archival research in early modern legal history.

Several of the chapters in this book have appeared in earlier versions in print. I am grateful to the editors of the *Journal of Medieval and Early Modern Studies*, published by Duke University Press, for their supportive and useful feedback on "Fighting Words: Witch-Speak in Late Elizabethan Docu-Fiction," revised as chapter 4 of this book. Their affirming interest in my work, seconded by the Society for the Study of Early Modern Women, which selected "Fighting Words" as best article in the field for 2000, assured me that the longer project was worth pursuing. I also wish to thank several presses for granting permission to reprint sections from the following essays, and the editors of the collections in which they appeared for scholarly support: "'There's Magic in Thy Majesty': Queenship and Witch-Speak in Jacobean Shakespeare," in *High and Mighty Queens of Early Modern England: Realities and Representations*, edited by Carole Levin, Jo Eldridge Carney, and Debra Barrett-Graves (Houndmills, UK: Palgrave, 2003), 151–68; "Tainting the Marvelous Monarchy: Witchcraft on the Jacobean Stage," in *Renaissance Refractions: Essays in Honour of Alexander Shurbanov*, edited by Boika Sokolova and Evgenia Pancheva (Sofia, Bulgaria: St. Kliment Ohridski University Press, 2001), 142–54; "Prophetic Cries at Whitehall: The Gender Dynamics of Early Quaker Women's Injurious Speech," in *Women, Gender, Radical Religion*, edited by Sylvia Brown (Leiden: Brill, 2007), 17–37.

Research and scholarly writing open up new ways of comprehending the world, but they also claim us from the world. During the years when *Words Like Daggers* claimed my time and attention, my family's unconditional love and support kept me energized and anchored. I do not want to measure love in terms of debt and credit and thus choose a different metaphor for the most significant acknowledgment of all: in the fabric of my life marked, during the writing of this book, with vibrant experiences but also with the deaths of my beloved sister and brother-in-law, Doug Baynton and Anna Baynton have been the strong warp that has kept me whole.

INTRODUCTION

Bitter Words and the Tuning of Gender

MIRANDA: Abhorrèd slave,
Which any print of goodness wilt not take,
Being capable of all ill! . . .
CALIBAN: You taught me language, and my profit on't
Is—I know how to curse. The red plague rid you
For learning me your language.
William Shakespeare, *The Tempest*

It is important not only to understand how the terms of gender are instituted, naturalized, and established as presuppositional, but to trace the moments where the binary system of gender is disputed and challenged, where the coherence of the categories are put into question, and where the very social life of gender turns out to be malleable and transformative.
Judith Butler, *Undoing Gender*

Generations of editors and directors of Shakespeare's *Tempest* have gone against the character assignation of the First Folio and attributed Miranda's verbal attack upon Caliban to her father, Prospero.[1] The reason? "Abhorrèd slave" has been deemed wording too unseemly for such a "precious creature" (1.2.350, 3.1.25). Indeed Miranda's words have a mutilating edge to them. She joins Prospero in calling Caliban "a slave"—the very word that, quite understandably, called forth the vicious curse with which Caliban burst onto the stage. Miranda's injurious appellation amounts to political denigration—exactly what Caliban attempted to reject when he taunted Prospero with the meagerness of the Duke's claim to sovereignty: "I am all the subjects that you have / Which first was mine own King" (1.2.341–42). Taken in context, Miranda's outburst deploys the discourse of gender identity and gender politics. Her words strike back against Caliban's equation of a sexual assault against her with securing his claim to the island: "O ho, O ho! would't had been done! / Thou didst prevent me; I had peopled else / This isle with Calibans" (1.2.348–50). The effect of Miranda's violent speech is double-edged: even as she rejects a victimized femininity, Miranda (like Prospero) provokes Caliban to curse—and to attain feminine gender qualities himself by virtue of wielding a traditionally feminine type of speech. In spite of Miranda's reverence for book culture, suggested by her reference to the "print of goodness" that Caliban lacks, "abhorrèd slave" derives its force from voice. To her father's demeaning speech she adds an extra aural punch. Prospero addresses Caliban as "Thou poisonous slave" and "Thou most lying slave" (1.2.319 and 344); Miranda replaces the sound of the Duke's hissing contempt with an explosive rumble, spitting out her revulsion into an adjective that needs no superlative degrees: "Abhorrèd."

While this verbal eruption of Miranda's is violent, her speech habits are not. She can hardly be labeled a scold. Yet even a single outburst of verbal violence on her part has important pragmatic and symbolic effects. It provokes Caliban to curse, which in turn incites a threat on Prospero's part that makes the Duke sound like a witch: "I'll rack thee with old cramps, / Fill all thy bones with aches, make thee roar / That beasts shall tremble at thy din" (1.2.368–70). Knowing how to curse—*really* knowing how to curse—appears to be instrumental for asserting both cultural authenticity and social power on the island, as Caliban recognizes: "I must obey. His art is of such power / It would control my dam's god Setebos / And make a vassal of him" (1.2.371–73). It has given Prospero the kind of control associated with Setebos, the supreme deity of the witch Sycorax, the island's previous and—in Caliban's mind—authentic ruler. But violent speech, including cursing, is also a treacherous instrument. It can assert the speaker's authority, and yet, as Kate Brown and Howard Kushner propose, it can as easily "demonstrate an incapacity for—or a criminal departure from—proper, purposive speech."[2] Or else, disappointingly, speech violence may threaten force and action but convey weakness and passivity, substituting—as Hamlet did—rhetorical and theatrical flair for physical violence.[3] Whether or not violent speech is pragmatically effective, its unabated edge easily slips out of the speaker's control and acquires its own quasi-autonomous agency. Habitually associated with the feminine since the medieval era at least, in the early modern era it proved capable of rendering the gender of both male and female speakers dangerously unstable, as this book argues.[4] It could beget violence, verbal and physical, in speaker and addressee, and quickly spread this violence far afield.

In the early modern era, violent speech, what Gertrude calls "words like Daggers" when describing Hamlet's rhetorical and perhaps physical assault against her in her closet, was renounced in sermons and pamphlets, vigorously disputed in courts of law, and dramatized in often contradictory ways in stage plays, ballads, and letters to religious communities. Typically it was gendered feminine, although men as well as women were capable of verbal violence and were found culpable for it. The law distinguished among scolding (associated with defamation and comparable to today's barratry); "conjurations, enchantments and witchcrafts" (discussed in chapter 4 under the heading "witch-speak"); and the "fond and fantastical prophecies" associated with high treason against magistrates and royalty.[5] Yet ministers, targets, and witnesses of injurious words had trouble telling apart the prophet from the witch or the scold. For instance, the traveling Quaker minister Barbara Blaugdone relates that during her mission to Cork in Ireland, she "was made to call to [her] Relations and Acquaintance, by the Word of the Lord, and was made to follow them into several Steeple-houses" where she prophesied. "The dread of God" that overcame her during these ecstatic prophecies, she continues, "made some of them to Tremble; and some said, I was a Witch."[6] Alexander Roberts, a Norfolk minister whose *Treatise of Witchcraft* combines demonological theory with docufiction about a local witchcraft court case, was one of many to claim a direct connection between scolding and witchcraft. He writes:

> Marie wife of Henrie Smith, Glover, possessed with a wrathfull indignation against some of her neighbours . . . often times cursed them, and became incensed with unruly passions, armed with a settled resolution, to effect some mischievous projects and designs against them. The divell . . . appeared unto her amiddes these discontentments . . . and willed that she should continue in her malice, envy, hatred, banning and cursing; and then he would be revenged for her upon all those to whom she wished evill.[7]

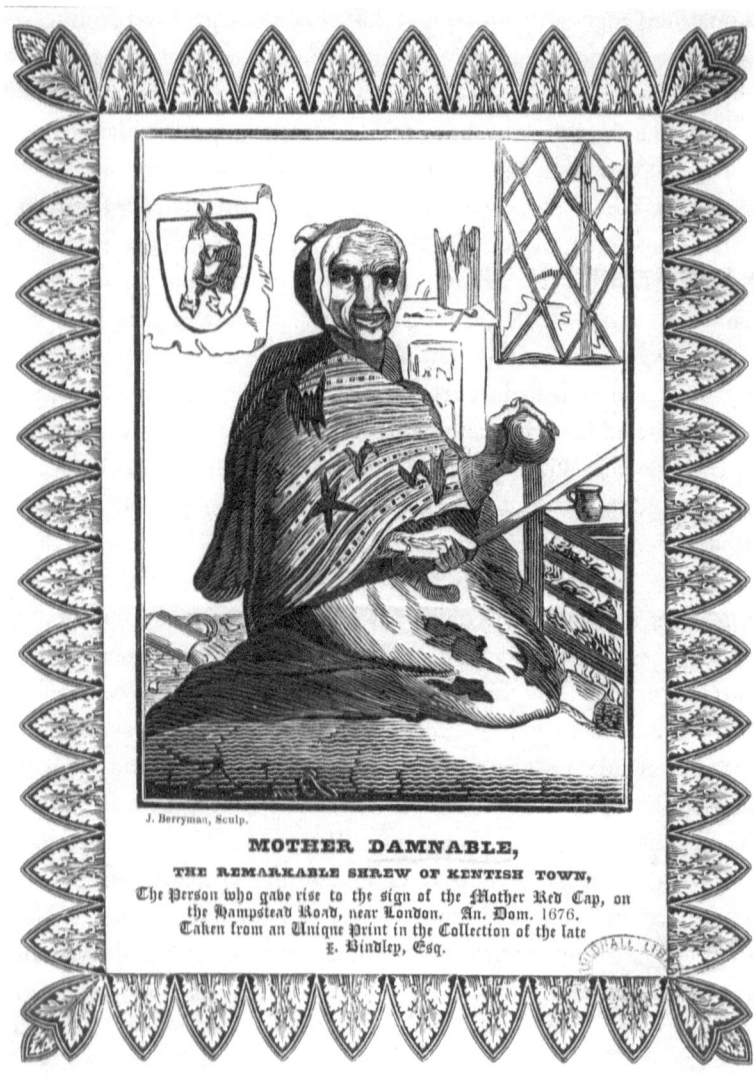

Fig. 1. Mother Damnable of Kentish Town (undated). Reproduced by permission of City of London, London Metropolitan Archives.

The semimythical Mother Damnable, also known as Mother Red Cap or "the Remarkable Shrew of Kentish Town," whose name until recently adorned a pub sign in Camden, London, exemplifies the way communal interactions with unruly women generated the conflated image of the witch, the prophet, and the scold (fig. 1). A witch by heritage and reputation, Mother Damnable was reportedly sought after for fortune-telling and healing. When she failed to deliver, she was ruthlessly taunted by her neighbors and in turn unleashed her tongue against them.[8]

Sometimes one type of verbal aggression was purposefully assigned a punishment meant for another type. According to the Quaker preacher Richard Hubberthorn, when during a mission to Oxford the Quakers Elizabeth Leavens and Elizabeth Fletcher spoke "the word of the Lord in boldness against the deceits of the Priests and people, in the Streets, in the Market-place, in the Synagogues, and in the Colledges," they "were mocked, buffeted, and shamefully used, being tied together at Johns Colledge and pumped, and kicked and buffeted, and thrust into a pool called Giles pool."[9] Leavens's and Fletcher's horrific treatment was a hybrid of the "ducking" with which scolds were punished in many cities well into the seventeenth century and the "swimming" of witches, usually with arms tied to their feet.[10]

Underlying both inadvertent and deliberate conflations of the fairly distinct types of feminine verbal violence was acute anxiety regarding its power to destabilize social hierarchies in general and, as I suggest, the category of gender in particular. This anxiety appears to have been justified.[11] Yes, documentary and dramatic narratives about aggressive and garrulous women often cast them as scandalous rebels against the social peace and gender norms and as reckless but ultimately unsuccessful usurpers of cultural authority. But there were contending narratives—sometimes in the same texts—that tell stories of the effective subversion and undoing of the normative restrictions of social and gender hierarchies. *Words Like Daggers* untangles conflicting and conflicted representations and interpretations of women's violent words in church and assize court "informations" and "examinations," as well as in documentary pamphlets, letters, and self-narratives composed between the 1590s and the 1660s. In the process I reconstruct, to the degree that it is possible, the speech acts of individual contentious women, such as the "vaunting and joyfull manner" in which Agnes Brampton of London threatened "that her husband shold not live above eighteen weekes," or the terrifying ritual curse "in

Welsh language" uttered by one Joanna Powel as she was "kneeling down upon her bare knees and holding up her hands," or the timing of Elizabeth Stirredge's "dreadful Warning" of imminent destruction leveled against justices of the peace assessing confiscated Quaker goods, which she sounded after silently staring down her opponents for nearly an hour.[12] These were powerful rhetorical performances, and I would argue that their dramatic potential was recognized not only by victims and witnesses of individual violent speech acts but also by theater professionals. Hence an important focus of *Words Like Daggers* is the manner in which the Renaissance stage, arguably the most influential cultural institution of the era, orchestrated and aestheticized women's fighting words, at the same time showcasing and augmenting their cultural signification and linking them explicitly to church and court politics.

Speech can be powerful, but it is fleeting. To assess the effects of women's violent speech as represented in the religious, legal, and theater discourses of the early modern era, I consider records from these realms with an ear for the interplay of words, sounds, physical performance, and locale. This performance-focused methodology is informed by Victor Turner's "processual symbology" and Judith Butler's treatment of speech acts as bodily acts. Like Turner, I approach violent speech acts with an interest in "events which may generate new cultural materials (symbols, metaphors, orientations, styles, values, even paradigms) as well as fashion novel patternings of social relationships with traditional cultural instruments." He understands these events to be performance situations that open up avenues for adding new signifieds to old signifiers by collective fiat and, more important for the purposes of this study, that enrich the public signification of symbolic action through the private construction of meaning. Turner maintains that individually construed shifts in public hermeneutics are possible "if the exegete has sufficient power, authority, or prestige to make his views 'stick.'"[13] Like Butler, I propose that even socially marginalized subjects can acquire such power thanks to the embodiment of the speech. For, as Butler argues, "the speaking body . . . exceeds its interpellation, and remains uncontained by any of its acts of speech." (Actors as well as political and religious activists across historical and geographic divides have been well aware of this.) In Butler's view, embodied speech has the potential to unsettle the dispositional *habitus* of the body, what Pierre Bourdieu describes as "embodied history, internalized as second nature and so forgotten as history." In the unpredictability of the speaking body rests its power to resignify dominant discourses.[14]

When scolding women, witches, or traveling ministers from a charismatic religious group such as the early Society of Friends poured out their intense emotions and desires, they used language characterized by *enargeia*. Classical authors, notably Quintilian, describe enargeia as the quality of speech that provokes imaginary seeing, making present to the mind's eye the (imagined) past or future and in this way transforming listeners of narration into witnesses. The enargaic effect is attributed to the choice of vivid narrative detail, with detail understood by the Greek rhetorician Demetrius to include not only visual description but also such aural elements as repetition, onomatopoeia, and cacophony.[15] While most humanist rhetoricians, including Erasmus, conflated enargeia (vividness) with *energeia* (animation), George Puttenham, in his ambitious *Art of English Poesy*, differentiated between the two in a manner most useful for this discussion of violent speech. Purposefully deviating from the visual connotations of enargeia, he associated the concept with the aural effect of language that works "alteration in the ear by sound, accent, time, and slipper [*sic*] volubility in utterance, such as for that respect was called by the ancients numerosity of speech."[16] Thus enargeia, as Linda Galyon clarifies, was a matter of sensory perception "operating only at the threshold of the ear," not to be confused with the representational vigor of energeia to bind things and words together on the cognitive level.[17] In Galyon's view, Puttenham's distinction between the two concepts elevated sound as a constitutive aspect of poetry. The reason: he considered the sensory "tuning" of poetic language, whether beautiful or ugly, to be indispensable for the "stirring to the mind" effected by poetry. For, Puttenham clarifies, "the mind is not assailable unless it be by sensible approaches, whereof the audible is of greatest force for instruction or discipline."[18]

From Puttenham to Stephen Greenblatt, scholars of English poetry have discussed enargeia as a hallmark of poetic achievement. They have associated the capacity of speech to engage and enhance sensory experience with the individual creative imagination.[19] *Words Like Daggers* demonstrates that enargeia was not the exclusive prerogative of poets and poetry. The well-developed sonic sensibilities of the early moderns were as readily affected by the enargaic howlings and incantations of witches, shrews, and prophets. This violent enargeia prepared targets and witnesses for a ready cognitive response to the energeic speech violence delivered through explicit or implied narratives.[20] The impact of violent speech was further strengthened by what Diana Taylor has termed its "animative" quality, the instance "when contentious speech breached not only the divide between the literal and the figurative, but also between the verbal and the physical."[21] Whatever the degree of intelligibility of women's violent speech, its embodied performative force confounded the sociolinguistic norms by which speech was regulated, and especially normative gender.

In telling the story of the confusion wrought by women's violent speech upon gender and other sociolinguistic categories, the chapters at the core of *Words Like Daggers* alternate their focus from analyzing the local effects of violent speech acts to examining the refractions of women's speech on the theater stages, where it was performed for thousands of spectators. The general trajectory of the book's narrative likewise emulates the expansive impact of women's fighting words. I begin by exploring verbal onslaughts by scolding women that upend social hierarchies in the family and the neighborhood and end with the contestations in the violent speech of female prophets of spiritual hierarchies.

In chapter 1, "Feminine Contentious Speech and the Religious Imagination," I map the narrative arc of the book in an analysis of the representation of fiery words in a single genre of religious writing. I demonstrate that, like their medieval predecessors, early modern divines were well aware of the propensity of violent speech to create chaos not only in local contexts—courtyards, alehouses, playhouses—but in the larger public sphere as well. In numerous sermons on the tongue, commentaries on the Epistle of James "to the twelve tribes that are scattered abroad" (1:1), ministers developed a stunning iconography of men with women's tongues and women with serpent tongues, of female speech splattering masculine humors around, of multigendered contentious speech threatening to become the soundmark of early modern communities. The fiery tongue, in these texts, had a grave and far-reaching impact. It poisoned speakers, addressees, and listeners; it ripped apart the social fabric of neighborhoods, cities, and even the commonwealth. But the cultural category that ministers claimed was rendered most chaotically unreliable by the fiery tongue was that of gender. In the sermons on the tongue, feminine-gendered contentious speech is shown as overpowering patriarchal efforts to regulate language. Furthermore its representations shed doubt on the binarism of gender.

In chapter 2, "Gender and the Narratives of Scolding in the Church Courts," I explore the kaleidoscope of local perceptions and outcomes of the type of women's fighting words labeled scolding. I examine church court depositions in defamation cases in an effort to reconstruct the semantic, stylistic, and vocal qualities of scolding acts at their points of origin. These witness depositions also help shed light on the ways that interested parties made sense of scolding and perceived its effects and significance. There was no social consensus on this type of verbal violence. Witnesses discuss scolding neither as uniformly uncontrollable and unreasonable nor even as inevitably notable. Scolding could be perceived as a distraction from daily activities, an interruption of night rest, an affront to honor, but also as a respectable claim to social authority, a valued social service, and even something akin to the voice of divine Law. It was understood to be viciously premeditated or, alternatively, as a devilish or divine possession. Collectively witness narratives in church court depositions in scolding and defamation causes point to the contradictory ways the vocal authority claimed by garrulous women could be used to uphold *and* to confound normative notions of gender.

In chapter 3, "Unquiet Women on the Early Modern Stage," the focus shifts from the legal record of scolding women to their stage representations. Here I explore the theater stereotype of the shrew, whose conflict with the stereotype of the shrew tamer instigated the dramatic action in many a popular comedy, from the Tudor descendent of the medieval morality genre, the anonymous *John John the Husband, Tyb His Wife, and Sir John the Priest*, through Shakespeare's *Taming of the Shrew*, to John Fletcher's *The Woman's Prize or the Tamer Tamed*. A useful tool for character recognition, the stereotype of the shrew by no means precluded possibilities for surprising exploration and improvisation on the part in performance. Certainly shrew plays ended with a restoration of the patriarchal gender hierarchy. Yet I suggest that between their metatheatrical plots and their textual clues for performance that blatantly contradicted historical penance rituals, these plays cast doubt on the viability of their reconciliatory endings. "Tamed" in only a provisional or illusory manner, theatrical shrews opened up for audience members livable models of gender fluidity.

In chapter 4, "Witch-Speak in Late Elizabethan Docufiction," I discuss Elizabethan pamphlets that documented witchcraft cases brought before the church and assize courts. Echoing the narrative protocols of the courts, the pamphleteers cast the witch as a clear and present public danger, a rebel against the laws of God and country. Yet they also documented how alluring witch-speak was. This violent and highly feminized discourse remained elusive and profoundly disturbing, yet it intrigued live and reading audiences and sometimes appealed to them. Pamphleteers thus fueled both public repulsion and public fascination with the fighting words of witches. Frequently they blurred a gender binary that denied social authority to outspoken women.

In chapter 5, "Courtly Witch-Speak on the Jacobean Stage," I analyze the politically compromising resonances of low-born witch-speak within the theatrical magic wielded by aristocratic characters on the Jacobean stage. In widely popular plays by Ford, Marston, Middleton, and Shakespeare, witch-speak is embraced by ambitious aristocrats and royalty as an effective vehicle for political power. Although the violent speech of historical witches was notably aestheticized and reframed in the drama of the era, its rhetorical edge remained unabated. Its dual-edged quality likewise endured. With alarming frequency witch-speak dealt an ethical blow to nobles and "marvelous" monarchs who used it, inviting socially diverse theater audiences to pass moral judgment on the court and the monarchy.

Retaining a focus on the court, in chapter 6, "Gender and Politics in Early Quaker Women's Prophetic 'Cries,'" I return to the drama of the historical record. I analyze the carefully staged manner in which women from the early Society of Friends delivered insurrectionary prophecies to the Lord Protector Oliver Cromwell and to King Charles I—men at the summit of political power. In sharp contrast to gender- and status-speech conventions, Quaker women prophets exercised remarkable composure, practicality, and toughness and often succeeded in the effective orchestration of their violent speech in unfamiliar and daunting soundscapes. They not only enriched the significance of feminine gender as inflected with powerful, if morally ambiguous, spirituality but demonstrated—at Whitehall palace—the political power of women's violent speech.

In the main chapters of this study I explore women's violent speech as articulated and contested *within* legal and political discourses. In the epilogue I take the opposite approach and reflect on the effect of violent speech *on* legal-political discourse. Focusing on the orchestration of Queen Margaret's avalanche of curses in Shakespeare's first tetralogy, I argue that her remarkable rhetorical violence generates echoes that render audible the inherent violence in the voice of the Law. Such violence, I suggest, is indispensable for the authority of the Law, but it also constitutes grounds for barring the Law from authority.

Methodologically *Words Like Daggers* bridges literary and historical studies by analyzing intertextual and performative borrowings in multiple directions among historical women, theater professionals, ballad writers, and pamphleteers. I apply performative and rhetorical analysis to historical documents and historicize the performative analysis of literary texts in their material contexts. As recent cultural historians of contentious women's speech and crime in the early modern era have perceptively argued, among them Bernard Capp, Marion Gibson, Laura Gowing, Tim Stretton, and Garthine Walker, legal sources and popular docufiction based on them often occlude and homogenize women's stories and voices in the service of institutional procedure, ideological agendas, and socioeconomic interests.[22] To compensate for such homogenization, I attend to the signs of interpretive conflicts regarding women's fighting words in these texts rather than to the resolution of the conflicts or to their moral glossing. Literary scholars writing on voice, agency, and gender in the era, including Gina Bloom, Danielle Clarke and Elizabeth Clarke, Elizabeth Harvey, and Carla Mazzio, point to the ease with which the relationship between voice and speaking subject is imagined as distorted or completely severed in early modern texts.[23] The Renaissance trope denoting the alienation of the speaking subject from vocal agency is the figure of Echo. In the tale from Ovid's *Metamorphoses*, the bodiless nymph Echo is doomed to pursue Narcissus and repeat the last words of what has been uttered. Her disembodied voice, write Clarke and Clarke, "is troped as feminine because of its emptiness, its belatedness and its inability to signify except in relation to an already established discourse."[24] But echoic voice is not merely derivative, nor does it do away with rhetorical agency. Rather, as Bloom has argued, it is "transactive and dialogic" and enjoys "a liminal kind of agency that is difficult to track and thus impossible to restrain fully."[25] Frequently and deliberately echoic, the voices of historical and theatrical scolds, witches, and prophets analyzed in *Words Like Daggers* gain in transgressive power as a consequence of loosening the ties between speech and individual speaking subject. Such loosening of speech-speaker ties, I propose, has two significant corollaries beyond the immediate rhetorical outcomes in the discursive situation at hand. First, it opens up possibilities for dynamic regendering and transgendering of speakers to match the perceived gendering of speech. (*Transgender* is used here in Butler's sense of "not exactly a third gender, but a mode of passage between genders, an interstitial and transitional figure of gender that is not reducible to the normative insistence on one or two."[26]) Second, it prompts a consideration of voice as the product not simply of the body but of the body as part of the soundscape. And once violent voices start re-sounding through voraciously and publicly consumed ballads, docufiction, and drama, how long before they become a constitutive part of a community's imagined soundscape?

Words Like Daggers

I

Feminine Contentious Speech and the Religious Imagination

In the third chapter of James's New Testament epistle to Christian believers, the apostle sounds a grave warning about the capacity of the human tongue to wreak havoc: "The tongue is a fire, a world of iniquity.... It defileth the whole body, and setteth on fire the course of nature; and it is set on fire of hell." To make matters worse, "the tongue can no man tame; it is an unruly evil, full of deadly poison." This devastating condemnation of the tongue follows a begrudging acknowledgment of the mighty power packed in this small organ. James's turn of phrase associates the tongue with the principal means of transportation in an age when domestic, foreign, and intercontinental travel expanded dramatically: "Behold, we put bits in the horses' mouths, that they may obey us; and we turn about their whole body. Behold also the ships, which though they be so great, and are driven of fierce winds, yet are they turned about with a very small helm, withersoever the governor listeth." Even as James compares the tongue to a horse's bit or a ship's rudder that steers them in the desired direction, he also charges it with the capacity to lead speaker and addressees—the entire social *and* natural world—into chaos and destruction. Unruly tongues, he goes on to explain, bring out into the world the "bitter envying and strife" hidden in the heart.[1]

The early moderns drew on a rich and strong discursive tradition of the "sins of the tongue" authorized by James's epistle. Edwin D. Craun traces the ecclesiastical beginnings of this discourse in thirteenth- and fourteenth-century pastoral manuals for confession. Starting in the late fourteenth century the ecclesiastical condemnation of deviant speech permeated the poetry of writers such as Chaucer, Gower, Langland, and the *Patience* poet.² By the end of the century, Sandy Bardsley contends, the ecclesiastical and poetic tradition of "the sins of the tongue" had gone viral. In the fifteenth century it permeated secular and church law courts; manor, borough, and guild administrations; and popular ballads and plays.³ Malicious slander, barratry, scolding, cursing, and prophesy continued as causes for legal action from the Elizabethan era through the Interregnum. In no small part the prominence of this discourse after the Reformation can be credited to the widely popular genre of sermons on the tongue, which gave an English habitation to James's admonitory epistle. In this chapter I expand the historical scope of Craun's and Bardsley's analyses by studying representations of contentious speech in Elizabethan and Jacobean religious commentators on James's epistle. Ultimately I argue that the cultural category the sermonists portrayed as rendered most chaotically unreliable by the fiery tongue was that of gender.

The "sins of the tongue" are defined with an insistence approaching exasperation in a host of sermons and other popular religious texts from the era. The issue was considered significant enough to be propagated throughout the realm by means of readings during Sunday services of the "Homelie agaynst Contencion and Braulynge." Included in a collection of homilies first published in 1547, shortly after King Edward VI came to the throne, and reissued several times during the reigns of Elizabeth and James, "Against Contencion and Braulynge" was among the twelve crown-endorsed texts that remained at the heart of Sunday and holiday services well into the seventeenth century. (One more, "The Homily against Disobedience and Wilful Rebellion," was added to the set after the 1570 Northern Rebellion.) The value placed by the governments of both Elizabeth and James on these texts' capacity to quell religious and hence political unrest made them the default liturgical choice over topical sermons by preaching ministers. The 1559 preface to the collection specifies that the homilies were to be read to parishioners "in suche order as they stande in the booke—except there be a sermon, according as it is injoyned in the booke of her Hyghnesse Injunctions, and then for that cause onely, and for none other, the readyng of the sayde homelye to be dyffered unto the next Sonday or holy day folowyng. And when the foresayde boke of homelyes is read over, her Majesties pleasure is that the same bee repeated and read agayne."⁴ A good Christian subject, then, was likely to have heard parts or all of the "Homelie agaynst Contencion and Braulynge" at least four times a year.

The homily's message was reinforced in other topical sermons and religious readings during church services. Among them is a sermon on "The Taming of the Tongue" by the charismatic and talented preacher Thomas Adams, whose patrons included Thomas Egerton, Baron of Ellesmere, Henry Montagu, first earl of Manchester and chief justice of the king's bench, and William Herbert, third earl of Pembroke. Although we cannot be certain that "The Taming of the Tongue" received endorsement by the court or by any influential aristocrats, its 1616 publication in a volume boasting that its title sermon, "The Sacrifice of Thankefulnesse," was preached at Paul's Cross suggests authority. Paul's Cross, after all, was what Ronald Bond has called "the principal pulpit in the land.[5] Another text in this genre is the sermon "The poysonous Tongue" by John Abernethy, Bishop of Caithness, organized like a medical handbook and included in his 1622 collection, *A Christian and Heavenly Treatise*. Clerical writers detailing the nature and danger of the fiery tongue feature the outstanding preacher William Perkins, leading Cambridge Calvinist and rector of St. Andrews, who coupled his call against the tongue's sins with specific strategies for its "wel ordering" in a widely reprinted treatise, *A Direction for the Government of the Tongue: According to Gods Word*. In 1619 George Webbe, Bishop of Limerick and later chaplain of Charles I, likewise attacked contentious speech in a pamphlet, this one modeled after common law court procedure and entitled *The Araignement of an Unruly Tongue*.[6]

None of these texts by high-powered men of the cloth visits the sins of the tongue upon the heads of female parishioners. Yet all appear to attribute feminine qualities to contentious speech, although, as I argue below, closer analysis renders such gendering more complicated.[7] Such propensity to gender fiery words as feminine is apparent when early modern authors interrelate the violent speech acts of scolding and what I have termed witchspeak—malevolent speech that was typically impossible to reconstitute but was credited with effecting physical harm or death. This connection was drawn time and again in the popular literature of the seventeenth century. Among the authors who highlighted it was Henry Goodcole, chaplain of Newgate jail and crime pamphleteer. Three times in his documentary pamphlet on the indictment, conviction, and jail confession of the witch Elizabeth Sawyer (1612), Goodcole singles out her "cursing, blaspheming, and imprecating" tongue as the "occasioning cause" for the devil's active interest in her. It was Elizabeth's fiery tongue, the minister-pamphleteer insists, that made her fall victim to the devil and caused the death of Agnes Ratcleife, whom Elizabeth bewitched. Furthermore her violent speech proved "the meanes of her owne destruction," as she uttered "most fearfull imprecations for destruction against her selfe" in the courtroom—imprecations that were promptly heeded by God.[8]

Even those of Goodcole's contemporaries who rejected his understanding of witchcraft concurred with him regarding the connection between witch-speak and contentious speech. The witchcraft skeptic Reginald Scot, for instance, asserts that the "chief fault" of witches "is that they are scolds."[9] In Wales litigation for scolding and witchcraft often overlapped. In 1670 one Welsh plaintiff, Sarah Poole, described the verbal onslaught of her longtime foe Elizabeth Parry to the Denbighshire justices of the peace in these terms: "Elizabeth Parry came not long ago to my house ... and scandalized me with most filthy and uncivil language and likewise kneeled down upon her knees and cursed me, whereupon I fell suddenly sick and so continued for seven days." Parry was said to have used a similar combination of scolding and cursing twelve years before, and reputedly Poole's child had died that very night, while Poole herself lapsed into a three-year-long sickness.[10] Welsh villagers and members of the English learned elite alike conjoined feminine scolding—the publicly provocative use of "filthy and uncivil language"—and feminine witch-speak. Goodcole, as we saw, was explicit about the lack of qualitative distinction between these types of injurious speech. Anxious about the possibility that scolds could easily turn into witches, he issued a stern warning in his pamphlet "to many whose tongues are too frequent in these abhominable sinnes."[11]

In chapter 4 I discuss the representations of witch-speak in pamphlets borrowing from early modern legalese as a high-profile crime defying patriarchal, Christian, and class hierarchies—what psychoanalytic critics refer to as the Law of the Father. Here and in the next chapter I analyze the portrayal, in religious and legal discourse, respectively, of the threat that contentious speech, usually labeled scolding, presented to the Law of the Father. For the early moderns, scolding was not mere outspokenness, forwardness, or incivility. A term more vehemently negative than in contemporary usage, it entailed habitual contentiousness and an assault on the peace of the neighborhood. In scolding, rhetorical aggressiveness was often hard to distinguish from physical aggressiveness. As Martin Ingram reminds us, the verb and especially the noun *scold* had "strong legal connotations." The "common scold" (referenced in court documents as *communis scolde, communis rixatrix, perturbatrix pacis, garrulatrix, obiurgatrix, calumniatrix*) was a technical legal term whose first record in the *Oxford English Dictionary* is dated 1467. Incidentally this first written record concerns a defendant named, like Shakespeare's "shrew," Katherine.[12]

Although, to use today's legal concepts, scolding could be a tort (an interpersonal offense) or a crime (an offense against the public), clerical as well as legal authorities of the era tended to view it as a crime, emphasizing its capacity to escalate to significant public proportions. In the opening part of the "Homelie agaynst Contencion and Braulynge," endorsed by the Tudor government, scolding and brawling are said to be more harmful than theft, for "a thief hurteth but him from whom he stealeth, but he that hath an evill tongue troubleth al the towne where he dwelleth, and sometime the whole countrey. And a raylinge tongue is a pestilence so full of contagion that Sainct Paule willeth Christian men to forbear the company of suche and neyther to eate nor drynke with theim." By the closing part of the homily "contencious wordes" transcend local contexts and become "muche hurtefull to the societie of a common wealthe" as a whole—a volatility that the emblem literature of the era also pointed out (fig. 2).[13] The homily's language of contagion and the emphasis on the threat to the polity at large indicate that clerical authorities (and likely the royal court) saw contentious speech in general and scolding in particular as a matter of dire public significance.

Semantics

Somewhat surprisingly the verbal phenomenon in such desperate need of chastisement and ordering lacks descriptive precision in these texts. More interested in the broad-stroke picture of the "evilfavoredness and deformitie" of unruly speech, authors of sermons and religious treatises pay scant attention to the specific "woordes of contencion" favored by parishioners; nor do they comment on the significance of these words or their figurative patterns.[14] The sermon writers in particular may have been wary of explicitly unraveling fiery speech in texts that were themselves meant for impassioned oral delivery. Instead they describe contentious speech in terms of absence.

Fig. 2. Emblem of the unruly tongue, engraved by Crispin de Passe. In George Wither, *A Collection of Emblemes, Ancient and Moderne* (London, 1635), 42. Photo courtesy of The Newberry Library, Chicago, call number Case folio W 1025.98.

Contrasting it to fervent preaching, Perkins calls it "rotten speach," "talke as is voyd of grace, which is the heart & pith of our speach." He goes on to emphasize its lack in the divine graces "which are to shewe forth in our communication, . . . Wisdome, Truth, Reverence, Modestie, Meeknesse, Sobrietie in judgement, Urbanitie, Fidelitie, care of others good name."[15] Such portrayal of the semantic content of contentious speech renders it impossible or at least unworthy to discuss, while clearly distinguishing it from the rhetorical aggressiveness of the ministers themselves. But it may also point to an important quality of contentious speech: its association with voice rather than sign, action rather than meaning.[16]

"Hot" and "Sharp" Voices

The divines readily elaborate on the aural matter of contentious speech. Hugh Latimer's terms of choice in describing it in the "Homelie against Contencion and Braulynge" are "hot" and "sharp." Early modern audiences of the homily would have surmised that hot words were made up of hot breath. Hot words thus both indicated a thermal imbalance in the speaker's body and contributed to this imbalance. This in turn signaled the speaker's inability to regulate the body humors, a point relevant to the discussion of the gendering capacity of contentious speech discussed below. "Stirred but with one litle woorde," Latimer exclaims, "how we fume, rage, stampe and stare like mad men." In addition to noting the brawlers' uncontrollable impulsivity, he points out the sharpness, or the malicious intent, of their speech. Contentious words, "more sharpe then any two edged swoorde," are clearly capable of wielding destruction.[17] Yet in considering these descriptors, we should entertain the likelihood that in an age much more attentive to sound than ours, *hot* and *sharp* also denoted the manner of enunciation: explosive, shrill, projective. Such manner is the opposite of the "meeknes and gentlenes" desired in civil communication, of the "soft" answers said to smother the fire of angry repartees in Perkins's treatise.[18] In contrast, words abruptly propelled by heated breath travel far, do not dissipate in a noisy environment, and reliably penetrate their addressee's ear. To an early modern mind, then, describing the sounds of contentious speech as hot and sharp could have gone hand in hand with viewing them as material vehicles for destruction, set into motion by an abrupt and uncontrollable discharge of choler through the speaker's breath.

The physical force of this discharge is suggested when words are said to have been spewed or sputtered out like venom, the breath mingled with saliva heavy with the words' malice. We get a sense of the velocity of such liquefied speech from Latimer's description of an imagined response to it: "Shall I be such ydiot and diserde to suffer every man to . . . spewe out al their venyme against me at their pleasure?" Adams, in his sermon, is at once more metaphoric and more literal when he describes the trajectories of poisonous words. They are said to poison their speakers first, for "they have speckled souls. Secondly, They sputter their venime abroad, and besputtle others: no beast can cast his poyson so farre. Thirdly, Yea, they would . . . poison Gods most sacred and feared name."[19] Not limited to one direction, explosive words are imagined here as scattering far and wide like shrapnel, their destructive potential widely dispersed. It is worth noting too that while these words are presumably propelled by the choleric heat of their speaker's breath—the light element associated with masculinity in the humoral physiology of the era—they are heavy with moisture, the heavy humor of female bodies. Acoustically, then, these descriptions render contentious words not so much feminine but rather as dually gendered.

They are also described as rash and rapid words, "multiplied" by their speakers. Enunciation-wise such multiplication entails short, machine-gun-like breath spurts, to use another metaphor from modern warfare. Considering the "most proper places" for evil tongue action—"*Ale-houses, Tavernes, Play-houses, Bake-Houses, Wooll lofts,* and *Gossip meetings,*" all of them noisy environments with reflective walls—rapid and forceful enunciation likely produced a dinging echo effect, adding to the overwhelming aural effect of contentious speech.[20]

The loudness of this speech is another quality noted with disapproval by the divines. Adams calls the actions of unruly tongues "roarings," and Abernethy compares it to the barking of city dogs, a truly clamorous sound in an age before the pervasive machine noises ushered in by the Industrial Revolution. Sounds of such volume have the capacity for carrying far. Indeed Adams envisions the "roarings" as reaching "the battlements of heaven" and shaking them, only to "waken an incensed God to judgement." Echoing the prophesies of Zechariah and Jeremiah, he renders the punitive divine counterpart of contentious human "roarings" as proportionate in volume: "*There is a curse that goeth foorth, and it shall enter into the house of the swearer,* and not onely cut *him off, but consume his house with the timber, and the stones of it.*"[21] God's curse is of a magnitude that shatters timber and stone, and its main material difference from human roarings appears to be the precision of its destructive force.

The divines' descriptions yield intriguing insights into the structural makeup of the "sputterings" of unruly speech—the early modern equivalent of what the psycho-acoustic scientist Pierre Schaeffer terms sound objects, the smallest self-contained acoustical objects of human perception. A sound object has a beginning, middle, and end. The onset portion is known as the attack, characterized by "a rough or dissonant edge to the sound," that is, by the predominance of noise over tone. The attack is typically followed by a "stationary or steady-state portion," known as the body. When sound weakens, the sound object enters the stage of decay, "usually combined with some sensation of reverberation."[22] As sound objects, hot, sharp, rapid, and loud "railings" would have been characterized by a sudden, forceful onslaught, the kind of attack perceived as startling and incomprehensible noise. Then they would reach a high-volume plateau, sustaining their energy for a considerable amount of time as roaring words multiplied. Because of the reflective qualities of the soundscapes in which these sound objects were generated, their decay would have been accompanied by echoed repetitions of the weakened sound. The echo effect would have further distorted tonal qualities and impeded comprehension, while prolonging the time span of the railings and imbuing the soundscape with fractured noise. Such an acoustic contour of contentious speech may also account for the divines' reluctance to dwell on semantic content. Clearly it gives a sense of the overwhelming impact of the fiery tongue, a recurrent motif in the sermons on the tongue.

Speech Acts and Their Effects

If the semantics of contentious speech is of little interest for the sermonists, while its aural qualities typically elicit brief caustic descriptions, the main focus of interest in their texts is pragmatics: the scope and effects of the poisonous tongue's injurious action. Earlier I noted Latimer's declaration that an evil tongue hurts not just an individual but also a city and sometimes the entire polity. Adams likewise imagines the injurious impact of the tongue to extend to "the whole world."[23] Abernethy refers to the wide reach of injurious speech in similar terms. The tongue, he says, "scourgeth mens good names"; it also "scorneth and scoffeth . . . and thereby is able to set a City on fire." Somewhat surprisingly he includes the injurious speaker among the tongue's victims. The railing tongue is "hurtfull to it selfe and to others," he claims, glossing the statement with a reference to Proverbs 17:4 ("A wicked doer giveth heed to false lips and a liar giveth ear to a naughty tongue").[24] While the biblical verse strongly implies that moral fallacy needs to be always already present for a "naughty tongue" to wield its destructive power, Abernethy charges the tongue with the autonomous power to create, or at least to maintain a morally depraved disposition within the speaker. Webbe likewise includes the defamer among the victims of the railing tongue: "An evill *tongue* doth murder three at once: 1. The partie whom he doth defame. 2. The partie unto whom hee doth defame him. 3. Himselfe that is the defamer." He goes on to develop an allegorical image from Solomon's Proverbs to support this point: "And therefore doth describe this bloudy tongue to bee always armed with a threefold weapon, An *Arrow*, an *Hammer*, and a *Sword*; an *Arrow* to wound the partie whom hee would defame in his absence whiles he is farre off; an *Hammer* to knocke him on the head with a false report unto whome hee doth make the report; a *Sword* to stab his own Soule in committing that evill which God doth hate."[25] According to such discussion by the divines, contentious speech wreaks havoc in the public (city and country) and the natural realms, as well as in the private realm (one's "own Soule"), perversely unifying them in its injurious impact. Furthermore it appears to function somewhat autonomously of the intent and direction given to it by the speaker. This of course raises important questions about the speaker's moral agency and responsibility.

What specifically do these authors maintain are the injuries wrought by evil tongues to the integrated natural-public-private realm? They claim that the destruction wrought by evil tongues was pandemic. One commonly used allegory is that of a contagious, incurable disease that destroys its carriers and all who come into contact with them. This is akin to the plague ravaging the crowded city, as the early moderns imagined it. Abernethy fleshes out this allegory, interweaving within his dynamic image biblical verses from the epistles of James and Paul, from Psalms, and the Book of Job:

> The disease of the tongue is a fierce malady, and hee that is affected with it, either can never hold his peace, or else never speake well. . . . Natu-

rally it is (as the lips are) uncircumcifed, polluted and uncleane, and becommeth at the last, *an unruly evill, full of deadly poison*: so inflamed thereby, that *it is set on fire of hell and setteth on fire the course of nature*. This poyson maketh the tongue to be so *poysonous*, that it is both in it selfe *poysoned*, and a *poysoner* of others. It is both *passive*, and *active*: it is inflamed, and inflameth others. It is *paralyticke* to all good, and furious to all evill. It defileth the whole body, and harmeth those that heare it, or of whom it speaketh: spowting out *Adders poison* from under their lips. A disease both noysome to others, and as dangerous to himselfe, as if hee had sucked the *poyson of Aspes*.[26]

Once again this description evokes the perception of contentious speech as an uncontrollable eruption of moisture-infused breath. The railer or scold is cast as both a victim and a propagator of social evil. As for the gender implications for the injurious speaker, they are complex. A scold is penetrated by the poison of unruly speech and herself penetrates others' vulnerable ears. A railer breeds poisonous words, but his words' poison operates independently of his will. As passive feminine victims of the "disease of the tongue," they are irrevocably corrupted; as active masculine propagators, they corrupt the entire social body. As in the case of the acoustic descriptions of contentious speech, an analysis of the divines' rendering of its pragmatic charge likewise suggests that the tongue's "sputterings" were viewed as dually gendered.

Prominent within Abernethy's pestilence image are two other common allegories of the destructive impact of evil tongues on the moral fabric of the individual and society: consuming fire and poison. As we saw in the discussion of the enunciative force of contentious speech, Adams also used the allegory of poison, but he was especially fond of James's notion of the tongue's "unruly fire." The evangelist, Adams reminds his audience, calls such speech "the 'fire of hell'; blowne with the bellows of malice, kindled with the breath of the devil. Nay, Stella hath a conceit, that it is worse then the fire of hell: for that torments onely the wicked, this all, both good and bad.... Swearers, railers, scoldes have hell-fire in their tongues." This is "such a fire," Adams concludes, "as sets the whole world in combustion."[27] Here is an image of the evil tongue as the instrument of apocalyptic destruction, recalling, for urban audiences, the fearful experience of rapidly spreading city fires. Yet the minister is by no means clear on the question of the origin of this all-consuming fire. Does it issue from the speaker's hot, sharp, and rapid words or with the breath of the devil said to kindle it? Are the producers of fiery speech imagined as feminized receptacles of the Devil's uncontrollable evil or as masculine disseminators of evil?

On a less vital level, though certainly fundamental, the ministers charged the evil tongue with undermining the reliability of language. It was said to blur the conceptual boundaries between such binary opposites as good and evil, confession and renunciation, truth and lying, healing and disease. Thus in Perkins's prefatory address to the Christian reader, the preacher exclaims, "What a shame it is, that men with the same tongue wherewith they confess the Faith and Religion of Christ, should by vaine and ungodly speech utterly deny the power thereof." Dwelling on the tongue's unreliable arbitrariness, Webbe weaves metaphors used in James's epistle of the tongue as a fountain of sweet and bitter water together with language from Proverbs to produce a long list of oxymorons: "It is a *Forge* both of *Blessing* and *Cursing*, It is a *Shop* both of *precious Balme* and *deadly Poyson*, It is the *Trouchman* both of *Truth* and *Error*: *Fire* and *Water* are enclosed in it, *Life* and *Death* are in the power of it; It is a necessarie good, but an *Unruly evill*, very profitable, but exceedingly hurtfull: wee cannot well want it, nor want woe because of it." Abernethy charges the tongue with intention to mislead, writing that it is "inclined to evil, and seeming to bee inclined to good." Adams chafes against the whimsical duality of this singular organ: "It hath no meane, it is eyther exceedingly good, or excessively evill.... If it be good, it is a walking garden, that scatters in every place a sweet flower, an hearb of grace to the hearers. If it be evill, it is a wilde Bedlam, full of gadding and madding mischiefs." The tongue's indiscriminate capacity to transform the world into a Garden of Eden or a madhouse is matched by its arbitrarily contrary effects upon the individual: "It ... purifieth, or putrifieth the whole carcasse, the whole conscience." Adams's verb choice in this statement is especially effective in rendering the tongue's swift transformation of good into evil, accomplished in this case through the addition of a single plosive consonant: "purifieth," "putrefieth."[28]

Modeled after criminal legal procedure, Webbe's pamphlet *The Araignement of an Unruly Tongue* focuses on injuries wrought by the evil tongue in the public sphere, at the same time dwelling on the tongue's capacity to confuse meaningful distinction and order. Here it is charged with overturning central hierarchies of power in households and neighborhoods. It is indicted on charges of high and petty treason, witchcraft, robbery, murder, and riot. When the unruly tongue presents itself as defender of the poor, women, and persecuted innocents, the narrating judge responds indignantly: "It is true indeed, thou naughty Tongue lendest shrewd wives a mischievous weapon to offend their husbands; Thou armest servants against their Masters, and settest neighbours together by the eares; Thou art an Abetter of all quarrels."[29] It seems that for this author the greatest injury of the unruly tongue is that it endows subordinates in key social units—the household and the neighborhood—with powers legitimately belonging to their superiors.

Injurious Vocal Agency and Gender

Given the key role played by the godly household in the political imagination of the era as the cornerstone of the ordered polity, one would expect that female verbal transgression of patriarchal authority—seduction, scolding, cursing, prophesying—would be the prime choice in the sermonists' blasts against contentious speech. In other words, however the gender of this *speech* may have been construed, we should expect that representative contentious *speakers* would have been routinely imagined as female. This is indeed the case in Adams's assertion that "woman, for the most part, hath the glibbest tongue." Webbe too singles out a female injurious speaker, Eve, when he reprises the biblical story of the Fall: "By the *tongue* of the *Serpent* was Eve seduced, and her *tongue* did seduce Adam."[30]

Yet a closer analysis of this rendition of Genesis 3 raises questions about both the gender of Eve's speech and Eve's agency as speaker. Does Webbe view Eve as a passive, feminine seduced or as an active, masculine seducer? Was Eve's *tongue* her own or the serpent's? What is the gender of the serpent, and is the masculine-feminine binary even applicable to it? As the agent *and* victim of contentious speech, a seduced seducer, Webbe's Eve is both masculine and feminine. And once the reader realizes that her tongue is (like) the serpent's, the question of Eve's gender becomes even more perplexing. Later on in *The Araignment of an Unruly Tongue* Webbe seems more assertive in gendering the scolding tongue (and, by extension, the scold) as feminine when he claims that "for incontinency it hath long since bin presented at the Spirituall Court, for there is no such common whore as the tong: It wil suffer any whosoever will, to lie with her." Yet here too the agency and gender of the contentious speaker is up for grabs. A bad tongue may be whorish and hence feminine when it wills the immoral actions of others and then yields to the immoral "will" of its victims. But are those who will multiply words with bad tongues masculine, as suggested by the Renaissance significance of "will" as aggressive "carnal desire," or feminine, as suggested by the pronoun Webbe uses to define the tongue?[31]

The divines' discussion of the injurious agency of contentious speech is more complex than attributing it to bad women. To questions of the speakers' gender and vocal agency it offers tentative and conflicted answers. The fiery tongue could feminize male and female speakers alike, but it also rendered its speaker masculine in its capacity to "beget" discord. As for agency, if scolds and railers were victims of their own devastating words, wouldn't their Satan-induced poisoned state, with its uncontrollable heat index, exonerate them from moral responsibility? Latimer seems to suggest as much and clarifies that losing control over one's tongue entails a loss of masculinity: "He that cannot temper ne rule hys awn yre is but weake and feble, and rather more lyke a woman or a child then a stronge man." A bit later in the "Homelie against Contencion and Braulynge" he frames the inability to regulate one's anger not in gender terms but rather "as a kynde of madness and that he whiche is angery is, as it wer, for that tyme in a phrenesie."[32] And whereas Perkins resolutely asserts his readers' Christian duty "not to raile again" when verbally abused, Adams is reconciled to the idea that it is beyond man's power, let alone woman's, to tame an unruly tongue. "God onely can tame mans tongue," he yields.[33] It appears that in the religious writings of the early modern era, fiery speech acts not only become emblematic of the systemic failure of patriarchal efforts to regulate speech; they call into question the very binarism of gender.[34]

The ministers distinguished between the agency of speech and that of the speaker, allowing for the possibility of gendering the two differently.[35] Symptomatic of the lack of control upon the body humors, possibly engendered by the Devil himself, fiery speech was readily associated with the "natural" condition of female bodies. This condition, as Gail Kern Paster memorably argues in *The Body Embarrassed*, was characterized by unruly passions and unregulated body leakages. Accordingly the vocal *product* of railing, unmanageable and moisture-infused, could be gendered feminine, whether or not its *producer* was female. Adams brings out the volatile femininity of contentious speech when he calls the tongue a woman's offensive weapon, for "a fire brand in a franticke hand doth lesse mischiefe."[36]

Yet such frantically uncontrollable speech, Adams continues, was by no means restricted to women, for "the Proverb came not from nothing; when we say of a brawling man, he hath a womans tongue in his head."[37] Nor did it automatically feminize its speaker. And herein the sermons on the tongue brought out a cultural apprehensiveness about the danger that fiery speech posed to hierarchical gender binarism. Granted that the sermons on the tongue construed contentious speech as a set of stylized performances of unreasonable passion, thus generating negative exempla of normative femininity. However, once we bracket the socially destructive effects of contentious speech, it is possible to conceive of the discharge of heated words through the orifice of the mouth as restoring the thermal balance to women's "naturally" cold and moist bodies. But contentious speakers were not solely women. And for men, a profuse discharge of the "air" of heated words was bound to lower dangerously the body's heat, generated by the male-making humor of blood.[38] Furthermore the divines' insistence on the power of contentious speech to poison its speaker implies that restoring the thermal balance of male bodies was imagined as a difficult if not outright impossible prospect. Their humoral balance impervious to the regulation of reason and experience, these men's tongues came to resemble unruly, leaky, sputtering female organs. At the same time, they retained their male generative potential. Here was a disturbing gender model of the contentious speaker indeed.

This reading of the volatile gendering potential of fiery speech opens up an informative parallel to narratives of sex transformation discussed in Thomas Laqueur's influential book, *Making Sex*. In them excessive body heat was deemed capable of transforming female bodies into male by forcing out the penis and testicles, imagined, respectively, as inverted uterus and ovaries in the Gallenic medical model. In my discussion, while contentious speech was never imagined as entailing anatomical transformation, it was viewed as capable of effecting similarly drastic changes to the speaker's gender. Hot words could feminize and they could masculinize. More alarmingly, given the contagious nature of fiery speech, unpredictable gender transformations were not limited to any single, exceptional speaker.

Ultimately the divines' portrayals of feminine contentious speech develop a hybrid iconography of men with women's tongues and women with serpent tongues, discharging choleric masculine humors across the soundscape while wreaking havoc on the elemental balance of the reason-controlled body. This is the damage to the speaker that sermon writers warn against. The multigendered speech acts of the fiery tongue are cast as capable of undoing normative sexual differences *and* confusing the gender of their performers. In a still broader sense they are portrayed as alarmingly generative. Saturating with noise and poisonous "sputter" the enclosed spaces in which they rebounded—"Ale-houses, Tavernes, Play-houses, Bake-Houses, Wooll lofts, and Gossip meetings"—contentious speech is imagined as heating the passions of those who frequented these places, unleashing the tongues of more and more community members. According to the religious discourse of the era, the avalanche effects of the fiery tongue threatened to become the soundmark of early modern communities and multigendered contentious speech—a most potent generative force. The question arises whether ordinary parishioners were in agreement as to whether violent speech was solely a force for evil and disorder.

2

Gender and the Narratives of Scolding in the Church Courts

Early modern sermons were by no means the only medium to address cultural anxieties about the effects of contentious speech upon individuals and communities. Between the mid-sixteenth century and the Civil War, historians agree, these effects were the object of numerous legal disputes. In an age described by J. A. Sharpe as "deeply litigious," defamation, a crime closely linked to scolding, was a leading cause for action in the church courts: the consistory courts of the bishops or their chancellors and the archdeaconry courts. Defamation, the public assault against one's all-important "credit," or reputation, was also prosecuted in city, borough, and manorial courts leet, as it had been in the late Middle Ages. Some cases made it all the way to the Star Chamber. A surge of litigation for defamation in the common law courts, among other reasons, occasioned a 1624 royal decree "for limitation of actions, and for avoiding suits of law."[1] Legal actions against defamation were undertaken throughout the country, although the patchy records of multiple jurisdictions impede statistical analysis of geographic distribution. Nonetheless historians have established that slander suits climbed steeply in the consistory courts of Canterbury, Exeter, Norwich, York, Chester, and Wiltshire; in London defamation cases jumped from a third of church court cases in the 1590s to three-quarters in the 1630s. Data specifically limited to female scolding from ecclesiastical and common law jurisdictions in various parts of England show a more irregular distribution of such prosecution, with some villages and towns avoiding it for years and others, like Nottingham and Manchester, emerging as hotspots.[2] Overall it appears that even if David Underdown's thesis about a general "epidemic of scolding" between 1560 and 1640 may have been somewhat exaggerated, public verbal attacks against neighbors and the general peace ranked high among litigation causes in the era.[3] The legal documentation offers rich ground for the analysis of perceptions of the social roles played by scolding and by scolds.

As was the case of the sermons, defamation suits show a discrepancy between the gendering of offensive speech and offensive speakers. Depositions for defamation in the Oxford church courts for the period 1603–22 list forty-three male and thirty-nine female defendants; in late Elizabethan Hertfordshire the numbers of male and female defendants in defamation suits were closely balanced; in Salisbury between 1615 and 1629 men outnumbered women by a ratio of 6:4 as defendants in slander cases.[4] Nevertheless among the multiple ways in which unruly tongues disturbed the peace of early modern neighborhoods and households, including "Swearing, Blaspheming, Cursed speaking, Railing, Slandering, Chiding, Quarrelling, Contending, Jesting, Mocking, Flattering, lying, dissembling, Vaine and idle talking," it was the speech of the "common scold" that became representative of verbal contentiousness.[5] By 1659 feminine scolding had acquired a proverbial status. "They scold," ran one of the sayings recorded in Howell's *Proverbs*, "like do many butter-whores, or oyster-women at Billingsgate." Such feminization of contentious speech had repercussions for legal action. Hardly any men were prosecuted as "scolds," in spite of the significant male representation among defendants in defamation causes.[6] In certain common law courts ducking and bridling, the punishments meted out for scolding, were applicable only to female defamers. The feminization of this type of speech violence rendered women representative criminal offenders, in spite of the fact that more men were charged with defamation.

Scolding speech may have been gendered feminine, but the rich records of the church courts indicate that participants in the litigation process construed the contentious *speakers'* gender and its relation to authority in vastly divergent ways. For all the extensive sermonizing against sins of the tongue, not all litigants and witnesses perceived contentious speakers as unambiguously malicious and destructive. (Perhaps this was one important reason for the sermonists' rhetorical zeal.) Exploring surviving depositions in defamation cases brought before the church courts, I attempt to reconstruct the sense that witnesses made of this speech, its vocal qualities, and the perceived effects of "fiery" speech acts on those who produced them and on their addressees.[7] In the outcome of this analysis I question claims that garrulous women were uniformly perceived as scandalous disturbers of the social peace, lacking in cultural authority. Certainly many were viewed as embodying feminine unruliness, but scolding was also seen as opening up livable opportunities for transgendered subjectivity of the female-to-male spectrum. In other words, in certain performance sites ambiguously gendered garrulous women could and did make viable claims to social authority.

An important caveat is in order. Although the church courts' documentation opens up insights into the historical makings of scolding, it by no means provides a direct, unmitigated record of the speech patterns and sounds produced by historical scolds. As Laura Gowing aptly cautions, "Justice in the church courts depended on storytelling"; frequently legal action was motivated by the opportunity to formally articulate one's version of events.[8] Accordingly in surviving depositions of participants in defamation law suits fiery words are the subject of storytelling, which in turn is affected by legal procedure, the memory and personal investment of witnesses, the protocols of representing oral speech in legal writing, and even the time crunch in which court clerks found themselves. Furthermore legal discourse followed established narrative protocols. These narratives had a common point of origin in the plaintiff's account of events known as the libel, which was itself likely to have been shaped by the proctors acting as ecclesiastical lawyers. The libel determined the questions (called interrogatories) posed privately to the witnesses of both litigants, thus providing direction and structure to the witness narratives.

But witnesses, some of whom had extensive litigation experience, could and did resist such narrative constraints. They generated narrative detail, conflated the questions based on the plaintiff's libel in their answers, and formulated completely new narratives for the consideration of the judge. Or conversely, witnesses, female and lower-class ones in particular, would self-censor their stories to maintain their moral reputation and avoid self-incrimination.

Witness narratives were further mediated when court clerks wrote them down as depositions. At this stage the clerks selected the spoken statements they considered pertinent to the case in question and conjoined them in interminable sentences. They interspersed the witnesses' speech with legal formulae: shifts of reported speech from first to third person, repetitive references to each character's role in the litigation process, summaries, stock phrases, and more.⁹

Still the depositions in church court defamation cases are indispensable for reconstructing at least fragments of the makings and effect of fiery women's speech. After considering the complex mediation of this speech, we can note phrases, statements, and descriptions of body language of marked individualistic flair. Oddly fitting within the stylistic registers of legalese and the witness narrative protocols, these are likely to be segments of contentious speech that impressed themselves onto witnesses' memories. Church court depositions are also invaluable for the light they shed on public attitudes to contentious speech and on the social roles of contentious speakers.

Depositions in church court defamation cases help us recover some of the semantic, stylistic, and vocal qualities of scolding at its point of origin. They re-present (make present, however tentatively and partially) the sense and voice of injurious speech. They clarify how interested parties perceived the pragmatics of contentious speech, its multiple rhetorical uses. Collectively they point to the contradictory ways the vocal authority claimed by scolding women could be used to uphold or to confound normative notions about gender.

Semantics

Unlike the clerical writers' evasive approach to the content of contentious speech, contributors to the legal record were understandably forthcoming about the meaning of language that landed women accused of scolding in front of the church courts. Most often at stake were assaults against sexual reputation or "honesty." Typically, though not exclusively, they targeted women. Since scolding was by definition a malicious speech act and scolds likely to favor hard-hitting vocabulary, we can surmise that broadly reported terms such as *whore* and *queane* indeed composed the basic arsenal of contentious speech.¹⁰ As Bernard Capp explains, the diminishing returns of overuse were countered by choices from an impressive lexicon of semantic variants, including "baggage, harlot, drab, filth, flirt, gill, trull, dirtyheels, draggletail, flap, naughty-pack, slut, squirt, and strumpet, generally heightened by adjectives."¹¹ Offending speech could be whetted through epithets. Whores were, among other things, common, base, arrant, strong, tempting, palsie-headed, curtailed (cart-tailed?), whott-tailed, "spanyell," Westminster, even Cannibal.[12] Queanes were said to have been impudent, drunken, coppernosed, pissabed, as well as scurvy rascal, stinking, and platterfaced.[13]

Male sexual "honesty" also came under verbal attack, if more obliquely and less frequently.[14] Gowing and Capp concur that typical taunts against men concerned their sexuality only indirectly. The familiar gibe of "cuckold" was a public declaration of a man's failure to discipline not his own sexuality but that of his wife. Terms like "bawd," "whoremonger harlot," and "whoremaster" slandered men by association with immoral women. "Rogue" and "knave" were commonly used, though they had such vague sexual connotations that they were not actionable in court. Still these terms and their rarer and more imaginative counterparts—"lecherous monkey," "bull of Bedlam," or "skipjack" (bigamist)—could wreak considerable damage to the social "credit" of married men and bachelors aspiring to married status.[15]

The preponderance of words in the "whore" and "whoremonger" lexicon of the depositions may well have resulted from existing limitations on the church courts' slander jurisdiction. It was restricted to spiritual matters, including sexual offenses, while allegations of property and personal crimes were supposed to be brought before the common law. In spite of these limitations, church court litigants and witnesses also reported, and the clerks recorded, assault words relating to theft, lying, drunkenness, ethnicity, witchcraft, professional incompetence, even murder. Thus Katherine Bllithman raised a hue and cry against Robert Byllye, calling him a "hold eyed lymber thief." Later she explained to the judge that Byllye "shuld recett certain corne of Sr Robert Brandlyng's, so moch as wold fine his house one hole yere." Alice Robinson extended her verbal abuse of Alexander Fetherstonhaugh to include his ancestors when she railed "that he was a thief and wold be hanged, as all his fore ellers was." Margaret Howhett publicly called Margaret Reed "a horse godmother water wych." Margaret Dawson declared Janet Gyllis a scold, characterizing her voice as "a barrel drome" and added "that she was ever ken for nought all the daies of hir lyf." Janet Piers loudly proclaimed that Jane Roberts from Poole, Wales, "went to the nayler's wife ... to be her midwife and shee did pull her gutts out and shee did die under her hands," contrary to witness testimony of the successful delivery.[16]

Scolding in the Church Courts 21

The vocabulary of sexual slander dominated church court records of contentious speech even in disputes having little or nothing to do with sexual honor. Thus when Agnes Aydon declared, in the midst of some street chiding, that Janet Clerk "hadd cutt a purse," one witness recalled her words as loaded with sexual innuendo: "Go thy way, like nowghth [*sic*] as thou art, and cut a purse, as thou haist doon before tyme, and thou may be duckt in Tyne, as thou haith beene." In one fell swoop Aydon conflated petty theft with whoredom (being "nought") and scolding, the latter by suggesting that the appropriate punishment for Clerk was "cucking" (or ducking). A similarly sexualized conflation of insulting terms is evident in Anne Shilton's denunciation as a "black-mouthed witch and whore." Drunken women were easy victims of sexual slander, as in the case of Joan Allan, who was called a "drunken bitch whore" and alleged to "entice all the young men about town to lie drinking and idling there with her" in her husband's absence. Even defamations involving charges of premeditated murder could involve an assault on sexual reputation. For instance, Catherine James was challenged by her neighbors Thomas and Catherine Davis thus: "Thou ould whore, thou hast poisoned thy husband [her deceased husband Robert Lloyd] and wilt poison him also [Catherine's second husband, Richard James]."[17] It may well be that sexually slanderous terms were seen as the semantic core of contentious speech because of the scope of church courts' jurisdiction. It is also the case that rehearsing the sexualized vocabulary of scolding and slander over and over again in the course of the litigation process solidified this semantic core.

Stylistics

Scolding may have been quite unimaginative in its reiterations of sexualized verbal abuse, but its stylistic aura was rich and creative, a quality frequently brought out in the legal documentation. Thus Richard Northcott, a witness in a 1665 defamation suit brought by Joan Drew of Okehampton, Devon, recalls the defendant Elizabeth Ebsworthy calling Drew "whore, drunken whore, and beggarly whore," as well as "a base scum'd bitch, and a base strumpet." These words, the court clerk noted, were spoken in the marketplace "in a very angry, railing and malicious manner and with an intent ... to take away the good name and reputation of her the said Joan Drew."[18] Clearly anger did not diminish Ebsworthy's vocabulary of abuse.

In a well-documented case from St. Alban's parish in London, Catherine Barnaby's pent-up anger at the Dickenson family and perhaps her own tragic personal circumstances are reported to have resulted in an impressive array of defamatory taunts. At Mistress Dickenson, Barnaby hurled the customary jibes of "a drunken Queane, and a coppernosed Queane" who "goest a drinkinge from house to house every daye." Adding dramatic flair to these terms of abuse, she asserted in front of the customers in Dickenson's shop that "that drunken quean ... hath made my husband spend 500 £ and hath nowe spent him beyond the sea, and ... shee keepes company with none but pedlars and Roagues and theeves." (Barnaby's husband in fact lived apart from her in a "garden house" in nearby Turnmill Street.) The final stroke aimed at Mistress Dickenson amounted to nothing less than an accusation of murder. "That Drunken Queane," Barnaby yelled, pointing to the girdler's wife from across the street, "hath murdered my child and smothered it in a rug." Barnaby called John Dickenson an insatiable whoremonger and disturber of the peace, one who "keepeth pretty wenches in his house and ... hath coaches coming and going at his bake dore att all hours in the night and ... hath such fidling and singeing and halloweing in his house she cannot sleep for it." Moreover she proclaimed him to be "a cheating knave and a cozening knave and that he getteth his living by cheating, bribing, cozening and buying of stolen goods, and that he brought a piece of stolen stuff to make his wife a gown."[19] While these remarkable narratives were not produced during a single scolding episode— Barnaby's "disquiet" speech troubled the Dickenson household and the entire neighborhood for seven years—their abundance and imaginative variety made redress by legal means difficult. To counter Barnaby's verbal attacks, the Dickensons, as Martin Ingram points out in his discussion of the case, would have had to start several suits in different courts, no small strain on their time and budget.[20]

As the Dickenson versus Barnaby case illustrates, elaborate detail was a favored stylistic strategy in defamation and scolding. Details were routinely used to substantiate an attack on an opponent's sexual reputation by professing personal knowledge of the setting or the financial circumstances of the alleged offense. For instance, Martha Morton of St. Oswald's in Chester aimed the customary "whore" insult at Judith Blenston and promptly added that Blenston "got eight shillings in one night for standing pimp to Mr Bradshaw." Anne Manning of Northmoor in Oxfordshire likewise deemed that providing financial detail would give an edge to her public insult of her sister-in-law, Alice Manning. To the sexual slur of "an ould whoore" delivered before no less than five witnesses in front of Alice's house, she added that Alice "went rydinge upp & downe the country after Robert Garrett, & . . . that she was the Millers whoore & that he the . . . miller had geven her tenne poundes to buy her a smocke." A woman from Loughborough was accused of being "naught with three several men in one night for three groats," and another one from Wittlesford was alleged to have paid with cheeses, venison, and a shirt for men to have sex with her. Male targets of scolding were similarly showered with shameful realistic details of their alleged transgressions. Thus the Leicestershire scold Grace Dorman called a neighbor who had chided her over some stray pigs a "pennycunt" because, she went on to explain to the puzzled bystanders, he had allegedly offered a penny to a beggar "to have been naught with her."[21]

As scolding bouts escalated, the realistic details used to enhance the more general terms of abuse coalesced into implied or partially developed narratives. Fragmentary as these narratives were, the notion of proof was central to them. Thus in 1635 Rosamund Mann of Barnby-on-the-Moor reportedly railed in public that one Bridget Hill was "a filthy jade," adding, "Thou art a common whore, thou laydest thine arse three times in an afternoon under another man's besides thine husbande. Thou art a tempting whore and I will prove it."[22] Factual precision about the number of sexual acts during the alleged transgression is here conjoined to the promise of a titillating tale to be shared with neighbors or judges at a later time. Sometimes defamers referred to inanimate objects as "witnesses" to the alleged acts. This strategy was used by Margaret Littleton when she told Mary Nicolls that "the yellow bedchamber" could tell she was a whore, and by Thomas Hoskins, who marveled that Helen Godderd was not pregnant, adding, "If the Watergate could speak it would tell may strange tales."[23] The tantalizing withholding of juicy tales by these defamers was an effective way to incite the curiosity and imagination of anyone who might have witnessed the altercations. At the same time, these instances of scolding seem to be shaped by the anticipation of proof to be provided in a legal setting.

Narrative-insinuating details were not always adequate for the scolds' rhetorical goals. This holds true for the culmination of the furious exchanges among Ann Hooper, Elizabeth Willey, and Elizabeth Eaton from the London parish of Stepney, which had started with the customary slurs about whoredom, illegitimate pregnancy, and symptoms of the pox. Eventually Eaton and Willey joined forces in a fully fleshed-out narrative of Hooper's transgression. "You whore," Eaton was said to have yelled at Hooper's window, "was not a Flemminge fetched out of bed from thee or leapt out of a window, when as you dwelleth at the next dore unto the Pope's Head in Wapping Wall?" Willey promptly added the financial detail that pinpointed "whore" to mean "prostitute": "You . . . lay with a Fleming for 2 s. and an Englishman for half a crown. I would have used my own countryman better."[24] In a few sharp statements Eaton and Willey sketched a sexual transaction set in a specific locale, which apparently violated norms of female behavior, trade tariffs, and national pride all at once.

Another stylistic element favored by contentious speakers was grotesque description. Thus when Beatrice Headon reportedly called Susan Westaway "a base whore, a common whore," she went on to claim that Westaway had "showed her cunt unto two of the constables of the same parish and told them that she had a chimney between her legs." No doubt appalled at hearing herself credited with a description of her own genitalia in terms that suggested both soot and indiscriminate traffic, Westaway promptly sued. Cartoonish grotesque was similarly tied to affront in Janet Wilkinson's address to Katherine Anderson as a "hange lipped witche." Moreover Wilkinson's slur appears to combine grotesque physical description with insinuation about the legal punishment for witches.[25]

Sometimes the scolds' penchant for realistic precision was cast aside in favor of the rhetorical effect of hyperbole. Such verbal extravagance could approximate proverbial expression, as in the affront hurled at Alice Richardson, said to have been "as common as the highway." Alternatively hyperbole was mixed with degrading humor, as when Joan Easton was called "the arrantest whore that ever had shone [shoes] of leather" and "an arrant whore as ever pissed."[26] As can be expected, hyperbole was frequently used to convey the sexual insatiability of the scold's target. Alice Johnson was said to have been "worse than a bitch, for that a bitch would take her kind at her time and then was satisfied, but no man was able to satisfy the filthy carnal lust of the said Alice." Jane Lloyd was defamed "in the open street at Ruthin, in the presence and hearing of many faithful subjects of the said lord King" as "a wicked witch . . . , wicked whore, proud bitch, lying under every bodyes breech under hedges, drunken whore, naughty queen that raisest ye husbands out of their beds from their wives to wander under hedges." Sicilia Thornton was dubbed "worse than a bitche thou goest sawghting [*sic*] up and downe the towne after knaves and art such a whott tailed whore that neither one nor two nor ten nor twenty knaves will scarce serve the [*sic*]."²⁷ In these and similar cases the scolds' hyperbolic defamations acquired Rabelaisian qualities.

Yet another favored stylistic feature of scolding was the symbolism of filth and beastliness. At vespers in the parish church of St. Andrews in London, Agnes Garrett publicly addressed Elizabeth Herbert as "filthy and naughty drab." Edith Busby and Jane Catesby chided each other while winnowing wheat in a street in Enstone; the latter called Busby "styncking jakes and shitton Jakes and filthy jakes" before throwing a stone at her head. Margaret Burrows charged Robert Shaw, a tallow chandler from Chester, in similar terms, calling him, among other things, "a stinking knave." He sued for defamation of his person and his trade. "Bitch," "cow," and "jade" were common derogatory terms, and even the occasional "bichefoxe" and "spanyell hoore" show up in court records. Sometimes dirt and animal symbolism were explicitly interwoven, as in the taunt hurled by Mary Woods at Jane Thomas: "Thou Jane art a Cuckin whore, and a dirty shameless mare." The association of pigs with dirt made them useful for the purposes of derogatory imagery, as in phrases like "dung-bellied drunken sow" and "swillbelly sow."²⁸ These affronts showcased the alleged moral depravity of defamation targets by denying them human status or by ascribing a repugnant sensory dimension to despicable moral qualities.

The symbolism of disease, particularly syphilis or "the pox," was yet another stylistic staple of contentious speech. A "pocky whore," a "burnarse whore," and "a blackarsed queane" were familiar enough jibes, and defamers were quick to attribute visible symptoms of venereal disease to those they targeted or to lay claims to personally available information. After Alice Francklin called Maud Spender of Coulston "a burnt tailed whore and a pocky whore," she hastened to elaborate that "the pox had eaten thee out if my sister had not holpen thee of them." During the neighborhood brawl in the London parish of Stepney, mentioned earlier, Ann Hooper chose to sting Elizabeth Eaton by specifying, "Thou art a Tinker's Trull, thou hast the Poxe in thy nose," while Hooper's husband, John, put down another neighbor, Elizabeth Willey, crying, "Thou hast forgotten since I sett up a Badstead for thee, when as I felt thee there was noe hair on thy private parts." At Bury St. Edmunds Faith Wilson charged a neighbor to "pull up your muffler and hide your pocky face, and go home and scrape your mangy arse."²⁹ Pox symbolism was well suited to the articulation of sexual slander and had the added bonus of conveying and inciting physical repugnance.

A more sophisticated stylistic choice was the hybridization of the symbolism of disease with that of Scripture. When Jane Whitefield turned on her own husband at a Cambridge fair in 1594, she called for "a pox of God on thee villain, thou hast been amongst thy whores." In a case brought by John Metcalfe against Anne Dixon contentious speech was tightly interwoven with prayer-like ritual cursing. Dixon was reported to have called Metcalfe "whoremaster, whoremonger and harlott and did sit her downe upon her knees and cursed and banned him, and his wife, and badd a vengeance light upon the wife of the said John Metcalf and upon that whoremaster and whoremonger harlott her husband ... and prayed God that they might never thryve." Sometimes it is impossible to distinguish among scolding, ritual cursing, and witch-speak. Such is the case of the fiery words attributed to Jonah Tebbe in a 1511 defamation case against her: "Fye on the, false horson churle, and I pray God the devyll of hell draw away thy body and sowle." At other times contentious speech referenced biblical narratives directly. When Alice Beck abused Dorothy Grundy's child, the mother's defamatory rhetoric borrowed from biblical narrative. After Beck "did cast down [the] childe in the durt and did trample it with her feete," Grundy stormed, "Is this naballs [Naboth's] vineyard that you deny my child water and use it so and if this be naball's vineyard and if you be Jezebell, God send you the reward Jezebell had." The biblical allusion, which would have been readily intelligible to the witnesses of this neighborhood brawl, casts the child as the innocent Naboth stoned to death at Jezebel's instigation. For Beck, Grundy invoked Jezebel's fate, to be eaten by dogs in her city. Of special interest here is the subject position that this contentious speaker constructed for herself. She was careful to use the conditional mood that was likely to render her insult legally nonactionable; caution, however, did not stop her from taking on the voice of the Old Testament prophet Elijah, as would the Quaker prophets discussed in chapter 7, when they publicly castigated men at the summit of political power.³⁰

A stylistic strategy related to Grundy's assumption of the voice of a biblical prophet was the dismantling of the distinction between literal description and figurative language in offensive speech. By far the most popular defamation was the threat to brand an opponent with the "whore's marke," a slit nose. As Gowing and Capp remind us, throughout medieval and early modern Europe mutilated noses were widely perceived as a shameful index of sexual promiscuity and sinfulness. Jealous wives in particular were lavish with such threats of their husbands' suspected mistresses. In 1579 Elizabeth Taylor of Leicestershire swore against a woman whom she called her husband's whore that she "would cut off her nose, wheresoever she met with her." Anne Browne of Oxfordshire vowed she would slit the nose of a young woman said to have ridden pillion behind Browne's husband if she dared do it again. Joan Hickmann threatened her London neighbor Joan Bird, whom she believed was "keeping her husband," that she would "slitt her nose and marke her for a whore."[31]

Like the common threats to scratch the face of alleged witches, which I will discuss later, such speech could slide into aggressive physical action, transforming the violent speech act into an animative. In 1618 Stepney Alice Squire declared that she had indeed given Katherine Berry a "whores marke" when she scratched her face. The animative deployed by Catherine Barnaby, whose multiple attacks against the Dickenson family of the London parish of St. Albans were discussed earlier, was more elaborate. She was said to "fall a scolding with her neighbours dayly and if that any of them do give her an answer she presently runneth and fetcheth a bottle [bundle] of hay and setteth it up and sayeth she cannot be Quiet for these roagues and Rascalls . . . she setts it up for them to scould at."[32] With this animative Barnaby not only emblematized her neighbors as scolds who would rail at a wisp of hay, but she likely infuriated them further, provoking "an answer."

Barnaby's choice of a material prop for her animative act was not coincidental. As an entry in a 1626 collection of "character" epigrams maintains, "There's nothing mads or moves [a scold] more to outrage than but the very naming of a wisp, or if you sing or whistle when she is scolding."[33] Barnaby's physical performance, then, was designed both to infuriate her addressees and to incapacitate a verbal attack on their part. Effectively she wrought havoc on her audience's field of meaning, their experience of their place in the world. As Slavoj Žižek explains:

An injurious word aims at bringing about in the other the breakdown of argumentation: its wound "corners" the other to such an extent that he is at a loss and can only counter my injurious word by having recourse to a violent *passage à l'acte*. This moment of perplexity, of the breakdown of the symbolic fiction, is the proof for me that the other exists for real. . . . Therein resides the double bind of the injurious word: it discredits in advance the victim's attempt to refute it via counterargumentation.[34]

Barnaby may not have been mentally stable, as Ingram suggests.[35] However, her adept use of a well-timed taunt and a well-chosen speech prop to confront the upright citizens with an image of themselves as the unruly Other speaks volumes about her stylistic aptitude, which was not limited to strictly verbal interactions.

Voices and Their Accompaniment

Although less detailed on the subject of acoustics than on the semantics of scolding, church court records shed important light on this issue. Similarly to sermon writers, witnesses in defamation cases refer to explosive, fiery speech. Thus William Hunt and Joan Hannes were said to have exchanged "hard and choleric words" as they chided from their respective yards. A witness to Prudence Higgins's scolding of Katherine Brown testified that she had spoken "in great heat of choler."[36] Choler, recall, is the fiery masculine humor that ministers writing on the fiery tongue related to explosive and projective enunciation. An excess of choler could transform a contentious verbal invective into an aggressive physical animative.

Another point of agreement between the legal record and sermons regarding the aural qualities of scolding was its loudness. When Elizabeth Raper railed at her servant Thomas Benbury about spending her money on maintaining his "strong whore," she managed to wake up a traveler staying at the Sign of the Swan, an Oxford inn. This traveler, one John Bean, testified that "he was lying asleep in a chamber" when he was awakened by "an uproar" between Raper and Benbury. The volume allowed him to recognize Raper's voice and understand her words. Margaret Shaw, who witnessed a brawl between Katherine Hanwell and Mary Walker at the butcher's shambles in Whitney, testified that although she was somewhat hard of hearing, she clearly heard Walker's words because they were spoken "very loud that one might hear her from one side of the street unto the other." What was audible to the hard-of-hearing witness must have been clamorous to those with normal hearing. A witness for Anne Burden in her suit against Elizabeth Anderson testified that when Anderson called the plaintiff "crowket handyd wytch," the words were spoken "audiently," so that "ther might many have herd them, beinge spoken so neigh the crose and in the towne gait as they were." The most clamorous voice I have identified belonged to Annie Wood, a scold who was "well whipped" and committed to labor in London's Bridewell Hospital in August 1559. Her railing "most unhonestly and slanderously upon this house [Bridewell] and Governor thereof" was gauged to have reached "the heryng of five hundred persons."[37]

The scolds' loud voices could be augmented by nonverbal noises, enhancing their performative effect. Thus Jane Robinson was said to have clapped her hands together before calling for "a carte a carte and a cucking stoole" for Helen Lo—a sound that elementary school teachers and public speakers to this day find effective in claiming the attention of a distracted or boisterous audience. Elizabeth Andrews, on the other hand, used nonverbal noise as the auditory equivalent of, literally, a punch line. After shouting, "Come out you whore and show your face, you base whore," in front of a house in Maiden Alley in London, she proceeded to smash the windows with her fist. Andrews's animative action embodied her verbal aggressiveness and added symbolic value to boot. As Capp points out, window smashing was "a traditional form of symbolic violence against prostitutes."[38]

Contentious Speech Acts and Their Effects

In spite of the semantic and auditory charge of contentious speech acts, some of the witnesses and even targets claimed that they could curtail the effects by "fortifying" their ears against the scolds' auditory assaults. Thus the Londoner Alice Stere explained that she stopped listening to a defamatory attack against a neighbor, and because "she was ashamed to hear such filthy words, [she] went immediately into her house and heard no more of their talk."[39] Stere was likely concerned about the possibility that opening an eager ear to "filthy words" or, worse, repeating them as a witness could damage her own reputation of "honesty." Some male witnesses, as Capp notes, claimed selective hearing when it came to women's disputes. A Cambridge chandler, for instance, testified that having been roused at midnight by an altercation between two women and "hearing them fall to scolding, he left them and went to bed." A Nottinghamshire man, summoned by a neighbor to witness how she was being abused, stayed put, "supposing it to be but a brawling matter." Another witness to the start of a quarrel never strayed from "his own business whereabout he was going, namely the fetching of water." Capp interprets these men's actions as belittling and even ridiculing the significance of women's disputes, but their disinterest may have had a different motivation.[40] The witnesses strike me as consciously heeding warnings given in many a sermon against listening too eagerly to the "fiery tongue" and thus augmenting its destructive impact on neighborhoods and beyond. Furthermore these model citizens may have claimed social authority by extolling their own willed resistance to contentious speech.

Even targets of defamation sometimes attempted to barricade their ears. When Mary Crooke staged a noisy assault on Anne Moxam's reputation in front of her house in South Wraxall, screaming "bobtail whore and whore bitch, saying that she was hot in the tail and had been and showed her arse before the king, and scratching at her . . . through the window said that if she had her forth, she . . . would pull her . . . in pieces and scratch out her eyes," Moxam stayed indoors without responding. Her choice was congruent with what Gina Bloom has described as the heroic code of female aural defensiveness, memorably illustrated by the chaste Lady in Milton's masque *Comus*. Unlike the Lady, however, Moxam was not attempting to elude seductive solicitation. In her case refusal to engage in a battle of words can be construed as active resistance against the socially corrupting venom of the "fiery tongue," a deflection of the provocation to assume the role of the scold herself. Heroic as such resistance may have been, it exacted a social price from Moxam; a disapproving neighbor scoffed that "she was a very coward that being overnight called so many whores she would not come forth of her house."[41] Crooke's violent speech had entangled her addressee in a double bind: the defense of silence did nothing to prevent public tarnishing of her character, while a spirited refutation would have discredited Moxam as a scold, if not worse.

The devastating effects of scolding were experienced viscerally by those it targeted. When Mary Tucker's sexual reputation was publicly assaulted, she "took great grief and went her way crying." Anne Burdett, who was publicly accused by a Leicestershire neighbor of abandoning a bastard infant in London some twenty years earlier, was left "extremely much dejected and impaired in her health." Other targets of scolding appear to have withdrawn within themselves, shunning even important Christian holidays and thus incurring the risk of ostracism and even ecclesiastical prosecution. Richard Easte of Suncombe in Oxfordshire reported "that he did not communicate this laste Easter byecause his conscience was troubled bye the ewill speeche of Katherine Ginacre, but doethe not refuse the Lordis table upon enie scruple in religion." Easte's testimony suggests that scolding inflicted a spiritual trauma upon him significant enough to make him ignore even legally mandated church attendance and thus risk an accusation of recusant Catholicism. Christopher Boreman of Southnewton, also in Oxfordshire, likewise found himself unable to receive communion "at Easter nor anie tyme since because ther was some controversie in lawe between this respondent and two other of his neighboures, and by that meanes he was not in perfyct love and charitie, and did not refuse to receave in contempte of the Queanes lawes."[42] Judging by these testimonies, not only did contentious speech jeopardize the spiritual well-being of its targets, but it also ripped apart the spiritual fabric of the godly community and undercut its spiritual revitalization.

Granted, the church courts never construed the effects of contentious speech in the calamitous terms that clerics used in their sermons to render the impact of the fiery tongue in their sermons. I have been able to locate a single reference to the propensity of contentious speech to provoke divine wrath, coincidentally not in a church court record. A Manchester court leet of 1620, to which Isabell Rychardson alias Walworke and Alice Worthington alias Greenehalghe were presented as common scolds, determined that "if theise and other abuses be not speedilye Reformed wee maye looke and Expecte that the great Stewart of heaven and earth will revenge theise and other the like synnes which Raigne amongst us."[43]

Nevertheless, like the sermons and the religious tracts, witness testimony credits scolding with the power to destroy the reputation of its targets and to damage seriously communal and family alliances. Again and again its targets are said to have suffered public humiliation or ostracism, legal prosecution, marital or economic hazards. Thus Edward Tile, a witness in a London slander case, deposed that after Dorothy Stockdale exclaimed that Robert Bridges "hast had to deale with fower women besides Hodgkins wife," he "and the rest of his fellowe Rulers [of the Company of Waterbearers] have putt the said Bridges out of their howse and sosietie." In the libel for the 1593 suit of Richard Ingram against Elizabeth Knowles, it was alleged "that by reason of the utterance of these defamatory words, the status, good fame and reputation of Richard Ingram are greatly and grievously injured and lessened among the good and substantial men with whom he had been of good fame and reputation, and in all likelihood they will be injured in the future." A 1602 Wiltshire case of sexual slander suffered by John Nicholas's wife and daughters cites testimony that the women could not "come in any company but they ... [were] laughed and jested at." In another Wiltshire case John Blathat accused Oliver Stoneax of having contracted the pox from a "Winchester goose" and challenged Stoneax to "show unto him ... his prick and he ... would show him ... his hand." Eager bystanders backed Blathat, urging that the target of his defamation "should be searched to see whether he had been burnt or no." Surely this must have been a humiliating and terrifying experience for Stoneax.[44]

In addition to the humiliation of the public affront, Blathat's challenge could have had serious legal repercussions for his target. As Christopher Haigh and later Ingram argue, public challenges to one's sexual honesty exposed the target of contentious speech to disciplinary (or "office") court action triggered by allegations of "common fame." Slanders of witchcraft or murder, for instance, could result in their targets' presentment in front of the secular courts. To forestall a disciplinary presentment a number of defamation victims brought their own "instance" cases to the church courts, using "one element in the legal process to protect themselves against another." But while the ultimate goal of interpersonal (or "instance") church court action was the reconciliation of the parties, the legal process itself undermined this outcome. Because of the lack of cross-examination, G. R. Quaife explains, "it was the task of the judge to evaluate the worth of each set of depositions." This strategy made discrediting the witnesses of the opposing party an attractive proposition.[45] It appears that church court action itself provided ample opportunities for intensifying contentious speech and expanding its scope beyond the scolding incidents that provoked the legal action in the first place.

In addition to sparking litigation, contentious speech could wreak havoc on the marital relationships and marital prospects of its targets, both men and women. For instance, a 1587 defamation of adultery in Minety caused "great strife... betwixt... Noble and his wife." Walter Longe's affront to William Burges of Semington, "thou art a wittol and canst not pull on a hose of [i.e., over] thy head for the bigness... of thy horns," reportedly led to the breeding of "much evil will between the said Burges and his wife even almost to the parting of them one from the other." Margery Hickes of the London parish of Abchurch was turned out by her husband when she was defamed by Helene Patteson; Hickes was eventually able to "justifie her good life by the testimony of her honest nighbors." Margery Newporte, a witness in another London case, repeatedly testified that after Margaret Herde declared that Margaret Hyde "use to ryde upon mens backes" and had a child in Wales prior to her marriage, Hyde's husband "do[th] think more hardlier of his wyffe then he was wont to doo, and doth bydd her Cleare her selfe of those speaches." In the Wiltshire record of 1615–29 discussed by Ingram, five defamation cases specifically mention the adverse effect of sexual defamation on the marital prospects of the plaintiffs, and three others suggest that this was a significant motive for legal action. Thus witnesses concurred that an accusation leveled against Thomas Shermore that he had fornicated with Agnes Archard was "a great blot and stain to him in the preferment of his marriage being a bachelor." When Anthony Ryder claimed that he had deflowered Jane Seymour, she was "like to be put by of a good match which otherwise had proceeded" in spite of her reputation as "a modest, civil and honest young woman."[46]

In discussing the effects of scolding as construed by the legal record, it is important to note references to its economic consequences. As Ingram contends, sexual ill fame by no means automatically precluded employment and commercial dealings, but defamation targets perceived matters differently. Thus Asa Scandaver of North Newton blamed his dismissal from the service of the Earl of Hertford on the public declaration by three women that he had fornicated with one Bridget Humphrey. William and Elizabeth Blandfield, an Exeter couple who sued Joan Creare for "slanderous, detestable and hateful words and statements" regarding Elizabeth's alleged theft of a silver cup, words uttered loudly and publicly, claimed that Creare's allegations had seriously hurt the family economy. The libel for this cause stipulated that not only was Elizabeth "in numerous ways injured and worsened in the good name, fame and reputation which she had... but also the aforesaid William had lost much gain and profit which he ... would have had and obtained by virtue of the buying, selling and exchanging"—all because of injuries to his wife's honor. The Blandfields gave a precise estimate of their losses, claiming "that they are the worse and have damage to the value of £20."[47]

In spite of the victims' emphasis on the economic and psychological damage wrought by contentious speech, it is not clear that such damage was the primary outcome sought by most scolds. More often they appear interested in controlling the hierarchy of social prestige (and, by extension, power) within the parish. In communities typically made up, in Ingram's description, of "neighbours of medium substance living cheek by jowl," scolds were eager to patrol the social status quo.[48] Hence new arrivals or those recently risen in the social hierarchy were regularly targeted by contentious speakers. When on Palm Sunday 1574 Cicely Goodman brought her husband his sword and cloak, this galled a neighbor enough to cry out, "Look where the naughty pack standeth, for naught she was before she came to the town, and naught she is still."[49] This public assault on Goodman's sexual reputation aimed to challenge the newcomers' flaunted gentility by inscribing it within an implied narrative of sexual misbehavior or perhaps even trade. Other instances of scolds claiming control over social prestige are documented in the numerous pew disputes heard by the church courts. Since church seating effectively functioned as a map of the parish's social hierarchy, pew disputes were essentially contestations of revisions to this map, revisions undertaken by church wardens to accommodate the upwardly mobile. Margery Hopkins of the Oxford parish of Saint Ebbe must have belonged to this group, likely by virtue of a recent marriage to a freeman of the city, and she proudly asserted her newly acquired status during a 1585 church court hearing. She had tried to get Barbara Nicolles to vacate the better part of a seat for her. When Nicolles, who "hathe sytt by the space of v yeares" in the contested seat, refused to budge, Hopkins called her "a basterd," prompting Nicolles's sharp retaliation, "Whosoever saithe that I am a basterde I saye she is a whore of her tong."[50] Arguably the defamatory words exchanged by the women in the midst of evening prayer aimed to strip their targets of the social status that entitled each to the coveted seat. If Nicolles was indeed "a basterd" she would not have had a valid claim to her family's seat; as "a whore of her tong," Hopkins would have failed to measure up to the social norm of the honest matron and thus she too would have been unworthy of the privileged seating.

In discussing the pragmatics of scolding we should note that it was not only female members of the community whose social ranking was challenged, a point to which I shall return later. When a woman from Wymeswold, Leicestershire, called her adversary "Lord Beaumont's whore" and "bid her get her gone to the lords who brought half crowns to her bedside," the lord's reputation did not remain unscathed. Even the moral status of ministers could take a direct hit from contentious speech. For instance, Venera Harwood from the Essex village of Northshoberie was presented for "rayling at [the] vicar in most base and contemptible manner, saying that she would never receave a cupp of salvacion at the hand of so damned a priest; and... comparing him to a dogg, with many other vile and contemptible termes." The libel for the case specified that Harwood persisted "obstinatlie in her malice," and it is plausible that there were those who listened closely to her scathing remarks.[51] In this direct confrontation, as in others, women used contentious speech to assert their view of the moral hierarchy in their communities and showed little consideration for the social privilege of those they degraded.

Gender, Social Authority, and Vocal Agency in Legal Discourse

"Gender," asserts Judith Butler, "is the mechanism through which notions of masculine and feminine are produced and naturalized, but gender might well be the apparatus by which such norms are deconstructed and denaturalized." Normative masculinity and femininity, she goes on to explain, do not "exhaust the semantic field of gender. Whether one refers to 'gender trouble' or 'gender bending,' 'transgender' or 'cross-gender,' one is already suggesting that gender has a way of moving beyond that naturalized binary."[52] Viewed through this theoretical lens, the legal contests over women's scolding can be construed as contests over a naturalized (and thus normative) gender binarism.

On the one hand, the courts could and did uphold normative gender binarism in decisions that cast scolds as bad women. The operative gendering mechanism here was their overtly and negatively feminized aggressive speech. Prompt equations were often drawn between scolding and that unique feminine transgression, whoredom. Among the many who made such connections was Elizabeth Hawle. When on the way to the Chipping Norton market her neighbor Elizabeth Clifton declared Hawle's son a bastard, Hawle immediately called her "a tib of the tonge." In the defamation case initiated by Clifton, at least three witnesses testified that a "tib" was a synonym of "whore."[53] Like many of her contemporaries for whom "a tib of the tongue" was an idiomatic phrase, Hawle readily equated her opponent's verbal explosiveness with the whore's socially injurious inability to control her insatiable body. Like whores, scolds were viewed as hyperwomen, their overbearing gendered performances threatening to unhinge social hierarchies and proper social subjectivity.

Because of their aggressive vocal agency, these hyperwomen were imagined as usurping male moral authority and social status; they were said to destroy social relationships, others' lives, and their own. As I posited earlier, scolding was perceived to tear asunder the social fabric of families and neighborhoods and to jeopardize the reputation and economic well-being of its targets. Witnesses also spun narratives about the scold as the malicious, irrational, sometimes crazed obverse of the (normative) social subject. This set of perceptions of scolding concurs with the sermon writers' allegorical descriptions of the fiery tongue as capable of poisoning speaker, addressee, and social environment. Accordingly the symbolism of the courts' punishments—public penance and (for defamers who refused public penance) excommunication, "ducking," carting, or bridling—makes it abundantly clear that no tenable social place was allowed for voluble hyperfemininity.

However, not all of the narratives generated during defamation cases cast scolding in such a dark light. A number of them portray the scolds' impressive vocal performatives as morally authoritative and even socially protective. Earlier I noted that women resorted to verbal violence to protect their own position within the delicate balance of social prestige in the parish. They were equally capable of couching their contentious speech as beneficial more generally for the institution of the family or their larger community. Such renditions of contentious speech acts, I would suggest, began to open up socially viable discursive positions for voluble women and to subvert normative gender binarism.

As surprising as it may appear, in these accounts of verbal contentiousness scolds get effectively transgendered through their speech, in Butler's sense of gender as a process and "a practice of improvisation within a scene of constraint," always done "with and for another." Transgendering entailed acting and being viewed not as hyperfeminine but as femininely impulsive *and* masculinely choleric, femininely unrestrained *and* masculinely authoritative. Butler contends that undoing normative gender restrictions can open up a new conception of identity "that has greater livability as its aim."[54] Indeed some legal narratives of scolding women appear to open up new conditions of livability for their transitionally gendered speaking subjects. In these narratives scolds occupy positions in the urban soundscapes as prominent as they are morally authoritative, positions of the kind typically reserved for socially privileged masculine speakers.

This was partly a function of sheer acoustic dominance. Scolds had no trouble raising their voices and nonverbal "accompaniment" above the daily noises of early modern neighborhoods. The sounds they made were sometimes described as "ringing." A witness of an outburst by one clamorous woman asserted that "all which were within a furlong of her might well hear"; it was also testified that "she hath made the street to ring." A London scold actually sounded a horn to attract an audience. In another case a male defendant, having been publicly called a "pricklouse," declared the woman who had attempted such defamatory counteraction "a tantarband and a tantarbawde whore."[55] His alliterative assault equated the sound of his opponent's voice with "tantara," or fanfare. As this sound is usually associated with military masculinity, its use as a descriptor of "whore" destabilizes the unambiguous gendering of the noun. Bells, horns, and fanfare are all acoustic signals with masculine associations, sharing the important function of warning. As R. Murray Schafer explains, in psychological terms signals "are figures rather than ground."[56] As psychological figures they compel conscious listening and restrict the possibility that listeners could "fortify" their ears against offensive speech.

Bell ringing and fanfare had other important associative meanings for the communities in which they were sounded. "The church bell," Schafer explains, "originally maintained both a centripetal and centrifugal function, for it was designed both to frighten away evil spirits and also to attract the ear of God and the attention of the faithful." As a community signal that "radiates sound uniformly in all directions," the bell marked the territory of the early modern parish. It called *in* the faithful neighborhood to services, but also served as an alarm signal for people to go *out* of their homes in cases of city fires, floods, and other catastrophes. The specifically directed and commanding sound of the horn was associated with the army bugle and the announcement of important events. Schafer traces the history of the horn to "a kind of magical device, used by early men to frighten evil demons. It was an aggressive, hideous-sounding instrument with supernatural capabilities."[57] The "tantara" or fanfare-producing trumpet is what the Hebrew Bible terms the shofar, one of the most ancient of wind instruments. The Lacanian psychoanalytic critic Mladen Dolar writes that the shofar is sounded "most often when a covenant has to be established or reasserted, the most significant being the moment of foundation of the Law when Moses receives the tablets of the Law on Mount Sinai." He goes on to explain that on this occasion the overpowering sound of the shofar remained inscrutable (literally, sense-less) to the people, but that it nevertheless performed as the indubitably present and terrifying voice of the Law underpinning the letter discernible only to Moses.[58] Associating contentious public speech with bell and wind instrument sounds amounts to an acknowledgment, albeit a resentful one, not only of its acoustic prominence but also of its important communal functions, such as warning against danger, mobilizing a neighborhood against it, and sounding the *voice* of the Law that underpins its legible articulation.

When an acoustic signal gets repeated frequently, it can turn into a soundmark, described by Schafer as "a community sound which is unique or possesses qualities which make it specially regarded or noticed by people in that community."[59] The narrow lanes and inner courtyards of the city, where stone walls reflected and magnified chiding voices, were extremely susceptible to sound marking by scolding. This was likely the case of the carpenter's yard in the London parish of Stepney, where Ann Hooper, Elizabeth Eaton, and Elizabeth Willey multiplied words, month after month, about each other's pox marks, the fatherhood of their children, and the preferential rate given to Flemings for sexual services. The relentless scolding of Catherine Barnaby, the Dickinsons' nemesis who haunted their street in St. Albans for seven years, is another good candidate for a neighborhood soundmark. Certainly the proverbially famous ringing voices of the Billingsgate oyster women were a trade soundmark of the market. Nor was this the only commercial area in London sound-marked in this fashion. A 1699 farcical dialogue dramatized "a Great Famous Scolding-match Between Four Remarkable Scolding Fish-women of Rosemary-lane, and the Like Number of Basketwomen of Golden-lane, Near Cripplegate." Golden Lane, where the Fortune Theatre stood, and Rosemary Lane, where in 1593 the Merchant Taylors' Company had built almshouses for women, must have been well known to the public for the vocal blasts of the "Tatterdemallions" selling their wares there.[60] Such soundmarks were hardly pleasing to the ear, but they were effective in summoning the communal attention of potential customers.

As scolding women mobilized public attention on issues of immediate importance to families and communities—illegitimate sex, disease, theft, violence—they took on the social role of moral vigilantes, self-appointed upholders of the Law. Scolding attacks, recall, could lead to presentment for disciplinary action in the courts; they also posed a more general threat to the reputation, or "credit," of their targets. I suggest that there were scolds who saw themselves as something other than the unwitting triggers of litigation. In their public performances these voluble women cast themselves as upholders and disbursers of justice, a quasi-masculine role modeled on legal procedure and carried out in the overpowering voice of a conqueror or the maker of divine Law. During church court hearings some scolds successfully continued to play the role of defenders of public virtue.

Cognizant of the importance of moral reputation for the effectiveness of verbal attacks, a number of scolding women assailed their targets' virtue while extolling their own as its polar opposite. For instance, Joan Searles taunted Thomasine Hayward in a manner attentive to both her own moral credibility and the all-important legal notion of proof: "I . . . did never play the whore with John Knights for a wastcoate and Holland smocke." Winifred Bland challenged Elizabeth Hollinshed in a similarly self-righteous fashion: "I never rode 12 myles on a bare horseback nor ever carried a payer of sheetes out of dores to Ned Bird." The attack on Mary Brasbridge's moral virtue was marked by a similar combination of precise realistic detail and exaltation of the scold's own virtue: "I never did as thou hast done, take up my clothes to my navel saying come and occupy me, and if thou once did occupy me, thou wouldest never care for thy wife."[61] Denigrating the moral status of legal opponents and their witnesses was a tried and tested tactic in church court litigation. Its deployment at the very beginning of verbal assault is one of several indications that early modern scolds saw themselves as the voice of the law. Some of their witnesses concurred.

Furthermore some scolds drew explicit connections between their assaults and legal punishments for immoral conduct. Agnes Blenkinsop threatened the singlewoman Margaret Nicolson thus: "Hyte hoore, a whipe and a cart and a franc hoode . . . , waies me [woe is me] for the, my lasse, wenst [wilt thou] have a halpeny halter for the to goo up Gallygait and be hanged?" Alice Flavell declared to her adversary that "she would hunt her up as dog would hunt a hare before she would leave her, and that she would have her whipped at a cart's arse."[62] Both women managed to combine, in the same breath, sexually suggestive contentious speech with specific descriptions of the punitive outcomes of legal action, effectively bracketing the two together.

Not only did scolding women model themselves and their victims as, respectively, judges and defendants in a legal cause; they also cast themselves as champions of the hierarchical order in the family and the neighborhood. One self-appointed defender of the patriarchal family was Mary Bradshew, whose curious verbal assault of Anne Baker in a busy street by the butchers' shambles in Oxford merits analysis. Bradshew, who appears to have known Baker only slightly or not at all, "openly" called her a whore for allegedly coming to Oxford to hang her own husband. A witness recalled Bradshew declaring, "Thou lovest an other man better than thy husband." Later Bradshew explained that Baker had prosecuted her own husband at the assizes. The scold's victim was confused and reportedly asked her assailant, "To whom does thow speake?" Another witness interceded to tell Bradshew, "You know not to whom you speake for this woman . . . is an honest woman." Indeed Baker had never brought her husband to court, although she had a history of quarrels with one William Baker Jr. Perhaps Bradshew took William to be Baker's husband. Her injurious tirade then would appear to have been fashioned as a violent public protest, which rendered an imagined legal action by a wife against her husband as treason and whoring.[63]

When Janet Dalton raised her voice against the man who had caused her falling-out with her husband, she cast him as a threat to her family and his own and as a public health hazard to the neighborhood. According to a witness, the Daltons were invited to one Sergant's house for supper, along with some friends who had been trying to help the family resolve an ongoing quarrel. As the company came upon Sergant in the street, however, Janet avowed "that she wolde nott go to supper with no such vile vyllands as he was" and added, "Falsh vile knave, thou wold have my husband to bring the pox to me as thou brought them to thi wife." She did not back down when Sergant called for witnesses to note her scolding and proceeded to call him "falsh pokye theiff," asserting "that she had said nothing but what she wold prove." Janet was indeed quick to follow up on her verbal assault with a lawsuit, which she brought against Sergant in the Commissary Court of Northumberland.[64]

Like Dalton, the Londoner Mary Sadde lent a double edge to her noisy attack in Horne Alley upon her nemesis Margaret Eddis, whom she called her "husband's whore." In a social atmosphere that, according to Gowing's perceptive analysis, "contained few avenues for condemning male sexual misconduct," Sadde declared to "a great company of people" her outrage that "her husband pawned her goodes and not soe much but her childrens clothes to maintaine" his mistress. Sadde's verbal assault was directed at "the other woman" rather than the adulterous husband. This choice predictably exonerated him from moral responsibility for his adultery but not from economic responsibility for the family. Sadde managed to cast herself as the reluctant guardian of the family economy, pushed into this position by a reckless husband. She went on to present her clamor as protecting the moral integrity of the Horne Alley neighborhood when she claimed that she would cleanse it of a known threat. "She had rousted her [Margaret] out of one place already," Sadde declared, "and yf she staied but till tomorrowe she wold roust her out of this."[65] To those gathered by her riotous speech she portrayed herself as a protector of the economic well-being of her family (her husband was said to have pawned *her* goods and *her* children's clothes) and of the moral well-being of the neighborhood, which she promised to rid of the alleged "whore." Scolding, then, was Sadde's means of making a public claim to economic and moral authority.

Fiery speech enabled women to bring abusive and adulterous husbands to public accountability. When Bridget Jewell, standing by a public pump in the middle of the street, pointed to Alice Bewe and railed that because of this "whore" she had "bene beaten almost blynde . . . these foure yeare," she was making a public claim about domestic violence even though the ostensible target of her violent speech was, once again, "the other woman." Her husband attempted to silence her, but she continued, redirecting her verbal assault to him and declaring, "I am the worsde for thee & thy kindred and s[h]albe whilest I lyve."[66] Janet Armestrong may well have been exposing to the public eye another domestic abuser as she exclaimed against John Hall "that he shuld have murdered and put down his two wyfes."[67] As these clamorous women ousted allegedly abusive husbands from their privileged positions as heads of the household, they simultaneously claimed the high moral ground as champions of the Reformation ideology of the companionate marriage.

Some scolds apparently felt secure enough in their position of moral authority to present a direct challenge to male social superiors whom they considered a personal or public threat. Among them was Jane Higges, who leveled multiple public accusations against Robert Williamson that he would have had her "to have bene naught with [him] & to have bene [his] whore." Higges used her fiery tongue to raise public awareness of Williamson's sexual advances, and she also undercut his sense of entitlement, sarcastically calling him "Sir Jacke" and "[w]ry Jack."[68] Furthermore she sought a powerful ally for her verbal campaign when she complained about Williamson to the local aristocrat, Lord Norris. Unlike female sexuality, routinely subjected to public surveillance in the era, male sexual misconduct was rarely a matter of public concern. Not so for this scold, whose boisterous public exposure of Williamson's attempts to turn her into a whore amounted to a quasi-masculine claim to social and moral authority.

Scolding women like Bradshew, Dalton, Sadde, Armestrong, and Higges were careful to give their contentious speech the veneer of moral respectability and social utility, but there were those who did not care a bit whether they alienated entire communities. For them the thrill of voicing what they may have perceived as the Law must have outweighed long-term considerations of social prestige and authority. Among such arguably sociopathic scolds was Margaret Challoner of Llandilo vaure, Wales. Sentenced to public penitence for scolding, she reportedly proclaimed that "it was none, but whores and rogues that caused her to be called in 'church.'" She then went on to evoke, in the enargaic fashion of scolding, an impressive image of the destruction that she was ready to wreak, declaring that "if she had bin present in church when she was called she should have gone nere to bre(ak) beene like to have broke his head, the old rogue." As the witness providing this information explained, by "the old rogue" Challoner meant "the curate of the parish."[69]

Margaret Jones of the Essex town of Alveley seems to have been similarly oblivious to the price she would pay for pitting herself against her community. When the minister reproved her for cursing in church, she lashed out at him, "sayinge God's wounds she would sweare in spite of his teeth; as she used much swearinge, so she layde violent hands and smote the vicar ... and followed him swearinge most devilishly, from one side of the towne to the other." Shortly after this mad chase, Jones "presumed to come to the [communion] table and there used her tongue, to the greate offence of all that were present; and at length when the communion was done, she stayed the going forth of the vicar, and rayled on him most shamfully."[70] The witness's evaluation of Jones's animatives as "devilish" pits her against the godly community whose ritual revitalization she sabotaged. Perhaps the parishioners refrained from interfering with Jones's verbal and physical violence because they perceived her actions as demonic, or they may have been struck by the potency of her voice. Challoner and Jones certainly challenged gender norms with their offensive vocal performatives and animatives, but it is hard to imagine that they managed to lay claim to moral authority or to shore up the conditions of livability of their lives.

Church court records yield a host of varied narratives about scolding, complicating an impression of this type of violent speech as uniformly uncontrollable and unreasonable. Scolding was portrayed as a distraction from daily activities, an interruption of sleep, a cause for public embarrassment, an affront to one's honor, a devilish or frenzied action. However, it was also seen as a puzzle, an incentive to call to account long-term moral offenders, a claim to moral authority, a social service, even something approximating the voicing of divine Law. It could limit, render impossible, or, conversely, enhance the livability of the lives of those who deployed it. On one end of the gender continuum, it was seen as a normative gendering mechanism that rendered garrulous women as negative exempla of hyperfemininity. On the other, it was perceived as opening up livable possibilities for a transgendered subjectivity of the female-to-male spectrum. The latter type of narratives from the church court depositions appears to contradict the spontaneous feminizing powers, which the authors of sermons and other religious texts attributed to the fiery tongue. In the religious discourse "hot" words were portrayed as threatening the masculinity of their speakers; in the legal discourse they were sometimes credited with the capacity to transgender female speakers. In both discursive fields offensive speech comes across as a vocal phenomenon capable of undoing gender binarism. This strong performative potential, along with the power to confound binary gender distinctions, made scolding immediately appealing to the theatrical cross-dressers of the early modern stage.

3

Unquiet Women on the Early Modern Stage

Given the public attention to women's contentious speech demonstrated in sermons and church court litigation, it comes as no surprise that women's "fiery" speech featured prominently in early modern drama as well. In the terms of humoral physiology, it was a hot issue. Like the sermons on the tongue, dramatizations of contentious women, typically, "shrewish" wives, explored the challenges of containing their fiery speech. Such exploration involved creating the recognizable stereotype of the shrew and pitting her against another stereotype, that of the shrew tamer, a part that provided exciting acting opportunities for the companies' male leads. But if character stereotypes propelled the dramatic action, performance clues suggested by the play text as well as the metatheatrical nature of plot development in the shrew plays afforded performance opportunities that complicated and questioned stereotypical gender binaries.[1] Like the oral stories in church court depositions, the plays brought out the protean power of speech to put to the test the hierarchical gender binary and offered live models of gender fluidity. So yes, in the ever-popular stage reiterations of shrew-taming narratives discussed in this chapter, "disciplined" garrulous women are reconciled with the families whose hierarchies they troubled, much in the vein of a masculinist wish-fulfilling fantasy. However, the nature of these stage reconciliations—illusory, arbitrary, or provisional—compromises the viability of the conciliatory mechanisms and opens up unscripted possibilities for the garrulous female characters. This in turn allows for nuanced acting opportunities and multiple ways of pleasing diverse theater-goers.

"Gender," Butler argues in a much quoted passage, "ought not to be construed as a stable identity or locus of agency from which various acts follow; rather, gender is an identity tenuously constituted in time, instituted in an exterior space through *a stylized repetition of acts.*"[2] The stylization of negative femininity through the many "citations" of scolding in performances of popular ballads and early modern plays must have been hugely influential. Ballads like "The Cruell Shrow: or, The Patient Mans Woe," "The Scolding Wife," "The new German Doctor; or an infallible cure for a scolding wife," "My wife will be my master; or, The Married-Mans Complaint against his Unruly Wife," "A Pleasant new Ballad you here may behold, How the Devill, though subtle, was guld by a scold," "A Merry Jest of a Shrewd and Curst Wife Lapped in Morels' Skin, for her Good Behaviour," and "The Scolding Wives Vindication: or, An Answer to the Cuckold's Complaint" all concur in portraying contentious speech as the hallmark of the unruly wife of the era.[3] Popular shrew plays, too, localized feminine contentions speech in the family. This is the case in *John John the Husband, Tyb His Wife, and Sir John the Priest* (based on a tale of medieval origins and first published in 1533), *Tom Tyler and His Wife* (a Tudor shrew farce of sufficient interest to early modern readers to merit printing as late as 1661), *The Taming of a Shrew* (printed in 1594, 1596, and 1607), its close relative by Shakespeare, *The Taming of the Shrew* (thought to have been performed as early as 1589, first published in the 1623 folio of Shakespeare's works, and reprinted in a 1631 quarto and subsequent folios), and the response to Shakespeare's comedy by John Fletcher, *The Woman's Prize or the Tamer Tamed* (ca. 1611).[4] The didactic value of these plays—that indispensable component of the early modern aesthetic of profit and pleasure—is perhaps best summed up by Sander the Player, from the anonymous *Taming of a Shrew*, who advertised his troupe's upcoming performance thus: "'Tis a good lesson for us, my lord, for us that are married men" (Induction 1.64). What was the lesson with which shrew-taming dramatizations engaged their audiences?

If popular literary texts agree in making scolding the distinctive speech act of the discontented wife, they diverge widely on how tenable they imagine the scold's identity to be in the long term. The desperate husbands in the play *John John the Husband, Tyb His Wife, and Sir John the Priest* and the ballads "The Cruell Shrow" and "My wife will be my master" believe this identity to be unassailable, barring divine intervention. As the speaker of the last ballad puts it:

Should I live as many Years
as never did king Nector [*sic*],
Yet do I greatly stand in fear,
my Wife would be my Master.

In the play *Tom Tyler and His Wife* the formidable scold Strife verbally and physically abuses her husband nearly to suicide, and that after a brutal beating by the railer Tom Tyler, who was supposed to silence her once and for all:

Ah, whoreson dolt! thou whoreson, subtle colt!
Son of an ox! Owe like you your knocks?
The piles and the pox, and the poison in box
Consume such a knave, and bring him to grave!
The crows and the pies, and the very flesh flies
Desire to plague thee. In faith, I will plague thee!⁵

In the play's final scene the raucous trio of chiding husband, his railing friend, the bully Tom Tylor, and Strife the scolding wife are enjoined to a friendly transformation by the character of Patience. Husband and wife kiss in reconciliation, but when Patience calls for a friendly kiss by Tom Tylor, Strife interjects, "I would he had kissed both the ends."⁶ It takes the entrance of Destiny—a divine intervention if there ever was one—to enforce a pledge of agreement. In "A Pleasant new Ballad" the shrew joyfully "kickt and prickt" the devil (who had transformed himself into a black horse) even as he tried to terrify her with the sights of the "paines" of hell "Ordain'd for Scolds so base." After she slit his ears with a knife, he rushed to return her home, "For hell will not be troubled / With such an earthly scold." The scold from the ballad "The Scolding Wives Vindication" eventually drops her noisy contentiousness, but not until she has substituted a husband who "nothing at all would do" with a sexually satisfying partner. Similarly in Fletcher's play *The Tamer Tamed* the "crying" country and city women who rally to the support of the protagonist Maria, heaving "stool on stool" and flinging "main pot lids," not only force Petruchio to ratify Maria's conditions of their marriage but also get to satisfy their appetite for wine, food, and pleasure (2.3.56, 2.5.150–68). Comparing "the shrewd Wives that are, or shall be planted in New-fond-land" to "mad-men, Drunkards, Children, or a Foole," the balladeer Robert Hayman concludes, "Mad men are bound; Drunkards are laid to sleepe: / Foles beaten are; Toyes Children quiet keepe: / I wish unruly Shrewes were turnd to Sheepe."[7] Plays and ballads like these suggest that, unlike other disturbers of the peace, a scold's identity was believed to be impervious to social pressure. In them, disciplining a scold remained a matter of wishful thinking.[8]

Other popular texts, however, portray scolding women who are "tamed," or broken, in the aftermath of physical and psychological violence. This is the case of the wife in the ballad "A Merry Jest," who is incarcerated in a basement, beaten bloody, and sewn up into the salted hide of Morel the horse. Another ballad, "The Scolding Wife," tells of a husband who calls on his friends to torture his outspoken wife. The men tear her clothes and hair and wring her arms "till out the blood did gush"; after chaining her in a dark house, the husband proclaims her mad and calls on the neighbors to help with the recovery of her wits. In the ballad "A Caution for Scolds" the wife is "conquered" by a "skillful Doctor" who binds her to a bed, shaves her head, lets her blood, and threatens to treat her "fits" by bleeding her further, this time by cutting her tongue. The "treatment" appears to be a development of the methods of a sinister German doctor featured in other ballads, who, after practicing in Poland and Spain, "cured" seven hundred London scolds in seven weeks by taking out "the Sting of the Tongue."[9]

"Treatable" or not, in these popular portrayals scolding is stereotyped as the conventional speech of the unruly wife. It solidifies a gender norm. Still, as Butler theorizes, "the practice by which gendering occurs ... is a compulsory practice, a forcible production, but not for that reason fully determining. To the extent that gender is an assignment, it is an assignment which is never quite carried out according to expectation."[10] Certainly this was true of dramatizing gender on the early modern stage. As the Shakespeare performance critic David Mann suggests, for theater practitioners a stereotype, especially one as simple as that of the shrew, "aids narrative compression and allows instant character recognition." But while stereotypes misrepresent and demean, Mann explains, for actors they present a challenge for elaboration, heightened emotion, and improvisatory animation. For the professional actors of the era dealing with a fast-changing repertoire, familiar stereotypes offered energizing challenges for exploration and improvisation. I would argue that experienced dramatists engaged similarly with the character stereotype of the shrew. Rather than using it as a simple building block of character and plot, they considered its creative potential and, as Mann writes, combined "traditional iteration with development and surprise."[11] To do otherwise would have alienated female audiences—something that playwright-shareholders had little financial incentive to do. In this chapter I demonstrate how the stereotype of the shrewish wife as developed in Shakespeare's *Taming of the Shrew* and its close relative, the anonymous *Taming of a Shrew*, resists full determination in the performed outcome of the play texts. Even though these plays were advertised through their titles as social satires dramatizing the "righting" of bad women, they end up dramatizing the provisional and illusory understanding of such "righting" and unsettling the stereotype of the scold.

Shrew Management

Audience expectations of hyperfeminine verbal violence and its public containment are activated as early as the titles of the two *Shrew* plays. But scolding as introduced in the Induction scenes is ambiguously gendered. Thus the opening salvo "You whoreson drunken slave" (Induction 1.1) in *A Shrew* is issued by the male tapster. True, in Shakespeare's play the drunk Christopher Sly is promptly countered by the Hostess; yet her threat, "A pair of stocks, you rogue!" (Induction 1.2), frames female verbal violence as congruent with the power of the law, not as challenging social order.

It is when the action of the *Shrew* plays crosses into the play-within-the-play that audiences are introduced to Kate's reputation as a scold and the expectation that she will get her comeuppance. She begins as a stereotypical character of the kind useful for policing "the gender boundary, pillorying women who transgress accepted norms," precisely the kind of female part that Mann claims was popular in theater productions since the mid-sixteenth century.[12] The stereotype is established before Kate gets to utter a single word on stage. In fact in *A Shrew* the discussion of her reputation as a "devilish scold" blatantly contradicts her decorous and silent public appearance on the way to church, taunting audience anticipation of her verbal violence (1.1.68). The "blunt"-spoken Ferando (Petruchio's counterpart in the anonymous play) is quick to declare a victory over "sharp"-tongued Kate in the decisively underwhelming courtship scene. Yet even as Kate protests against marrying "this brain-sick man," she confides in an aside that she's tired of having "lived too long a maid" and is ready to "match him too" (170–71). Her decision to "match" Ferando may be a solution for the stagnant marriage market in Athens and can be interpreted as intent to reform her ways. Yet between the pun of "match" on "rival," or its now obsolete significance of "to encounter as an adversary, to fight," and Sander's laughing pronouncement to Ferando's face that his master "spoke like an ass to her," expectations that Kate's scolding will cease upon the "match" appear doubtful (192).[13] In Shakespeare's play Gremio declares that Katharina is "too rough" for him and, in a rare salvo of punning witticism, says she is one not to court but "to cart" (1.1.54–55).[14] By the time Katharina addresses her father with the respectful "I pray you, sir," she has already been denied participation in the romantic plot and deemed a better fit for a prospective narrative of legal correction. However, the incongruity of having the legal punishment of carting threatened by Gremio's impotent pantaloon character raises questions about the viability of containing contentious speech, similarly to the anonymous play. This theme is poignantly revisited in the closing scene of *The Taming of the Shrew*.

Historically carting was indeed a punishment used to regulate the sexual and verbal transgressions of women. City, borough, and manorial courts leet of the late medieval and early modern eras used it for convicted prostitutes and scolds, a choice that matched perfectly the semantic ambiguity of the early modern notion of the "tib" (or whore), who could be either "a tib of the tongue" or "a tib of her body," and, as church court testimonies suggested, for a number of good Englishmen was both.[15] The close relative of carting was "cucking" (or ducking), specifically reserved for scolds. Though symbolically effective, carting and cucking had the potential of spinning out of control. Certainly they were not the kinds of rituals that boded well for the public peace. Therefore the mitigation-bent church courts, which heard the bulk of the cases related to scolding and defamation, preferred the similarly humiliating yet much more controlled punishment of public penance for convicted offenders.[16]

In the two *Shrew* plays the management of the woman with the fiery tongue bears some broad similarities to church courts' actions. Gremio's pipe dream of punishing Shakespeare's Katharina by carting never pans out, but in both plays Kate is subjected to a series of public humiliations. Each of these occasions functions as public testimony of her verbal contentiousness, equating it with negative femininity. We recognize testimonies of this nature from depositions in church court defamation suits of the sort discussed in the previous chapter. Shakespeare's Hortensio publicizes that Katharina has a bad reputation throughout Padua "for her scolding tongue" (1.2.94); Polidor from *A Shrew* is considerably more emphatic when he declares that "he that hath her shall be fretted so / As good be wedded to the devil himself, / For such a scold as she did never live" (1.1.50–52). Ferando concurs. So does Shakespeare's Petruchio, even though he is newly arrived in Padua and has never witnessed Kate speak: "I *know* she is an irksome brawling scold" (1.2.178, emphasis added). On the wedding day Petruchio's lateness leads Katharina to believe that his proclamation of the wedding banns was nothing but a public ridicule of her reputation as a scold: "Now must the world point at poor Katharine" (3.2.18). When the groom finally arrives, his attire described as "base" in *A Shrew* (2.1.142) and "mad" in Shakespeare's play (3.2.114), to say nothing of his notoriously diseased horse, further demean Kate as at best worthy of the craziest of husbands. At worst, as LaRue Love Sloan suggests, the image of "a horse that, notwithstanding its dropsical diseases, has repeatedly fought the bridle and refused to submit to 'the manage' of the rider" functions as a "preemptive Skimmington ride," the public shaming ritual used to punish husbands unable to control their wives by having them paraded through town seated backward on a horse or ass. In this scenario Kate would be publicly declared an unmanageable shrew even before the wedding.[17] Along similar lines Ferando in the anonymous play explains that his ragged costume is meant to provide protection against Kate's prospective assault upon him: "When my wife and I are married once, / She's such a shrew, if we should once fall out / She'll pull my costly suits over mine ears" (2.1.114–16). The wedding ceremony itself, ruthlessly botched, promises to go down in Paduan history as commemorating the comeuppance of the scold, for "such a mad marriage never was before" (3.2.172).

The narratives and spectacles that publicize Kate as a stereotype of negative femininity to the community at large have their domestic counterparts in the household.[18] Take, for instance, Curtis's inquiry preceding his mistress's arrival at Petruchio's house, "Is she so hot a shrew as she's reported?" (4.1.15), or Grumio's story about her impromptu "cucking" in a "miry" place when her horse collapsed, pinning her underneath (54). In *A Shrew* Polidor's boy raises the specter of Kate's reputation as he taunts

Ferando's servant Sander: "How wilt thou do, now thy master's married? Thy mistress is such a devil as she'll make thee forget thy eating quickly; she'll beat thee so" (2.2.21–23). Later another servant of Ferando's, Tom, confirms Kate's reputation: "They say she's a plaguey shrew" (3.1.5). Such "evidence" of Kate's verbal and physical violence (she is a scold because she has been repeatedly discussed, ridiculed, or punished as one by her husband and the community) may be considered circular today but was convincing by early modern standards. It is informed by and reinforces normative gender binarism, according to which women wielding verbal power were stigmatized as unnatural usurpers of male authority.

On stage and off, the circulation of stories about shrew management by public humiliation not only identified but also controlled female contentious speech. To an extent. Dramatic action (like church court testimonies) shows how shaming a woman as a scold can indeed forestall her lashing back verbally. To charge back at accusations of scolding, after all, is to demonstrate their aptness. Thus in *A Shrew* Kate remains remarkably composed when Valeria, disguised as a music tutor, urges her to play her music lesson and suggests that if the sound of music has tamed "savage beasts," it may affect similarly "she whom nought can please" (2.1.1–6). Ignoring the thinly veiled insult, Kate responds matter-of-factly, "It is not matter whether I do or no, / For, trust me, I take no great delight in it" (9–10). It is only after Valeria proceeds with an unseemly sexual joke that Kate loses her composure. Shakespeare's Katharina likewise appears to be cognizant of the need to restrain her speech in public. When Hortensio publicly declares that she would not find a mate unless she "were of gentler, milder sort," she couches her outrage as a conditional statement rendered by a hypothetical third person:

I'faith, sir, you shall never need to fear;
Iwis it is not halfway to her heart.
But *if it were*, doubt not her care should be
To comb your noddle with a three-legged stool
And paint your face, and use you like a fool.
(1.1.61–65, emphasis added)

Quite apart from the constraining effect on the scold, early on in Shakespeare's play shrew-shaming stories upholding gender binarism are shown to have additional social benefits. They defuse the interpersonal, interfamilial, and domestic tensions wrought by Katharina's sharp tongue. They provide some emotional compensation to the Paduan "mates" for the verbal and physical abuses they endure. They establish the head of the household, Petruchio, as a capable rhetorician, one who knows how to shape speech and spectacle as stinging offenses and yet manages to tread clear of the crime of publicly defaming a Baptista daughter even as he "ropes in" his problem wife.

But public shrew shaming is also shown to have its limits and liabilities. As the plays' "tamers" (Ferando, Valeria, Sander in the anonymous play; Hortensio, Gremio, Grumio, Petruchio in Shakespeare's) assault Kate's honor or delight in imagining or plotting physical assaults against her, they act as contentious speakers themselves, even if they stop short of defamation. Furthermore their verbal assaults on "the shrew" threaten the communal peace. As ministers preaching on the capacity of the "raylinge tongue" to "beget, cherish, and increase publicke Discord" knew too well, responding to contentious speech in kind inevitably aggravated this socially destructive phenomenon.[19] Particularly problematic would have been the fanning of the flames of discord by servants in the two *Shrew* plays, notwithstanding its comedic effect.

In their sermons, as we saw in chapter 1, men of the cloth struggled unsuccessfully to find a comprehensive solution to the problem of the fiery feminine tongue. They lamented the weakness of will power or the sheer frenzy that rendered the tongue uncontrollable and called on God to tame the "unruly member." Confronted with scolding and defamation suits in the parishes, the ecclesiastical courts offered a pragmatic solution to the problem: the sentence of public penance. Though not frequent (most defamation cases never reached a verdict), penances are described with painstaking precision in court verdicts. Successfully performed, a penance reintegrated into the Christian community the perilous rebel against social hierarchies (and her family). Refusal to perform resulted in the excommunication of the guilty party. Thus whether the offender was welcomed back into the fold or expelled, social peace was declared. Like shrew-shaming storytelling, the textual protocols of the penance reinforced normative gender binarism that denied outspoken women vocal authority. Ironically, however, penances relied on women's voices to institute the social peace. And unlike verbal protocols, voices were as unreliable as were their auditory contexts. The last scene in the *Shrew* plays aptly dramatizes the difficulties of orchestrating a penance.

The notion of penance is explicitly introduced in Shakespeare's play by the old pantaloon Gremio. Not long after suggesting that Katharina should be carted, he goes on to protest that Bianca's confinement within Baptista's house would make her "bear the penance of [Katharina's] tongue," while a penance is more appropriate for Baptista's elder daughter, "this fiend of hell" (1.1.89, 88). But Gremio does not initiate a legal process, let alone pursue it to its end. As long as Katharina is taken out of the marriage market, where she vehemently publicizes the inadequacies of eligible bachelors, no Paduan appears too eager to press charges against a Minola daughter, whether she bruises their egos or breaks their pates. In both plays Petruchio too appears to be as aware as any litigious Londoner of the ultimate need for a broad social reconciliation with his contentious wife, or else the reign he has so "politicly begun" would quickly prove troublesome (4.2.157).[20] Considered in this light, Gremio's hunch about the benefits of a penance (though not of carting) appears to be close to the mark after all. Among the available means of managing Kate's fiery tongue, a public penance comes across as a good reconciliation strategy. A fully fleshed ecclesiastical court scene, of course, goes neither with the foreign setting of the shrew plays nor with the regulations of the master of revels. Still the final scenes in the two plays bear distinct ritualistic similarities to staging the penance that would have been exacted of a convicted scold. In both church court ritual and the plays' scenes, the offense is summed up and renounced and the social reintegration of the penitent shrew acknowledged.

The most prominent event in the last act of the anonymous play and Shakespeare's is Kate's long and carefully attended speech, a speech whose language is heavily indebted to the church court-mandated ritual of the penance. But in the penance scene Kate does not undo her female subjectivity, as Lynda Boose contends, nor is she ultimately transformed into what Pamela Allen Brown describes as a "second Grissel." She does not, pace Emily Detmer, "like a victim of the Stockholm syndrome, . . . [deny] her own feelings in order to bond with her abuser." The final speech does not slot her securely into the hierarchical order, per Gary Schneider's interpretive model. Nor is Kate's rhetorical performance "little more than property in the leading actor's bravura," as the latter presumably basks in the demonstration of Ferando's/Petruchio's effective taming methods, as Mann suggests.[21] Functionally Kate's final speech turns out not to be a penance after all, even though textually it resembles one. Two factors contribute to this effect: in Shakespeare's *Taming of the Shrew* the performance clues embedded in the speech, which, I suggest, exceeds the normative vocal constraints of gender binarism; in the anonymous *Shrew* play the framing of the scene and the plot parallels this framing generates.

The Ritual of the Penance

To gain a sense of the way Kate's public penance fails to fulfill the function of its script, we must first analyze the performative qualities of this ritual. They can be derived from the painstakingly precise descriptions in the legal documentation of the church courts, worth quoting at some length. In October 1621 the archdeaconry court of Nottingham stipulated:

> The said Elizabeth Tuttie shalbe present in the church of Mattersey aforesaid at Morninge prayer upon the Sundaye nexte followinge the receipte heereof & then & theare havinge a white sheet about her ~~& a white rodde in her hande bare headed bare legged & bare footed~~ shall ~~kneele~~ stand on somme forme in the sighte of the congregacion till the Gospell be reade & a sermon or homilie ag[ainst] [MS torn] & sclanderers & [MS folded] & then and theare shall saye after the minister as here followeth
>
> Good people whereas I forgettinge my duetie to almightie God by my evill life have given occasion to be presented for a greate disturber of my neighbours & speciallie of my Minister beinge my nexte neighboure & for a notorious swearer & greate curser of my owne husbande & children & for my prophaninge of the Sabaoth by bakinge I doe here before you all acknowledge & confese my faulte & am righte hartelie sorie for the same beseeching god and you all whome I have heerebye offended not onelie to forgive me & take example by this my punishment not to offende in the like but also to ioyne with me in hertie prayer to the throne of the almightie for the assistance of his holie spiritte that I never doe the like againe sayinge as our saviour Christe hath taughte us *Our father which art in heaven etc.*

And she is [to] certifie the performance heereof under the hands of th[e M]inister & churchwardens at the church of Eastretford the xxxth of this instant October together with thease presents Given the ixth of October 1621.[22]

This court sentence specifies not only the time, place, and text of the penance but also the "costuming" of the offender, her gestures and body actions, and where the punishment would fit in the order of the church service. The legal formulae prescribed for Tuttie's sentence are instructive. She was to wear a white sheet but was spared the white rod, uncovered head, and bare feet required of, say, penitent adulterers. A sentence issued by the same court for the convicted male defamer Charles Shawe calls for similar "linen apparel." Neither Tuttie nor Shawe were ordered to kneel before the congregation. The female offender is required to "stand on some forme," while the male is not. Possibly this was because, unlike Tuttie, Shawe was tall enough to be visible to the entire congregation. Other offenders were explicitly instructed to utter their confessions "with a loud voice," again likely to ensure that their penance was audible to the entire congregation.[23]

In both Tuttie's and Shawe's cases the content of the penance is carefully synchronized with the theme of the respective Sunday service. Shawe's recitation was to follow "the reading of c. 3 of the Epistle of St James" about the fiery tongue, while Tuttie's was to fit in after the Gospel reading and a homily whose title, not completely legible in the manuscript, appears similar to the crown-endorsed "Homelie against Contencion and Braulynge," discussed in chapter 1. Furthermore each penance script seems designed not only to acknowledge specific details about the offense but to connect to the focus of the service in which it was inscribed. Thus Shawe was enjoined to apologize "for slaundering one Bartram Midforde, namely in that I called him openly 'beggerly harlot and cutthrote,' sainge that he was a 'covitous snowge, and such as he by Godd's worde aughte to be weded out of the Coomenwelthe.'" This detailed personal apology was to be followed by language loaded with biblical references. "I acknowledge," Shawe was to say, "that thus to slaunder my Christian brother is a heinous offence, first towards God, who haithe straightly forbidden it in his holy lawes, accomptinge it to be a kynde of murderinge of my neighbour and threatninge to punyshe it with hell fire and the losse of the kyngdome of heaven."[24] The wording here is reminiscent of both the story in Numbers 14:36–37, where Moses's slanderers are stricken by the plague of God, and of the familiar image of the tongue as "set on the fire of hell" from James's epistle, which the congregation would have heard immediately prior to Shawe's penance.

Similarly after Tuttie publicly confessed her offenses and apologized for them, she was to offer a prayer, in which she was to be joined by the parishioners "for the assistance of [the] holie spiritte that I never doe the like agayne." The inherent difficulty of curtailing "bitternesse, anger, railing and blasphemy" would have been underscored in the homily preceding her penance. The communal prayer, on the other hand, appears designed to function as the kind of response enjoined in the culmination of a homily like the one "agaynst contencion and braulynge": "Above all thynges kepe peace and unite: bee no peace breakers, but peace makers."[25]

Carefully orchestrated in this manner, the church ritual of the public penance amounted to a resounding declaration of the restored communal peace. Conditions for this peace varied. The one constant was that offenders bore the financial burden for reconciling the community. Having lost their legal case, they were responsible for compensating the witnesses brought in by both sides and for all other court expenses. The price they paid in humiliation is not to be ignored. Some courts demanded a straightforward promise that offenders would refrain from divisive scolding in the future. Such was the wording chosen by the Consistory Court of Ely, which in 1595 prescribed that Elizabeth Bowltell and Katherine Oliver would end their respective penances by promising "by God's help never to offend hereafter in the like againe."[26] The Durham court that sentenced Charles Shawe made provisions for a more elaborate promise: "I fully intende to amende my outeragious tonge and wilfull behaviour, as maye please Almightie God, satisfye the Quenes lawes, and tourne to yur example and myne owne sowles health."[27] The language of this penance suggests an idealized image of a parish of law-abiding and morally exemplary believers, capable of providing the peaceful support needed for healing the offender's soul. The implication is that without the example of the godly community, the transgressor's intent to keep the peace may not suffice. Elizabeth Tuttie's penance ends by having her lead the congregation in the Lord's Prayer, the ultimate communal peace declaration. It appears, then, that in spite of the abject position in which church court sentences cast convicted scolds and defamers, the penance performed by these offenders was ceremonially indispensable for inaugurating the public peace. Tuttie's example indicates that in some cases, the script of the penance went as far as supplanting the abject part of the offender by the speech act of Pauline ministry.

Katharina's Subversive Penance

The final speech of Shakespeare's Katharina is certainly ceremonial. Its whopping forty-four lines are delivered at the culmination of the long-delayed wedding feast supposed to usher in the domestic and the larger public peace: the new peace in Baptista's household now that the daughters have been married off, the hard-won peace in Petruchio's household, the peace among the various competitors for Bianca's hand, between masters and servants, between generations, between Paduans and outsiders. Katharina has been called in by the men who have testified publicly against her and judged her a scold; she has been given a prompt: "I charge thee tell these headstrong women / What duty they do owe their lords and husbands" (5.2.134–35); she is expected to voice the script on wifely obedience familiar to all assembled from scripture, sermons, and conduct books on marriage. As she has been declared (by reputation, if not by court verdict) to be a "brawling scold," this script is also supposed to include a specific apology for her verbal acts of violence. Properly enacted, Katharina's penance would seal the rift between her troubled history and the future, as befits the genre expectations of comedic reconciliation. For spectators of the ritual on stage and off, it would reinforce the moral ideals and gender binarism that they are supposed to uphold.

If she were *not* to deliver her penance, Katharina would face the dramatic equivalent of excommunication, an exclusion from what Ingram calls "the communion of the faithful," in this case the private club of the richly born and well-connected Paduans. She would certainly lose the title of mistress of Petruchio's household, not without damaging its reputation. As Ingram explains, the penalty of excommunication extended to "those who consorted with excommunicates, bought and sold with them, or gave them succour or harbour."[28] Thus Petruchio, having just won the wager, would risk being ostracized unless he annulled the marriage. All of this would not only spoil the romantic plot but explode the myth of social, domestic, and (perhaps most detrimentally for the mercurially minded suitors) the financial well-being of the community celebrated at the wedding. The dramatic stakes in this scene of *The Taming of the Shrew* could not be higher.

Katharina's penance is not Shakespeare's only dramatization of this last resort to suture social rifts, and the precedent does not bode well for hopes riding on the vocal performance of a penitent woman. In a moving scene from *The Second Part of King Henry VI*, Eleanor Cobham, the ambitious wife of the Duke of Gloucester (the second man in the realm after the king), appears on stage dressed in a white sheet, barefoot, with a burning taper in hand and a schedule of her crimes pinned to her back.[29] This elaborately staged public penance and the concomitant exile to the Isle of Man is Eleanor's sentence for treasonable necromancy. A bit earlier in the play she appeared in her garden ordering accomplices to conjure spirits with the purpose of prophesying the death of the king and high-ranking nobles. The seriousness of Dame Eleanor's crime precludes her restoration to court, but her life, her hope for spiritual salvation, and any chance that her husband might have of reclaiming his status at court, to say nothing of the reconciliation among the testy political opponents, all depend on how faithfully and effectively she performs her penance.

Physically Eleanor's performance starts out convincingly: coming up to her husband en route to St. Paul's, she earnestly describes her shame, her tears, and her "deep-felt groans" (2.3.31–33). But contrite suffering—described and enacted according to the implied stage directions—quickly gives way to spiteful sarcasm of the duke and wrathful indignation leveled at the witnesses of her penance:

> Sometime I'll say, I am Duke Humphrey's wife,
> And he a prince and ruler of the land:
> Yet so he ruled and such a prince he was
> As he stood by whilst I, his forlorn duchess,
> Was made a wonder and a pointing-stock
> To every idle rascal follower. (42–47)

Once unleashed, Eleanor's sarcasm quickly escalates into a doomsday prophesy about Gloucester: "But be thou mild and blush not at my shame, / Nor stir at nothing till the axe of death / Hang over thee, as, sure, it shortly will" (50–52). Clearly the penance has disciplined all of Eleanor's body except for her tongue. As for her conscience, she declares herself incapable of a spiritual renewal. Exiting the stage, she proclaims, "My joy is death" (88) and avows that shame has become ingrained in her: "My shame will not be shifted with my sheet: / No, it will hang upon my richest robes / And show itself, attire me how I can" (107–9). Two scenes later Eleanor's prophesy comes true, as the Duke of Gloucester is murdered by order of the enemies she had warned him against. All in all, the episode dramatizes a penance botched by unrestrained female speech. In its outcome, not only is the duchess rendered a social and spiritual antisubject, but the fragile web of courtly allegiances has been ripped apart, undoing her powerful husband.

In its precipitous disintegration, Dame Eleanor's penance recalls that of the historical Mary Frith, better known as Moll Cutpurse, the seventeenth-century transvestite and thief dramatized by Middleton in his comedy *The Roaring Girl* as well as in Nathan Field's comedy *Amends for Ladies*. In a letter to the English ambassador to Venice, the London gentleman John Chamberlain describes how "this notorious baggage ... wept bitterly and seemed very penitent" when she was brought to Paul's Cross, "but yt is since doubted she was maudelin druncke, being discovered to have tipled of three quarts of sacke before she came to her penance." The fiasco of Moll's penance, Chamberlain informs his friend, was partially the result of the poor orchestration of the event. "She had the daintiest preacher or ghostly father that ever I saw in pulpit," writes he, "one Rattcliffe of Brazen Nose in Oxford, a likelier man to have led the revels in some ynne of court then to be where he was, but the best is he did extreem badly, and so wearied the audience that the best part went away, and the rest tarried rather to heare Mall Curpurse then him."[30] The contrast between the "ghostly father" and the bulky penitent, between Moll's noisy wailing and his dainty preaching must have been truly comical. When Chamberlain gloats that "the best is he did extreem badly," it is clear that, like the rest of the crowd, he was more affected by the entertainment value of the performance than by Moll's allegedly successful social integration.

Unlike Eleanor's or Moll's penance, Katharina's is a success, by communal standards. It is dutifully carried out to its finale. It is orderly, albeit with a twist. Most likely Katharina enters wearing the "honest, mean habilments" that Petruchio deemed best for the occasion, having destroyed his wife's fashionable dress in the clothing lesson scene (4.3.162). Given the contrast with the festive attire of the other wedding guests, such costuming would be the functional parallel of the penitent's white sheet. But she also wears a hat—probably the very same "bauble" that Petruchio mocked earlier in front of the haberdasher (82) and to which she clutched as she declared, "Love me or love me not, I like the cap, / And it I will have, or I will have none" (84–85). Confusing the humiliation effect of the penitent's costume, such mixture of styles recalls the "mad attire" worn by Petruchio himself in the wedding scene, especially given the association of baubles with clowns. In the announcement of Petruchio's arrival at his own wedding on a diseased horse, his bizarre mixed-up costume was meant to poke fun at the reputation of the bride. Quick to forestall ideas about the possible significance of Katharina's mixed-up costume, he commands, "Off with that bauble. Throw it underfoot" (5.2.126). Katharina, the corrected penitent, complies, but the performance genre of the penance has already been muddled.

If wearing the "bauble" may have been Katharina's choice, the overzealous Petruchio introduces an additional incongruous component to the penance ritual. His prompt asks her to combine repentance (for her offenses and her failure to live up to the model of the dutiful wife) and judgment (of Bianca and especially the widow, as falling short of this model). When Katharina is given her cue to speak, the stage direction "Enter Kate, Bianca, and Widow" implies that she does not face the onstage audience by herself but is flanked by Bianca and the widow, whom she had been commanded to bring forth from the parlor and, if necessary, to "swinge [i.e., thrash] . . . soundly forth" (5.2.108). Petruchio's prompt and the blocking it entails allow for two performance options: either Katharina is speaking *for* the group of penitents, or, like a minister, she is giving the lines of the penance text *to* the women by her side. In the first case her speech pointedly renders her the only woman worthy of social reintegration, given the other women's unwillingness to face the wedding guests, Bianca's public affront to her husband as a "fool" (133), and the widow's pointed refusal to heed the script of wifely obedience. In the second scenario we witness "Katharina Minola, / renowned in Padua for her scolding tongue" (1.2.93–94), reading a penance script to women who have never been "published" as scolds. This is Pauline ministry, far exceeding the leading role in a common prayer assigned to penitents like

Unquiet Women on the Early Modern Stage 61

the historical Elizabeth Tuttie. Neither of these options bodes well for extinguishing the fire of contentious speech in Padua nor for the eagerly awaited social reconciliation.

The major deviation from the historic model of the public penance of the convicted scold is the loosely scripted nature of Katharina's performance. All she has available to construct her ceremonial penance is knowledge of conduct book rhetoric on domestic duties and her practice echoing Petruchio's rhetorical strategies in the sun-and-the-moon scene (4.5). There, as Megan Little has argued perceptively, Kate was "given her first rhetorical exercise: to exchange the moon for the sun, a man for a woman." She quickly masters the strategy of antiphrasis (expression by the opposite) and goes further. When Petruchio asks her to address an old man as if he were a young gentlewoman, she demonstrates mastery not only of antiphrasis but also of another of Petruchio's ceremonial oratory tools, the paradoxical encomium.[31] Back in Padua Petruchio had wooed her tongue-in-cheek, applauding her "mildness praised in every town," her "virtues" and "beauty" (2.1.189–90). Now, when he asks her for a "maidenly" embrace of Vincentio, Kate complies and goes on to lavish ironic hyperbolic praise upon the bewildered old man: "Young budding virgin, fair, and fresh, and sweet" (4.5.37). In the scene from the anonymous play, Kate's paradoxical encomium is even more elaborate, demonstrating her minute attentiveness to language strategies. It builds on the mineral imagery that Ferando used in his fantastical description of the "lovely maid" and weaves in falcon and sun imagery from Kate's own "taming" experience:

> Fair lovely lady, bright and crustalline,
> Beauteous and stately as the eye-trained bird,
> As glorious as the morning washed with dew,
> Within whose eyes she takes her dawning beams,
> And golden summer sleeps upon thy cheeks;
> Wrap up thy radiation in some cloud,
> Lest that thy beauty make this stately town
> Inhabitable like the burning zone . (4.1.35–42)

The rhetorical points scored by Kate in this scene are many: she pleases Petruchio's whim, impresses her male on-stage audience (Petruchio and Hortensio in Shakespeare's play; Ferando and Sander in the anonymous), and takes a jab at the vacuous language of courtship. The effect of Kate's rhetorical fireworks on Vincentio in Shakespeare's play is difficult to judge, as Petruchio is quick to take over and reestablish reality: "This is a man, old, wrinkled, faded, withered" (4.5.42). Perhaps we may take a cue from the anonymous play to discern it. There Kate's speech destabilizes the Duke of Sestos's notion of self: "What, is she mad too? or is my shape transformed" (4.1.44). In the stars-and-the-moon scene Kate's deployment of male ceremonial oratory affects the gender roles of several participants in the exchange. Without breaching the decorum of wifely obedience, she lays a claim to male ceremonial oratory, and in the scene from the anonymous play manages to destabilize the male identity of the Duke of Sestos. In her final speech, I would contend, Kate similarly subverts and surmounts both the oratory of penance and gender binarism.

All the components of penance are present in Katharina's speech: the acknowledgment of offenses, the personal apology, the appeal to the righteousness of the godly community. But they are curiously delayed, strangely sequenced, and shifted into dizzying perspectives. Instead of an apology, Katharina opens with a direct, personal attack on the widow:

> Fie, fie! Unknit that threatening, unkind brow,
> And dart not scornful glances from those eyes
> To wound thy lord, thy king, thy governor.
> It blots thy beauty as frosts do bite the meads,
> Confounds thy fame as whirlwinds shake fair buds,
> And in no sense is meet or amiable. (5.2.140–45)

To the references to the widow's being past her summer-season prime, Katharina adds an offensive simile of a muddy, contaminated fountain, one that "none so dry or thirsty / Will deign to sip or touch one drop of it" (148–49). She goes on to sermonize on the relationship of husband and wife as modeled on the relationship of the self-sacrificing, caring monarch and his obedient subject: "Thy husband is thy lord, thy life, thy keeper, / Thy head, thy sovereign; one that cares for thee" (150–51).

It is after delivering her sermon on marriage hierarchy and before listing her offenses, that Katharina utters an apology: "I am ashamed that women are so simple / To offer war where they should kneel for peace" (5.2.165–67). Yet this is no personal apology. It is far from clear that she is aligning herself with the "simple" women of whom she is ashamed, given the use of "they" in the second part of this sentence. Attending to Katharina's shifty rhetoric in this section, Little raises a provocative question: "Has Kate been perfectly tamed, becoming a puppet that even persuades other women into subjugation? Or, is Kate instructing women that they are 'simple' when they employ inexpedient rhetoric, launching a Ciceronian 'war' instead of mere ornamental and feminine 'tribute of true obedience'?"[32] It appears to me that the botched penance script of Kate's final speech calls for a performance in which she wages a very smart war of words. The rhetorical weapons she deploys against the women who have ridiculed and shamed her are "simple" in the sense of "direct." Against the men who have constrained her into performing a penance, she deploys subtler weapons: fragmentation of the implied script of the penance, punning, and parodic hyperbole.

After a nod in the direction of listing her offenses—"My mind hath been as big as one of yours, / My heart as great, my reason haply more, / To bandy word for word and frown for frown" (5.2.174–76)—Katharina finally arrives at the culmination of her penance, where she is to call on the goodwill and moral example of the godly community. She urges her reluctant copenitents, "Then vail your stomachs, for it is no boot" (180). Editors routinely gloss this charge as "Lower your pride," in accordance with the *Oxford English Dictionary* meaning of the verb *vail* as "lower in sign of submission or respect." However, in the late sixteenth century *vail* was also used in the sense of "to be of use or service; to avail or profit," which would render "vail your stomachs" as "make use of your stomachs, pluck up your courage." This meaning, interestingly, is documented in the *Oxford English Dictionary* with a literary quote from 1592, close to the conjectured first performance of Shakespeare's *Shrew*: "What booteth it of Gentries brag to boast, What vaileth it, old ensignes foorth to show?"[33] Is it giving up pride, or is it an act of courage to place a hand under Petruchio's foot? Is Katharina urging a peaceful yielding to the morally superior master of the household? Or is she acknowledging the courage it takes to trust him with her public display of moral integrity (or arguably, moral superiority)? The performance choices are balanced, but given the moral authority that Katharina claims for herself in the scene, I believe the latter option is more justified.[34]

Kate's choice of body action at the end of her speech, going down on her knees to place her hand "below [her] husband's foot," certainly exceeds the requirements listed in penance scripts for convicted scolds. Kneeling for forgiveness, bareheaded and barefooted, was reserved for penitent fornicators and adulterers, not for penitent scolds. Is this a preemptive penance on her part for some possible adultery in the future? Is she playing upon Petruchio's insecurities? Katharina's hyperbolic body language appears to take Petruchio aback: "Why, there's a wench!" exclaims he and ends her public performance with the kiss required by the comedic genre (5.2.184). The rest of the male spectators' responses indicate bewilderment—not unlike Vincentio's bewilderment in the-sun-and-the-moon scene, before he mustered the wit to laugh at the joke at his expense conceived by "fair" Petruchio and perfected by "merry" Kate. Lucentio's comment that it is "a harsh hearing when women are toward" may well apply to both his "toward" bride and the paradoxical encomium qualities of Katharina's performance (187). He is, after all, the male character who happens to be most widely read in the liberal arts, including rhetoric, and should have no trouble identifying parody. Hortensio, never particularly insightful, takes Katharina's kneeling to be the culmination of her submissive penance, but Lucentio, in the play's last line, suspends rational judgment, calling such taming "a wonder."

Does Katharina's exuberant performance in her final speech serve the discursive goals of the penance: reintegration of the offender into the community and restoration of the communal peace? Only partially, and only temporarily. Certainly she earns public acclaim for her impressive improvisation on the theme of the penance. Unlike the stereotypical scold or, for that matter, any scold or defamer from the historical record, the welcoming of this offender back into the fold comes with a financial prize for her. Shakespeare's is indeed a make-believe world, not only when it comes to masculinist wish-fulfilling fantasies for containing the contentious female but also in respect to women's wish-fulfilling fantasies for social and financial profit. But Kate's final speech alienates Bianca and the widow. Furthermore in its wake Petruchio, too eager to claim his wife's performance as *his* victory, widens the social rifts among the new families as he retorts to Lucentio and Hortensio, "We three are married, but you two are sped" (5.2.189).

As for the "slotting" of Katharina into the patriarchal order that her penance was supposed to effect, she juggles learned masculine rhetoric too adeptly for such slotting to be secure. A testimony to her discursive mastery is Petruchio's demonstrated belief in the sincerity of her penance. Like Vincentio, who had to chuckle when Katharina called him a "budding virgin" or else he would have demonstrated laughable ignorance of the purely performative nature of the paradoxical encomium, Petruchio has no choice but to validate his wife's over-the-top penance. Failing to do this would cost him dearly. Worse, it would sever his connections with the world of Paduan abundance as the husband of an unrepentant scold. So for her gender-bending rhetorical mixture of feminine verbal contentiousness, masculine sermonizing, and a corporal rendering of the paradoxical encomium, Katharina does not get the boot at the end of her speech, but rather a kiss.

"To Sleep, Perchance to Dream"

Wish fulfillment is, of course, the stuff that comedies, or "pleasant conceited" histories, are made of. What is curious about the shrew plays is how persistently they remind spectators of the illusory nature of their wish-fulfilling taming plots. Such persistence works effectively with what Mann describes as the propensity of Elizabethan dramaturgy "towards disengagement from the character," toward encouraging "the appreciation of acting as a skill, as a piece of artifice."[35] But it goes further than performance convention. Reminders of the characters' fictional construction in the shrew plays are not limited to the occasional metatheatrical remark or to drawing the audience's attention to the actor in such framing devices as prologues and epilogues. They are essential to the plot, and thus it is not just characters but the dramatic action of the taming whose illusory quality is highlighted.

A number of significant contemporary productions have shown Kate's penance as the culmination of a plot focused on illusion making. Tori Haring-Smith points out in her study of the stage history of *The Taming of the Shrew* that since the 1950s directors like George Devine, John Barton, Maurice Daniels, Trevor Nunn, Clifford Williams, and Michael Langham underscored the play-within-the-play structure, play-acting, and the interaction of Sly with the players, making Shakespeare's *Shrew* "a play about plays—a statement about the theatre and the power of theatrical illusion."[36]

In 1978 Michael Bogdanov's production opened with a statement about theater illusionism. Here is how Haring-Smith describes this opening:

> As the last members of the audience were being seated, a drunkard began to argue with one of the usherettes. "I am not having any bloody woman tell me what to do," he yelled. He eventually climbed onto the stage and started a riot that completely destroyed the old set, revealing a bare stage with iron staircases, scaffolding, and catwalks.... Only then, as the audience began to hear familiar dialogue, did they realize that the drunkard was Christopher Sly.... While Sly watched the first scene between Lucentio and Tranio, the usherette, now dressed as Katharine, walked across the stage and Sly slunk off after her. When he reappeared, he had been transformed into Petruchio. This doubling established the main play as a male chauvinist fantasy, the longed-for revenge of Sly upon stubborn women.[37]

As befit Bogdanov's concept of the play as Sly's make-belief, Katharina's last speech was rendered with utmost seriousness; in Haring-Smith's description, she "seemed to relish her new servitude in a perverted way." Such an overzealous performance of Kate's penance, the famed theater critic Michael Billington wrote, disturbed Petruchio and perhaps even humiliated him—a choice that probably has to do with the director's attentiveness to modern audiences' discomfort with domestic abuse and its effects.[38] But an overzealous delivery of the speech also fits well with the significance of play-acting in the play as a whole. The play-within-the-play dramatizes a popular story about the wished-for "righting" of the contentious wife and sets the performance of this fiction within another illusion, Sly's entertainment as an aristocrat. Like the rest of the low-born sleepers who get treated by lords and princes to a noble status in a popular Renaissance genre indebted to the *Arabian Nights*, Sly willfully embraces the illusion.[39] When offered wanton pictures from Ovid's *Metamorphoses* and an attractive wife, he decides to "let the world slip; we shall ne'er be younger" (Induction 2.133–34). No matter that the pictures were a crude substitute for the classic narrative, and the wife a transvestite page; Sly goes for the self-deluding dream.

At the end of the play Shakespeare chose not to take the spectators out of the dream of the tamed shrew by closing the frame story. However, as I have argued, in the last scene of his play he construed a dream on the verge of morphing into a nightmare of communal strife and hotly contested family hierarchy. In *The Tamer Tamed; or, The Woman's Prize*, a sequel responding to Shakespeare's *Shrew*, his younger collaborator John Fletcher offered his vision of the postpenance shrew. According to Fletcher's "book-ending" of Shakespeare's play, the taming of Kate's fiery tongue was only a temporary illusion. Petruchio remembers his married life with Kate thus:

> Had I not ev'ry morning a rare breakfast
> Mixed with a learned lecture of ill language
> Louder than Tom o' Lincoln, and at dinner
> A diet of the same dish? Was there evening
> That e'er passed over is without "thou knave"
> Or "thou whore" for digestion? (3.3.157–62)

Tranio likewise recalls how Kate "out of her most abundant stubbornness, / Out of her daily hue and cries upon him— / . . . turned his temper / And forced him blow as high as she" (1.1.17–20). Noisy scolding was as emblematic of Kate and Petruchio's household as the ringing of Tom o' Lincoln, the great bell of Lincoln Cathedral, was of the parish. Furthermore, much as the divines' warning against the fiery tongue feared, Kate's "sermonizing" has unleashed a feminine tongue in Petruchio, who is said to "blow as high as she." That Petruchio was "forced" to develop such a feminine attribute suggests something about his wife's masculine qualities.

As for the anonymous *Taming of a Shrew*, Kate's penance is rendered completely illusory in the frame that encloses the plot. In the last scene Sly is awakened by the Tapster and heads home to tame his wife in the manner of the dream he believes he has had. The Tapster follows him, anticipating another noisy entertainment by a scolding wife. While a number of modern productions have borrowed from this scene to render the illusory quality of "righting" the shrew, it often goes unnoticed that in the anonymous play Sly never hears Kate sermonize on gender roles in the family. The last he sees of shrew taming is the practical joke played on the Duke of Sestos in the sun-and-the-moon scene. He is taken off-stage, in a drunken sleep, following the reconciliation of the duke with his son. In this play the penitent shrew—who here gets to rehearse the story of Genesis—is part of a fictional entertainment designed for the Lord. It is instructive to consider the difference between the two visions of the tamed shrew performed, respectively, for Sly's and for the Lord's entertainment. To Sly the players give a trickster who is ready to call the sun the moon, as her husband bids her, and who mercilessly mocks a stranger from a higher estate. To the Lord the players offer a cash-winning sermonist.

On the Renaissance stage garrulous women disturbed the domestic and communal peace and thwarted desired romantic and economic alliances. "Taming" them was stereotypically portrayed as essential to the resolution of the dramatic conflict. However, "tamed" theatrical shrews bore little resemblance to the penitent scolds of the legal record. Whether through the performance suggested by the play text or through the conspicuous framing of the main plot, compliance with the gender binary in the final speeches of these multivalent characters was rendered provisional and illusory. Like some historical shrews, Shakespeare's Katharina would have performed her way on stage into a transgendered vocality, at once masculinely choleric and femininely impulsive, mixing catcalling and male rhetorical flourishes, abiding by the precepts of feminine subservience while laying claim to legal and moral authority. Fletcher determined that there was too much rhetorical energy and acumen to Kate's character to have her restrain and soften her speech after the wedding. And through his elaborate framing device, the anonymous author of *The Taming of a Shrew* satirized the success of shrew taming as an illusion custom-made for audiences eager to suspend disbelief. In the case of Kate, the most long-lived shrew of the early modern era, what Butler claims about sexuality holds true for the articulation of her gendered subjectivity. She could have been portrayed as undone by the precepts of gender binarism in the patriarchal manifestoes that she is coerced to recite. (Several memorable modern productions of the play have her follow this route.) But performance clues in the dialogue presented the young male stars who performed the shrew with much more challenging and exciting acting opportunities.

4

Witch-Speak in Late Elizabethan Docufiction

Judging from the variety of early modern publications documenting and commenting on contemporary witchcraft cases, the latter half of Queen Elizabeth's reign can be justly called the era of the witch.[1] Demonological treatises, tracts on prophecies and demoniac possessions, the lone spiritual memoir, and a good number of news pamphlets on prominent court cases all attempted to make sense of this elusive phenomenon, signaling a public obsession with a relatively infrequent and prominently gendered crime. In most cases writing about witches was based on documentary evidence from criminal investigations and trials. This was overwhelmingly the case for the Elizabethan news pamphlets. Yet even for the "Witch County" of Essex, the numbers of witches and their victims in the popular press were significantly higher that those in surviving indictments in assize records, suggesting that in the late 1500s public knowledge of witchcraft, an overwhelmingly female crime, was actively shaped not so much by the courts as by pamphlet writers.[2] It would be useful, then, to examine pamphlet representations of witches in order to understand the most widely circulated notions about the makings of the witches' destructive acts. In the process it is worthwhile attending not only to the pamphleteers' dominant structural and stylistic choices but also to discursive elements in these popular texts that appear to be at cross-purposes with their ostensible rhetorical goals. These, arguably, are the textual remains of historical witch-speak.

As Stuart Clark has explained, writing about witchcraft for the popular public was an important ideological enterprise. Witchcraft—"overthwartness made systematic, unruliness or overturning taken to ritualistic lengths"—was rendered a "necessary evil" that, in the prevalent antithetical thinking of the era, defined the institutions of God's order and the monarch's by providing their negative image.³ In the period's language of contrariety, which defined good through evil, order through disorder, soul through body, male through female, and the ordered commonwealth through demonic tyranny, witches epitomized the inversion of natural, patriarchal, Christian, and estate order. No ordinary criminals, they were, to quote the impassioned writing of one pastor-demonologist, "most wicked runnagates from the fayth, false forswearers of Gods power, traytours of the majestie of God, most vile starters aside."⁴

But such inversionary thinking, Clark explains, entailed a constant and ultimately destabilizing semantic exchange between the two terms of the antithesis. The "superior" term was completely dependent for its meaning on its "inferior" partner and could never be affirmed without evoking precisely what it sought to suppress.⁵ In the context of the cultural beliefs and practices of courtroom attendants and pamphlet readers of the middling sort, the semantic dependence of the superior term frequently translated as an enhanced interest in the forcefulness of its privative or inferior partner. Indeed the witches' words recorded in the popular pamphlets wielded a performative force that, I argue, provoked interest, admiration, and sometimes even the approving laughter of both courtroom audiences and readers from the middling social estates.

The pamphleteers, like the magistrates, judges, and clerks who produced the court documents on which these popular writers drew, tried hard to demystify, order, and circumscribe the slippery rhetorical phenomenon of witch-speak. Its manifestations, described below, included effectively staged and endlessly variable disturbances of signification, equivocations, moans, giggles, and incantations of intangible form but unmistakably material impact. Though lacking in authentic creative power, witch-speak nonetheless possessed the affective power to induce fear and wonder, to make believe. It was, literally, overspeaking, getting the upper hand in a verbal strife, exerting control over a performative context, and asserting oneself over one's superior in the social or gender hierarchy. When Elizabethan and some Jacobean pamphleteers, driven by conflicting ideological and marketing impulses, attempted to dissipate the mysterious force of witch-speak, they frequently succeeded in preserving it.

A discussion of witch-speak and its performative force allows us to refine and develop further the strong thesis of the feminist historians Christina Larner, Marianne Hester, and Anne Barstow that witch hunts were women hunts, "sexual violence against women within a context of male supremacist social relations." The important ideological ramifications of this thesis have been pursued by Diane Purkiss in a discussion of the witchcraft persecution during the English Civil War. This persecution, she claims, was a vehicle utilized by parliamentarians and royalists alike for the assertion of a masculine military identity.[6] Yet in their efforts to expose the full terror of female persecution that cemented the historical foundations of the modern nation-state and the reformed church, these feminist historians have underplayed the witches' memorable performances in the local contestations of power. Court records and the Elizabethan pamphlet literature building on them provide numerous reminders that witches were not just unfortunate victims or helpless scapegoats for cultural anxieties, created by a changing social and belief system.[7] These sources describe women who, once identified as witches, contributed to a frightful dialectic of fighting words and acts.[8] They lashed out with curses and spells against the neglect, maltreatment, and brutality of social superiors, exercising what one anthropologist has called the "negative power" to make trouble.[9] Legally witchcraft was defined as *maleficium*, willfully inflicted harm. In an effort to restrain the witches' force and their perceived avidity for the property and control over the well-being of others, the community matched the witches' fighting words with harmful physical acts: commoners brutally beat suspected witches, scratched and drew blood from their faces in order to alleviate the suffering of alleged victims, set fire to their thatch roofs to see whether they would be summoned home by demonic confederates, dunked them in water with their thumbs tied to the toes of the opposite feet and condemned them if they floated up for a gasp of air, and flocked to grisly public hangings.[10] Each act of identifying and punishing the witch was an exercise in culturally or legally sanctioned violence, circulated farther afield through popular print. This violence was not simply a matter of the disciplining use of punishment by the monarchy. It was diffused throughout the communal and legal structures of early modern England.

Building on the records of church and assize courts, the Elizabethan pamphlets' popular "texts of horror" intertwine two thrilling stories. In one of these stories zealous moral reformers impressed upon their unredeemed popular audiences witchcraft as an inverse model of proper social conduct. In this narrative, incidentally, witchcraft was indispensable for the conceptualization of social structures. Yet even the most zealous of reformers were bound by commercial considerations since they had to sell their ideological wares to audiences ready to pay cash for a good thriller. Hence the pamphleteers' interest in stories about a relentless clash of wills, in which the underdogs could prevail, if briefly, over their superiors. In this type of narrative women—who were brought to court as witches but who also accounted for most of the witnesses and virtually all the examiners for the witches' mark—participated actively on both sides of the divide, but female power was frequently linked to witchcraft.[11] Thus the Elizabethan pamphleteers used witchcraft as a tool of (negative) sociocultural definition, but equally important, they helped incorporate the witches' *resistance* to communal, institutional, and state violence into the conceptual construction of the English polity.[12] The principal vehicle through which witches challenged the right over the supernatural claimed by religious reformers and the consolidating absolutist regime was witch-speak: the performative use of language involving some combination of the following components: powerful if elusive figuration; refreshing, disturbing, and cynical laughter; and uncanny manipulation of the interlocutor.

As I attempt to reconstitute the witches' fighting words and deeds surfacing in court records and Elizabethan docufiction, I also reconceptualize the vocal agency of these unruly women. Their agency was not limited, as one might infer from Sharpe's discussion of female involvement in witchcraft court cases, to fighting other women over the control of healing practices, child rearing, and child care.[13] The witches' words, distorted and reordered but widely circulated by means of the pamphlet trade, evoked a history of insurrectionary speech that had an impact beyond the female sphere. Thanks to the popular press, their ridicule of social betters and their victories over learned opponents reached and fascinated expansive reading audiences.

The Makings of Witch-Speak

The most powerful weapon of the witch, the early moderns agreed, was the word. The influential *Guide to Grand-Jury Men* by the prominent controversist and clergyman Richard Bernard lists a host of verbal formulas in the arsenal of bewitchment techniques. "Cursing and banning, and bitter imprecations," "threatnings with curses," "Charmes and Spels, the words thereof being repeated," "certaine formes of words like prayer, using the name of God, and the Lord Jesu, or the Virgin Mary," "praising and . . . words of commendations"—witch-speak was endlessly variable and, we shall see, difficult to distinguish from other performative utterances.[14] In the terms of J. L. Austin's language theory, what witches said (the *locutionary act* of meaning production) was not all that important; it was the power of the utterance to affect their interlocutors (the *perlocutionary act*) that could be a matter of life and death. Whereas the actual *content* of the witches' words was rarely clear or even significant, few early moderns dismissed the emotive *force* of witch-speak to bring forth the acts it enunciated.[15] What were the means through which witch-speak acquired the force to enact what it named? Did this force reside with the "one" speaking out, or was it a purely discursive phenomenon? In other words, whether it was an imagined or real evil that was effected by witch-speak, was the infliction caused by the utterer or by the utterance? Or, to recall Butler's query in regard to injurious speech in general, was "a community and history of such speakers not magically invoked at the moment in which that utterance [was] spoken?"[16]

The most conspicuous—and terrifying—aspect of witch-speak was its mysteriousness. By virtue of belonging to the realm of the supernatural, the transformation of the witches' words into deeds always took place behind the scenes. The "diabolical" forces they employed were inaccessible to mortal eyes. A witch did not even need to be present at the scene of the crime. Her words were constructed as witchcraft only retroactively, from the faltering and interested memories of victims, in witness depositions shaped by court protocols. No matter how abundant or cohesive witnesses' and victims' evidence in a particular witchcraft case, invoking supernatural forces through witch-speak remained an intangible, inaccessible, and hence uncontrollable act. The one precise record of witch-speak in an Elizabethan pamphlet, to my knowledge, comes up in the jail examination of Elizabeth Stile of Windsor at the end of Richard Galis's 1579 pamphlet: "Their words of charme weare these, *come on let us go about it*, and presently they were changed into a new shape." The statement is, however, dubious at best, since throughout the pamphlet the one witch credited with shape-shifting is "father Rosiman alias Osborne"; none of the female witches are described as capable of taking on nonhuman form. Neither is the shape-shifting charm cross-referenced in the other pamphlet featuring a confession by Elizabeth Stile, the 1579 *Rehearsall both straung and true*, although the content of the confession matches the one in Galis's pamphlet.[17]

The knowledge of witchcraft resisted the standardization of print, overlapped with "natural" quick wit and sharp tongue, and was transfused along informal channels of family and neighborly or personal affinity, typically managed by women. Early modern writers on witchcraft often voiced their exasperation with the impossibility of furnishing noncircumstantial evidence of these criminal (speech) acts, evidence demanded by the English common law tradition.[18] Even John Gaule, a partial skeptic on the issue of witchcraft, demanded the relaxation of standards for "palpable evidence for conviction," referring to witchcraft as "an abstruse mystery of iniquity."[19] This "abstruse mystery," I propose, was a matter of effective performative improvisation and the kind of enargaic rhetoric that rendered troubling metaphors literal in a sonically suggestive or overwhelming manner.

Among the "ragged" mistresses of enargaic witch-speak who effectively breached the boundary between metaphor and reality was the Arundel woman Susanna Wilson. In 1602 she was tried by the archdeaconry court of Chichester on several counts of adultery, defamation of another townswoman, and violent abuse of a woman servant. According to the testimony of witnesses, Susanna had completely reorganized the patriarchal household economy. To cavort with her lover, Thomas Page, she locked her husband into his chamber for hours. She refused to eat with her husband and even forced him to pay for his meals "as though he were a stranger," while she lavished money, food, and sexual favors upon her lover. Even more alarming than James Wilson's well-known humiliation, however, is the report that his wife threatened that unless "the saide Thomas Page ... did resorte unto the house of the saide James Wilson her husband the saide Susanna *woulde make all the vaynes in the harte of her saide husband to ake*."[20] Given Susanna's reputation for malevolent power, the broken heart metaphor she evoked acquires a particularly sinister ring. Her words assert her powerful sexuality and worldly ambition, while also claiming the supernatural power to carry out what they portray in vivid detail: to wring with deadly pain each artery in her husband's heart.

Until 1990, when the case against Susanna Wilson was discussed by the West Sussex historian George Hothersall, her powers of figuration remained unknown outside her neighborhood and the Chichester ecclesiastical court.[21] The speech of other witches, however, reached wider audiences thanks to reporting pamphleteers. A 1593 pamphlet on demoniac possession inflicted by a Warboys family of witches upon the members of Robert Throckmorton's family records a similar instance of enargaic sliding of literalness and metaphor into witch-speak. A section of the pamphlet likely authored by Henry Pickering, uncle of the possessed Throckmorton children and a Cambridge scholar, reports that when the chief suspect, Mother Samuel, was confronted by him and two of his fellow students, she became "very loud in her answers and impatient, not suffering any to speak but herself." Admonished that she should "keep the woman's virtue and be more silent," she countered "that she was 'born in a mill, begot in a kill, she must have her will,' she could speak no softlier." The booming voice of the suspected witch and the rhyming dimeter of her speech must have struck Master Pickering as peculiar enough to merit a description including a direct quote in his account of the encounter. Just as memorable were Mother Samuel's fighting words with which she countered the Cambridge scholar's threat that if she did not confess and repent, "he hoped one day to see her burned at the stake, and he himself would bring fire and wood, and the children should blow the coals." Informed by Continental notions of witchcraft as heresy, Pickering's fulminations are themselves attempts at enargaic figuration. But Mother Samuel proved more adept at building enargeia: "I had rather," she fired back, ". . . see you doused over head and ears in this pond!" In contrast to the rambling description of the scholar's malicious "hope," the witch's spit-in-your-eye counterattack evokes the effects of her "evil will" as at once imminent and corporally specific. Moreover she fits her vision of Pickering's infliction into the very surroundings of this exchange, which unfolded "in the street hard by a pond."[22]

The shift from prose to verse meter and the merging of metaphor and literalness in enargaic figuration do not fully account for the rhetorical power of witch-speak to turn words into deeds. Like scolding (and song), witch-speak derives much of its force not from the signification of the word itself but from the manner of its utterance. It is an instance of intensified language, the kind of language that quite literally has more body, what Butler describes as "injurious speech" that confounds social-linguistic speech norms.[23] Uttered as loud incantatory howlings or as low mumblings, witch-speak intensified its injurious power through the visual impact of "glowing eyes" and the suggestion of sinister rituals through posture and movement. In this respect it verged on Taylor's notion of the animative, the shifting of speech into physical action that, as we saw, also characterized some instances of scolding.[24]

Elleine Smithe, one of the Essex witches whose trial documents are paraphrased in a 1579 pamphlet, was reported to have been outraged at her stepfather's request for the money she had been given by her dead mother, herself executed as a witch. An unnamed "informant" explains how "in fallying out [with her stepfather] the saied Elline *in greate rage saied unto hym*, that it had been better for hym, had he never fallen out with her, and so it came to passe, for the same Jhon [*sic*] Chanundler confessed before his death, that after that same hower that she had saied so unto hym, he never eate any meate that digested in hym." While Elleine's words may well be classified as a threat, the informant cited in the pamphlet clearly associates their injurious effectiveness not with their content but with the enraged and loud manner in which they were spoken.[25]

Sometimes it was the very quality of the soundmark produced by the witch rather than any of her actual words that was credited with injurious power. Such was the case of Margaret Landish, who in 1645 demonstrated witch-speak in the courtroom, paradoxically, when she refused to confess that she was a witch. She proceeded to produce "a strange howling in the court to the great disturbance of the entire bench." On the other side of sound intensity, incomprehensible "murmurings" were also seen as the soundmark of witch-speak. Mother Staunton, whose 1579 assize trial is reported in the pamphlet featuring Elleine Smithe, was said to have gone "her waie murmuring" after she was denied some yeast by the wife of one Richard Saunder. As a result of her murmurs, reportedly a "yonge child in the Cradle was taken vehemently sicke, in a merveilous strange maner."[26]

The bodily force of witch-speak did not depend exclusively on the sound of the witches' utterances. Expressions and gestures were also important. In 1601 Alice Walsh of Wearmouth testified in front of the church court in Durham that her neighbor Alice Colier had poisoned a cow and caused it to miscarry. Walsh blamed this misfortune, among other things, on Colier's "glowing eyes." In 1663 a charge of witchcraft arose in a church court case brought by Ann Wright of Nantwich against Mary Briscoe. In the course of the witness examinations, Briscoe was reported to have "candled her eyes upon [Wright's twelve-year-old daughter] like a cat as big as two saucers." The girl fell into a trance, was afflicted by fits and swellings for the next thirteen weeks, and eventually died. Briscoe's facial expression may well have been meant to scare the girl out of her wits. Saucer-size eyes, we learn from a 1649–50 assize court deposition by Dorothy Rodes of Bolling (another mother whose daughter was allegedly a victim of witchcraft), were associated with the appearance of the dead supernaturally come back to life. In one of several frightening encounters with an alleged witch, Dorothy's daughter, Sara, claimed that she had also seen the witch accompanied by a woman who had been dead for two years. When her mother appeared incredulous, Sara explained, "A, mother, but she never rests, for she appeared to me the fowlest feinde that ever I sawe, with a paire of eyes like sawcers."[27]

Early witchcraft pamphlets whose authors aimed to impress documentary truthfulness upon their readers also recorded instances of witch-speak enhanced by expression and body movement. Mother Staunton, the Essex witch featured in the 1579 *Detection of Damnable Driftes*, whose murmurs were mentioned earlier, was one of those masters of staging body movement. When Robert Cornell's wife repeatedly denied her milk and eventually "barred the doores against her," the old woman "satte doune upon her heeles before the doores, and made a Circle upon the grounde with a knife. After that she digged it full of holes with in the compasse, in the sight of the saied wife, her man, and her maide, who demandyng why she did so: She made aunswere, that she made a shityng-house for her self after that sorte, and so departed." This scatological explanation of the witch's emulation of a well-known ritual of devil conjuration proved immediately effective. The following day the wife of the house "was taken sicke, and began to swell from tyme to tyme, as if she had been with child, by whiche swellyng she came so greate in bodie, as she feared she would burste: and to this daie is not restored to healthe."[28]

Figurative witch-speak was sometimes used in the metatheatrical format of formal cursing, first discussed in Keith Thomas's magisterial work on early modern supernatural beliefs. Instances of formal cursing described in court records reveal that such imprecations were typically delivered in ritual form, with the woman either kneeling or standing with her arms raised, publicly calling out for divine vengeance against her offenders. Thus when in the summer of 1596 the unnamed wife of Maurice Jones of Barking was asked to help one Robgentes's wife with prayer and medicine for stomach pains, she "fell downe upon her knees, & after many curses & evill speeches, praied, that the said Robgentes wife might never be cured; but that she might abide the extremest tormentes that ever was abidden." A few years later the widow Helen Hiley of Wetherby was reported to have gone to her next-door neighbor John Wood "and kneeled downe upon her knees and said a vengeance of god light upon the[e] Wood... and all thy children, and I shall trulie pray this praier for the[e] so long as I live." In Wales, where, Suggett points out, formal cursing was widespread, "on occasion an obscene frontal expression of insult and protest was addressed to the malefactor by the female cursers who might bare their breasts or raise their skirts." As was the case of other instances of witch-speak, the sound volume and physical performance of formal cursing had injurious effect in spite of the unintelligibility of the words. In 1617 Joanna Powell of Westhide "did curse John Smith, one of the churchwardens... in Welsh language, kneeling down upon her bare knees and holding up her hands, but otherwise the words he could not understand."[29]

The murmurs, howlings, imprecations, and vocal and corporal figurations of witch-speak reportedly hurled the enemy's violated body to the ground, racked it, burned or froze it, caused suffocation and bloating, crippled the legs and the arms.[30] This verbal violence could be conjoined with physical assault. One witch, notorious for both verbal and physical aggressiveness, was the above-mentioned Mother Staunton of Wimbush. She reacted with "greate anger" when the wife of Robart Petie denied her "diverse thynges, whiche she demaunded at once, and also charged with the stealing of a Knife from thence." Elleine Smithe of Maldon, who reacted "in greate rage" when her stepfather "demaunded certaine money" she had received from her deceased mother, was also reported to have given "a blowe on the face" to Widow Webb's daughter, "offended" that the girl had quarrelled and fought with her daughter. Ursley Kempe, arraigned at St. Osyth in 1582, was said not only to have cursed her sister-in-law but to have viciously attacked her. Lawrence Kempe, Ursley's brother, testified that "his saide wife did tell him that two yeeres before, shee mette the said Ursley his sister upon Eliotsheath, & that she fell uppon her, & then tooke up her clothes and did beat her upon the hippes, and otherwise in wordes did misuse her greatly."[31]

Linked to violent and degrading body acts, witch-speak could also be related to laughter, though the kind of laughter that plays with dangerous subjects. In 1593, according to the documentary pamphlet *Witches of Warboys*, the eighty-year-old Mother Samuel declared that she was pregnant in order to avoid hanging as a witch. This "set all the company on a great laughing and she herself more than any other because (as she thought) there should for that cause no judgment have been given." The pamphleteer interprets the condemned witch's laughter as comic credulity, but Mother Samuel may have been making a sinister joke. Earlier she had explained to her examiners that the alleged victims of her witchcraft were no longer plagued by chicken-like spirits believed to be her familiars because "the said dun chicken with the rest are now come into her, and are now in the bottom of her belly, and make her so full that she is like to burst."[32] If she believed she was pregnant with these demonic spirits, carrying the pregnancy to term would have had distinctly unpleasant consequences for her persecutors, a prospect Mother Samuel would have had good reason to laugh about as her trial was about to wrap up.

As Gibson has pointed out, the use of humorous anecdotes when describing witchcraft became an established practice in the narrative-driven (as opposed to documentary) subtype of witchcraft pamphlets prevalent after 1590 and into the Jacobean era.[33] It is not clear whether the witch jokes in these pamphlets had any factual basis, but the pamphleteers presented them as genuine, which suggests that readers readily established a connection between witchcraft and fierce humor. A 1606 pamphlet records "a homely tale" of this comic sort, singled out as the culmination of a long list of *maleficia* carried out by Johane Harrison and her daughter. Johane's humorous, if vicious, retaliation for the "scurvy" jests of a local drunkard, the pamphleteer tells us, "made al the bench to laugh," and is worth quoting at some length:

> Now this Good-fellow (not enduring to looke upon a bad face but his owne, especially when he is Cup-shot) called aloude to her, Doe you heare Witch, looke tother waies, cannot abide a nose of that fashion, or else turne your face the wrong side outward, it may look like raw flesh for flyes to blow maggots in. Stil as the Witch was ready to reply, he would crosse her with one scurvy Jest, & between every Jest drink to her, yet sweare, God damn him: she should starve ere she should have a drop on't, since the pot was sweet hee'd keepe it so, for should but her lips once looke into the lid on't, her breath's so strong, & would so

stick in the cup, that all the water that runs by Ware would not wash it out again. At last the witch got so much time to cal to him, Doest thou heare, good friend (quoth she) that thou throwst in thy drink apace, but shall not find it so easie comming out."

When the drunk went out to urinate, he found "a red lump as big as a cherry" on the tip of his "nose." (Could this be a pun on or misprint for "hose," easily recognized by early modern lovers of jest?) Understandably "the sight thereof drave his hart to an ague, & his tongue to an alarum."[34] The jester paid with physical suffering and public humiliation for his abuse of "the Witch." Here, as elsewhere, witch-speak is portrayed as comic improvisation. Its comedy, however, provided humiliation without blessing, purging without regeneration, havoc without renewal.

If witch-speak acquired its material force through a volatile combination of enargaic figuration and improvisational performance, who did this force reside with: the individual witch, the discourse of witch-speak, or the historical community of its speakers? Early modern skeptics like Reginald Scot and George Gifford seemed to believe that this affective force was a feature intrinsic to the discourse of witch-speak. It is "the *fables* of Witchcraft," Scot claims in the opening of *The Discoverie of Witchcraft*, that "have taken so fast hold and deepe root in the heart of man, that fewe or none can (nowadaies) with patience indure the hand and correction of God." These fables, he continues, have fixed themselves in the heart, to the effect that the world has become "*bewitched and over-run* with this fond error."[35] Malevolent power, in his view, issues from deceptive stories, rather than, as was commonly believed, from autonomous demonic agency wielded by witches. The famous witchcraft skeptic denies witches any meaningful performative agency and portrays them instead as pitiful melancholiacs, toothless, bleary-eyed, and generally contemptible.

Scot's ascription of performative force (or, to be more precise, the counterfeiting of autonomous injurious power) to stories about witchcraft rather than to the speaking subjects of witch-speak is motivated by his desire to demonstrate the inanity of witchcraft persecutions. Indeed how does one persecute an injurious utterance? Where and when does the persecution of words that are injurious in themselves begin and end? And yet, while this erasure of the injurious power of witch-speak is effectively designed to get the witches off the hook of legal persecution, it also denies them whatever claim to social power and pleasure they might secure through their successful wielding of performative (injurious) speech.

I would insist, contra Scot, that witches did have the power to injure with the sounds, words, gestures, and movements that made up witch-speak. But this power rested with no single witch. The moment of the witch's injurious utterance was a moment of what Butler refers to as "a condensed historicity . . . an effect of prior and future invocations that constitute and escape the instance of the utterance."[36] The force of witch-speak, in other words, is accrued over time and is the effect of its historicity. This force is directly linked to the linguistically encoded memory of trauma inflicted by a *series* of injurious speakers. So even though witch-speak depends on the individual subject for its efficacy, it does not originate with any single subject.

The *speaking* subject of witch-speak (as opposed to its *collective* subject) does have agency, but this is the performative agency of a dissimulator or an improvising actor rather than that of an author. The success of the witch-speak performative, somewhat like the performatives of jesters, is not the success of an individual intent to govern the action of speech. As injurious speakers, witches have responsibility, but this is a citational responsibility for the renewal of the linguistic, sonic, and corporal tokens of their historic community.

In this line of thought, each court deposition and examination concerning witchcraft, and each of their subsequent incarnations in popular print, charged the individual witch as responsible for a *history* that she conjured up as a speaking subject. The history of witch-speak in turn was criminalized precisely through the persecution of subjects who could be charged with its injurious force. By substituting individual agency for a collective historical agency, the legal system and the popular press of early modern England treated the witches' injurious speech practices as the criminal discourse of individually culpable agents. They thus transformed a history of social opposition into a criminal act.

Discursive Ordering: Witchcraft in the Press

The Elizabethan public's fascination with witchcraft was neither spontaneous nor unmediated. Through the 1590s the witch was largely the product of the legal system and the proto-journalistic pamphlets. This would change in the early seventeenth century, when the pamphleteers' moralistic digests of witness "informations," pre- and posttrial "examinations," and occasional sensational countryside witch story were supplanted by the excitement of literary tragicomedy, melodrama, and demonological scientific inquiry. The result, discussed in the next chapter, was the proliferation on page and stage of more spectacular and sensational witchcraft representations, indebted to the witch-speak of historic witches but also to Continental lore and classical witchcraft tales.[37]

Through the 1590s, however, the witchcraft genre par excellence remained the pamphlet. Unlike scolds, murderous wives, "monstrous" and monster-bearing women, and other real-life female criminals, freaks, and prodigies beloved of the popular press, the witch appears to have been given a voice in just one Elizabethan broadside ballad.[38] There may have been some sixteenth-century witchcraft docudramas, but if so, none of them survives.[39] Surviving texts indicate that a full-blown theatrical documentary presentation of witchcraft had to wait until the Jacobean era. In the meantime the representation of witchcraft was confined primarily to the genre of the pamphlet, best known for its tight focus on a single event, its coherent if lengthy argument that discouraged the spawning of secondhand versions, and, above all, its moralistic didacticism.

Elizabethan pamphleteers set out to assign a shape to volatile, improvisational witch-speak that was at once recognizable and tantalizing. Oftentimes rushing to capitalize on public interest in a controversial trial or witch execution, they typically relied on ready-made protocols of legal proceedings against witchcraft. They transcribed available pretrial "informations" by victims and witnesses as well as witches' "examinations," or else paraphrased court testimony and gossip while mimicking the distinctive features of legalese and flaunting the orderliness of their presentation of events. Reproduced in a form that would have been familiar to many involved in the trials, witch-speak acquired a tangible shape in the pamphlets that could be understood, ridiculed, condemned, appropriated. Once the witches' acts were stripped of voice, expression, gesture, and the relevance of locale, their performative power was extinguished. Imprisoned in quotes, bewitching speech lost its sting and became a sign of criminal and sinful depravity. Nevertheless the pamphlets contain numerous indications of the bad fit of the "straitjacketing" of witch-speak in this genre.

A curious event reported in the pamphlet on the bewitchment of children from the influential Throckmorton family illustrates the transfer of elusive witch-speak into the shape of the written confession. During a Christmas Eve service, Mother Samuel was successfully pressured to confess her responsibility for the children's possession in front of the parish members. But later she withdrew the confession and, in spite of threats to be taken for an examination to the bishop of Lincoln, would only "confess" to the children's father in private. After a series of failed attempts to secure her public confession, Master Throckmorton recruited the help of his brother-in-law and rector of Warboys, Dr. Francis Dorington.[40] The minister came up with a strategy to quell the old woman's equivocations as well as local rumors that she was a victim of aristocratic malice. He resorted to "recording" techniques; he took down in writing the confession that Mother Samuel made "something coldly" to him, then went over the script in front of several witnesses, planted under the window of the examination parlor.[41] In the pamphlet Mother Samuel's witch-speak is thus reported in the form of a written "translation" of her testimony, which we have good reason to suspect was shaped by the effort of the Cambridge-educated minister to counteract her "coldness." This translation itself gets reported in a pamphlet unifying into a seamless third-person narrative the accounts of at least five "authors," all of them men of learning and authority.[42] However well Mother Samuel may have remembered her verbal acts, which had likely triggered the children's possessions, all that the pamphlet offers its readers is the report of a translation, not the authentic speech of the witch, nor even the report of that speech by the (presumably) witnessing pamphleteer. Dorington, like the pamphleteers, refused to take into account the witch's protests against his text, when Mother Samuel "would fain have denied all again." Yet one wonders what text she would have agreed represented her "confession" to Throckmorton truthfully.

Reducing witch-speak to formulaic reports by authoritative men was one means of taking the sting out of women's fighting words. Another was enclosing them within what Deborah Willis describes as didactic "frame stories," at once connected to the story of local witchcraft and separate from it.[43] In a diegetic move typical of the genre, witchcraft pamphlets would open with generically diverse prefaces, which could include epistles to the reader, dedicatory epistles to patrons, exhortations or epigrams in verse form. In them, the discussion of witchcraft is typically subsumed under a moralistic call against "godles actes," "the fruites of Papistes and papistry," general impiety, or lack of religious or civic vigilance.[44] As Gibson usefully points out, the description of witchcraft in the prefaces of Elizabethan pamphlets is so general that they could easily introduce "any pamphlet about crime or sin."[45] Such abstract moral or legal reformism is at odds with both the localizing precision of pamphlet titles and the factual detail in examinations and informations quoted or paraphrased in the pamphlet's bodies. In contrast to such meticulous care, the prefaces tie the very particular power struggles of the witches to larger narratives about the urgent necessity for individual and communal reform.

Thus the author of "The Epistle to the Reader" in the 1566 pamphlet *The Examination and Confession of Certaine Wytches at Chensforde* defines the pamphlet's rhetorical goals thus: "By thadmonition of this littel boke [let us] learne in such sorte to keepe our soule, by fixed and assured faith in Christ, from the stinking puddle of filthy pollution." John Phillips, who contributed a verse "exhortacion to all faithfull men" to the prefatory materials of the same pamphlet, concluded with a series of calls to "swearers," "whoremongers," "such men as delight in sinne," and "filthy swynishe dronkardes" to change their ways.[46] Similarly W. W.'s dedication to "the right honourable and his singular good Lord, the lord Darcy" in a lengthy pamphlet on the 1582 St. Osyth witchcraft trials sets out the reformers' task in practical detail:

> If there hath bin at any time (Right Honourable) any meanes used, to appease the wrath of God, to obtaine his blessing, *to terrifie secreete offenders by open transgressors punishments, to withdraw honest natures from the corruption of evil company, to diminishe the great multitude of wicked people, to increase the small number of virtuous persons, and to reforme all the detestable abuses* which the perverse witte and will of man doth dayly devise, this doubtlesse is no lesse necessarye then the best: that Sorcerers, Wizzardes, or rather Dizzardes, Witches, Wisewomen (for so they will be named), are rygorously punished.[47]

In this offensive for the reformation and salvation of the reading public, witches are cast as a negative example to be exposed and shunned at all costs, yet they are also subsumed within a larger set of "offenders," "evil company," and "wicked people."

Although the authors of the witchcraft pamphlets insisted on their truth value, in the opening addresses witches' names were often completely suppressed and their actions made indistinguishable from other sins and crimes. Whatever the particular transgression of the local "problem women"—typically asserting themselves before their social and economic superiors or breaching the norms of the patriarchal household—it was subsumed under the heading of a much more nebulous complex of irreligious or criminal traits. The discrepancy between the witchcraft narratives in the prefaces and the pamphlets' main body, however, remains quite palpable. In my view, it highlights the difficulty of fitting witch-speak into a sequential narrative format, abstracted from the local context of injurious utterances.

Another dimension of the straitjacketing of witch-speak into pamphlet form was the emphatically orderly character of their presentation. Driven by a desire to impress the truthfulness of their narratives but also to emulate the finality of legal decision making, pamphleteers were eager to reproduce, or at least imitate, the style and order of legal documents. Thus Thomas Dawson, the printer of the pamphlet on the notorious St. Osyth witch trial, advertises in the title that this "Recorde, of the Information, Examination and Confession of all the Witches" was "written orderly, as the cases were tryed by evidence." The author W. W., who may have been the witches' examiner, Justice of the Peace Brian Darcey, or someone writing for him, must also have been convinced of the importance of presenting the examinations in the order in which they were taken. He drew attention to this order in the dedicatory address to the young Baron Darcy: "This I speake (Right Honorable) upon a late viewe of tryall, taken against certaine Witches in the countie of Essex; the orderly processe in whose examinations, together with other accidents, I dilygently observing and considering their trecheries to be notable: undertooke briefly knit up in a fewe leaves of paper, their manifolde abuses."[48]

The legal documentary sources of the pamphlets provided another means of making witch-speak predictable and thus less threatening: encasing it in legal formulae that strung the witches' improvisatory variations in repetitive patterns. Examination reports listed witch acts one after the other, aiming for the persuasive effect of *copia*, with little attention to the language of interpersonal conflicts. Instead repetitive connectives shaped malevolent speech acts as identical. Mother Waterhouse's confession in

The Examination and Confession of Certaine Wytches at Chensforde (1566) is representative of this strategy:

> *Fyrst,* she receyved this cat of this frances wife in the order *as is before sayde*....
>
> *Then* when she had receyved him she (to trye him what he coulde do) wyld hym to kyll a hog of her owne which he dyd, and she gave him for his labour a chicken, which he fyrste required of her & a drop of her blod....
>
> *Also* she saythe that another tyme being offended with one father Kersey she toke her catte Sathan in her lap and put hym in the wood before her dore, & willed him to kyll three of this father Kerseys hogges, which he dyd, ... and she rewarded hym *as before*, with a chicken and a droppe of her bloud....
>
> *Also* she confessed that fallying out with one widow Gooday she wylled Sathan to drowne her cow and he dyd so, and she rewarded hym *as before. Also* she falling out with another of her neyboures, she killed her three geese *in the same manner.*
>
> *Item,* shee confessed that ...
>
> *Also* being denyed butter of an other ...
>
> *Item* fallinge out with an other ...[49]

Neatly drawn-up lists, in which the names of the witches were coordinated with the witnesses who testified against them and their alleged victims, regularized the long and confusing accounts of "sundry enformations, examinations, and confessions." One such reading aid to keeping track of the witches' maleficia and perhaps memorizing their negative example is the addendum summarizing the *True and just Recorde* of the St. Osyth witch trial at which Lord Brian Darcy had presented thirty-eight testimonies, detailing the bewitchment to death of twenty-three people and the spells cast upon numerous other villagers by no fewer than thirteen accused witches. In this digest, neatly organized columns, reminiscent of the graphic arrangement of commonplace books, match the source of information with the name and number of each witch, her alleged criminal actions, and her victims. Curiously the list order is far from perfect. A few entries before the end of the numbered witches list the author shifts to a narrative description of their familiar spirits, only to recall Margery Sammon, a witch he had omitted. He gives her a number and lists the names of her two spirits but fails to ascribe any crimes or victims to her. A few lines farther down, as the column arrangement resumes, the name of Annys Glascocke shows up, unnumbered and lacking any reference to crime, victims, or familiars. Presumably it was added after the pamphlet had gone to the print shop. The same woman is listed again, this time as Annis Glascoke and with a description of her crime and victim, in what appears to be another hastily added entry.[50] Clearly, fitting witchcraft into a diagrammatic format presented significant challenges to author and printer alike.

In its attempts to unravel and categorize witchcraft, the popular press was working hand in hand with the judicial system. The two institutions strove to expose the perverters of moral order, to raise religious and civic vigilance against criminal sinfulness, and to purify the Reformed community. But the dissemination of this ideological message of the godly was only part of the pamphleteers' business. Driven by marketing demands, they were willing to search far and wide to provide entertainment for their readers. As one preface author put it with unusual metaphoric panache, the ideal pamphlet would offer both "holsome hearbes of admonitions for the unwarie, and carelesse, and soote flowers to recreate the wearied senses."[51] Searching for the right marketable combination, pamphleteers mixed the legalistic molding of witchcraft as a willful and persistent attack upon English morality and social hierarchy with descriptions of deviant and sometimes morbid sexuality.

Thus even though, according to the legal record, native English witches from the Elizabethan era were not in the habit of holding demonic orgies, the press churned out Continental and Scottish witchcraft tales with an explicit sexual component. For example, the North Berwick witches from the 1591 pamphlet *Newes from Scotland* allegedly "confessed that, when the Devil did receive them for his servants, and that they had vowed themselves unto him, then he would carnally use them, albeit to their little pleasure, in respect of his cold nature: and would do the like at sundry other times." The examination report of Agnes Sampson, the oldest witch, supplies a more lurid description of this carnal usage: "Forasmuch as by due examination of witchcraft and witches in Scotland, it hath lately been found that the Devil doth generally mark them with a privy mark, by reason the Witches have confessed themselves that the Devil doth lick them with his tongue in some privy part of their body."[52]

Such descriptions conjoined foreign-born notions of oversexed devils copulating with witches during their sabbath with a native English fascination with the witch's mark as an object of sadistic eroticism. The obsession with the witch's teat is demonstrated in the 1589 pamphlet on the Chelmsford witches. In the section on the examination of Joan Prentice, one of defendants in the trial, we read how her familiar, "a dunnish colloured Ferrit" with "fiery eyes," appeared in her bedchamber and managed to scare her into letting him suck her blood even though Joan initially refused to jeopardize her soul in this way. The narrative focuses closely on physical experience: "The saide Ferret replyed and saide, I must then have some of thy blood, which she willingly graunting, offered him the forefinger of her left hand; the which the ferret tooke into his mouth and, setting his former feete upon that hand, suckt blood thereout, in so much that her finger did smart exceedingye." The pamphleteer then fleshes out in similar physical detail the familiar's "courtship" of Joan:

> Item, the said examinate saith further that about one moneth after, the said Ferrit came again unto her in the night time as she was sitting upon a little stoole, preparing her selfe to bed-ward, as is above saide: Joan wilt thou goe to bed, to whome she answered yea, that I will by Gods grace, then presently the Ferret leapt up upon her lap, and from thence up to her bosome, and laying his former feete upon her lefte shoulder, sucked blood out of her lefte cheek....
>
> Item, the saide examinate furthermore saith and confesseth, that the saide Ferret divers times after appeered unto her alwaies at the time when she was going to bed, and the last time he appeered unto her was about seaven weekes last past, at which time she going to bed, the Ferrit leapt upon her left shoulder, and sucked blood out of her lefte cheeke, and that done: he demaunded of her what she had for him to doo?[53]

Apparently Joan's familiar—a creature of oral fixation—was obsessed with the witch's teat located on Joan's cheek. Or at least the pamphleteer and the maker of the title page woodcut, which shows Joan in a breast-feeding posture with her familiar ferret reaching up to her face, agreed that portraying the witch as the object of the devil's oral sexual desires would attract and gratify reading customers (fig. 3).

¶ The Apprehension and confession of three notorious Witches.

Arreigned and by Iustice condemned and executed at *Chelmes-forde*, in the Countye of Essex, the 5. day of *Iulye, laſt paſt*.
1 5 8 9.

¶ With the manner of their diuelish practices and keeping of their spirits, whose fourmes are heerein truelye proportioned.

Fig. 3. Title page illustration from *The Apprehension and Confession of Three Notorious Witches* (London, 1589). Reproduced by permission of the Trustees of Lambeth Palace Library.

The sado-erotic fascination with the witch's teat was not restricted to living bodies. The 1593 pamphlet on the Warboys witches narrates how, after Alice Samuel's execution, the jailer stripped and examined her corpse, finding "a little lump of flesh, in manner sticking out as if it had been a teat to the length of half an inch." The examination was not court-ordered; it was also more than casual. At first the jailer and his wife were somewhat hesitant to disclose their finding since "it was adjoining to so secret a place which was not decent to be seen." Nevertheless they decided to share their discovery with the attending crowd:

> In the end, not willing to conceal so strange a matter, and decently covering that privy place a little above which it grew, they made open show thereof unto divers that stood by.
>
> After this the jailer's wife took the same teat in her hand and, seeming to strain it, there issued out at the first as if it had been "beesenings" (to use the jailer's word) which is a mixture of yellow milk and water; at the second turn there came out in similitude as clear milk, and in the end very blood itself. For the truth of this matter, it is not to be doubted of any, for it is not only the jailer's report unto all that require of him, but there are forty others also in Huntingdonshire of honest conversation that are ready to confirm the same upon their own sight.[54]

The jailer and his wife were not the only ones to partake in and encourage public indulgence in gruesome eroticism. In his meticulous report of the grim details of handling Samuel's dead body, the pamphleteer utilized it to entice a much larger audience than the original forty witnesses.

As Peter Lake writes, pamphlets, those creatures of ideology but also of the market, presented outlandish and violent acts ostensibly for moral instruction "but also to shock, titillate and engender that *frisson* of horror laced with disapproval which allows both pleasure and excitement at the enormities described to be combined with a reconfirmed sense of the readers' own moral superiority."[55] The Elizabethan reform, through the documentary witchcraft pamphlets of the era, of a superstitious and morally lax populace depended on a mixture of flaunted documentary truth-value and the sado-erotic appeal of strategically exposed female bodies. This reform, however, was also interwoven with and continuously undermined by the pamphleteers' interest in the reverberations of witch-speak.

The Allure of Witch-Speak

Unlike the ornate oratorical rhetoric of most Elizabethan pamphlets, as Sandra Clark points out, witchcraft pamphlets contained a high proportion of eyewitness reporting.[56] The pamphlets may indeed have aimed at condemning the disturbing speech acts of the witches as so much sinfulness while titillating their audience's morally dubious reading tastes, but they were also unabashedly exploitative of popular speech and rites. I now turn to an examination of the *failure* of the popular press to completely regiment the discursive transgressions of local "problem women" as abominable and self-destructive Satanic acts. In this section I attend to the cacophony of voices in the Elizabethan witchcraft pamphlets and to the witches' inventiveness, wit, and daring, which on a number of occasions gleefully subverted the rhetorical efficacy of the godly pamphleteers. Resonating in the popular wares of the Elizabethan witch-hunting press, witch-speak frequently implicated readers in the mischievous delight that witches took in their jokes and on occasion made a stubborn return into the daily speech of some commoners.

Witch-speak was spectacularly slippery in its denotation. For instance, witches could be confusing name-shifters. Thus T. I., author of the 1595 double feature *A World of Wonders*, tells about one Mother White-coate of Barking, Essex, "alias mother Arnold alias mother Glassenberry."[57] A true juggler of identities, this witch must have shifted names depending on the community she associated with or upon her role within it. Her indictments too bear marks of the uncertainty of her name, for, as Gibson explains in the preface to her edition of the pamphlet, in some of them "the name 'Arnolde' has been written and then scratched out."[58] In effect the pamphleteer's desire to designate the witch's identity by supplying the whole list of names by which she was known only underscores the impossibility of this enterprise. As readers, we remain uncertain about the number and identity of the witches featured in the pamphlet, especially since some of the victims suffered after exchanging bad words with Mother White-coate's unnamed daughter. This, of course, was precisely the position in which early modern villagers found themselves in their encounters of women dabbling with the supernatural.

Untutored and evasive, the utterer of witch-speak not only shifted names but was also in the habit of disappearing. The witch-hunting press never offered a successful resolution to the question of the origin of the demonic craft. Of course, Satan was believed to be at the bottom of this "plague," but the testimonies of the witches also alluded to human tutors. These human ringleaders of the Satanic network were remarkably difficult to track down. For instance, the author of *The Examination and Confession of Certaine Wytches at Chensforde* relates Elizabeth Frauncis's pretrial confession to Dr. Cole, archdeacon of Essex, and Justice of the Peace Henry Fortesque that "she learned this arte of witchcraft at the age of. xii. yeres of hyr grandmother whose nam was mother Eve of Hatfyelde Peverell disseased."[59] It is probably no more than a coincidence that the first witch featured in an Elizabethan documentary pamphlet should have been named Eve. It is no coincidence, in my mind, that Elizabeth Frauncis brought up a deceased person as the source of supernatural knowledge. Like Eve from the Book of Genesis, Eve of Hatfield Peverel could no longer be summoned by a human court to answer for her deeds.

The same was true of another witch credited in two pamphlets as a tutor in the dark arts. According to the record of the jail examination of Elizabeth Stile, alias Rockingham, of Windsor in the 1579 pamphlet *A Rehearsall Both Straunge and True*, "Mother Seidre dwelling in the Almeshouse, was the maistres Witche of all the reste, and she is now deade." In his autobiographical pamphlet Richard Galis likewise reports the death of a witch he calls "Audrey the Mistresse," apparently the same leader of the group of witchcraft suspects that included Elizabeth Stile, as well as Mother Dutton and Mother Nelson.[60] While Galis attributes Audrey's death to either her grief at having been publicly "schooled for... lewd behaviour and idle life spent to no profit" by the minister or to "the inward gnawing of conscience," neither he nor the anonymous author of *A Rehearsall Both Straunge and True* mentions any confessions by Audrey the Mistresse/Mother Seidre. As in the case of Eve of Hatfield Peverel, the mystical moment of the first initiation into the demonic trade remained inaccessible to those involved in the investigations and trials as well as to the readers of the two pamphlets.

Alice Samuel, of the Warboys witches in the 1593 pamphlet on the Throckmorton children's possession, likewise told a story about the disappearance of her initiator in witchcraft. During her examination by Francis Cromwell, bishop of Lincoln, and Justice of the Peace Richard Tryce she explained that she was taught how to call her familiar spirits by a mysterious "upright man" who showed up one day at her house. Mother Samuel took her time before she came up with a description of the stranger. She went to an adjoining chamber to consult privately her familiar spirits, and only after audibly charging them three times to reveal his name did she finally report that he was called Langland. This is information dubious at best, not only because of the uncertain chain of reporters but also because no witness actually heard the name uttered by the spirits, even though Mother Samuel's charge to them was apparently clearly audible. Mother Samuel could (or would) not tell where Langland dwelled, then reported that her spirits, upon another consultation, had first said that he had no dwelling, and had later on added "that he went the last voyage beyond the seas."[61] Was she referring to a voyage to the New World? Was the stranger alive or dead? Was he real or a figment of her imagination? Was she consciously playing the part of the spirits' confidante and perhaps mistress, or was she hearing voices? In any case, in the story she told her examiners William Langland was just as impossible to track down as the deceased Mother Eve and Mother Seidre.

If the stories told by and about witches in the pamphlets were remarkably elusive about the human agents of witchcraft, this was certainly also true of the witches' familiars. They were often ascribed shape-shifting capacities. In a pamphlet record of a pretrial examination, the Essex witch Elizabeth Frauncis talks at length about her familiar, the talking, wish-fulfilling "white spotted Catte" Sathan. This cat, which she said had provided her with sheep, a lover, an abortion, a husband, and the means of dispatching a fickle lover and a troublesome infant, seems to have come straight out of a Puss-in-Boots folk tale, as Gibson rightfully notes.[62] Sathan was even capable of turning into a toad to fit in her husband's shoe, where it struck him with lameness at her demand. After fifteen or sixteen years of service, Frauncis gave away Sathan to her neighbor Mother Waterhouse, whom she had instructed in the art of witchcraft. Mother Waterhouse, in her reported examination, stated that she was "moved by povertie to occupie the wol" from the cat's box. So "she praied in the name of the father, and of the sonne, and of the holy ghost that it wold turne into a tode, and forthwith it was turned into a tode, and so kept it in the pot without woll." But this was not the end of the transformations of Sathan the cat. Jone, Mother Waterhouse's daughter, told the examiners that the one time she had seen "the thinge" held by her mother, "that was in the likenes of a tode." However, when Jone decided to improvise a revenge on a neighbor's child and called Sathan, it "came to her (as she sayd) she thoughte out of her mothers shewe frome under the bedde, in the lykenes of a great dogge." By the time this familiar went out to torment little Jone's enemy, Agnes Brown, the dog had grown horns, a detail to which Agnes later testified at the trial.[63]

Occasionally a witch would tell a story about merging with her familiars into a single grotesquely misshapen body. The Warboys witch Alice Samuel told her examiners that the dun chicken believed to be her familiar had ceased to plague the children of the Throckmorton family because it had come into the bottom of her belly. Earlier Mother Samuel had complained to Robert Throckmorton of a stirring and "a marvelous great pain" in her stomach caused by a swelling "as big as a penny loaf," which, she suggested, was an evil house spirit that "is gotten into my belly."[64] In both stories she portrayed herself as victimized by the spirits and enduring pains similar to those of the possessed children. Furthermore the stories precluded the possibility of anyone witnessing the shape and actions of the familiar spirits sheltered within the body of the victim-witch. As Mother Samuel's narrative deflects the responsibility for bewitching the children upon the allegedly present yet intangible familiars weighing down her body, elements of merry jest and fabliaux begin to surface in her tale. Alice Samuel's body bulging with chickens—whether they were the food she so eagerly devoured at the Throckmorton's table or the pregnancy she unsuccessfully pleaded in order to escape hanging—can easily figure comic abundance of the Gargantuan type rather than threat. As Purkiss has noted in her study of witchcraft representations, the intangible familiar, so threatening to the well-being of the household, could also partake of the character of the exuberant carnivalesque.[65]

As suggested by Alice Samuel's imaginative play with the notion of the ingestible chicken familiars, humor was another aspect of witch-speak that thwarted its regimentation for the moralistic and market purposes of the pamphleteers. Practitioners of witch-speak appear to have had a taste for practical jokes combining humiliation and physical suffering, yet amusing for those witnessing them. Two such jokers, whose tricks provoked contagious cruel laughter bound to reverse the moralizing momentum of the Elizabethan pamphlet, were the name shifter Mother White-coate and her daughter. Their "manifolde mischiefes" not only tipped the balance of social power in rural Barking, Essex, in their favor but also provided comic diversion among their neighbors. When George Male, a local man of property, chased Mother White-coate and her daughter from his door and refused to give them alms, he was not cursed in some vague, general manner. The women's threat was specific, finely synchronized, and quite funny in the rough, bawdy manner of slapstick comedy. Mother White-coate "threatned that shee would set a Bee in his tayle the next time. Yea and that a singer sayed the daughter," playfully suggesting the comic tale about Male's "tail" that was in the making.[66] Whether through natural or supernatural means, the threat came true, and George Male must have become the occasion of quite a few snickers as he frantically scratched his itching bottom, dressed up in an expensive new outfit. "So not long after he determining te ride, put on a new payre of hose with a double rugge in them prysed fortie shillings, the first day of his riding he was so tickled in the buttocke, that he scratched through all, both hose and lynings and such a hole in his flesh, that it was not whole a moneth after."[67]

Mother White-coate was apparently quite adept at comic witchcraft. Another example of her supernatural jokes, this time with a morbid quality, involves the suicide attempt of William Daulbie, a friend of the Male family. This time the witch was repaying Daulbie for his own practical joke of tripping her in front of her neighbors during a Rogation week procession. As soon as she got up she sought Daulbie among the throng of people and "taking him by the hand thanked him for her fall, and sayd she would be even with him." Indeed she figured out a match to his practical joke. On his way to Barking, Daulbie came upon the witch as "she sat a praying under a tree, and so passed by her, and so went home, where beeing not a quarter of an houre, but Daulbie was so miserably vexed, that he sought to kill himself, thrust his hedde into the swelling tubful of swines meat, where he had smothered him self if help had not prevented it."[68]

Both episodes of T. I.'s pamphlet narrative capture something of the crude slapstick humor of the situation. As readers chuckle at the sight of George Male ruining both his clothes and his social image, and at the ridiculous image of Daulbie making—quite literally—a pig of himself, and a dead one at that, they inadvertently echo the laughter of the witch and perhaps quite a few of the events' original witnesses. At least for the duration of the comic effect, live and reading audiences find themselves in the position of content beneficiaries of witch-speak.

Other witches with a penchant for publicly humiliating practical jokes were reported to have devised classic comic numbers. The confession of the notorious Dr. Fian, "Register" of the North Berwick witches who allegedly attacked James VI of Scotland, featured in a 1591 pamphlet, includes a story about a Scottish witch with a keen sense of humor. While this story could have been made up by the doctor after the brutal torture to which he was subjected, it is also possible that it was the creation of the unnamed and unprosecuted witch who had set up the practical joke. Given reading skills that match her noble status, she could have been inspired by a similar episode described in Apuleius's *The Golden Ass*, a popular reading among the early moderns. When this mother of a young gentlewoman discovered that Dr. Fian planned on using "conjuring, witchcraft and sorcery" "to obtain his purpose and wicked intent of" her daughter, she herself provided the three pubic hairs he had asked the young woman's brother to steal, except that they were taken from a heifer's udder. Dr. Fian was thus able to perform his magic trick—only to find himself ardently pursued by a cow in heat, "to the great admiration of all the townsmen of Saltpans, and many other who did behold the same."[69] In this reported event the witch garnered public admiration and moreover was never examined or prosecuted for her craft. Within the pamphlet too her humorous story provided readers with much needed comic relief from the gruesome descriptions of "grievous" torture used to extract the confessions of the North Berwick witches. Later it was quoted as a supernatural number in George Gifford's influential *A Dialogue Concerning Witches and Witchcrafts*, reissued twice during Elizabeth's reign. Halfway into James's English reign, the visual comedy of this scene was revived once again in the popular play *The Witch of Edmonton*, whose urban and courtly audiences must have joined the on-stage witnesses of the joke, "ready to bepiss themselves with laughing."[70]

Occasionally tales of witty witches, likely informed by real witches' reputation for throwaway humor, found their way into the commercially successful jest books that provided diversion and conversational prompts to gentlemen of leisure. Admittedly, few Elizabethan jest book compilers considered witches laughable, even though jest books abounded in jokes about such serious topics as image worship, robbery, executions, and death. One of the exceptions was Anthony Copley, an impoverished distant relative of Queen Elizabeth. In the section on felons and thieves in his collection *Wits Fittes and Fancies* (1596), Copley includes a tale of a hardy witch who uses her wit to get out of the obligation to pay for the sign shaming her for her crimes: "An old woman was whipp'd at a Carts taile for baudrie & witch-craft: And after was done, the Hangman demanded of her his fees & charges: namely, he reckon'd unto her (amongst other things) what the paper and the picture she wore on her forehead all the whipping while cost him. All too deare a paper, so (said the Witch) but hold heer thy reckoning for this once, & see thou keepe that paper for me till the next time."[71] She is going to be back, the unrepentant witch quips, as she publicly makes a fool of the hangman waiting to be reimbursed for his expenditures. And she is going to pay for the public spectacle of her punishment at her own rate and on her own time.

Funny Elizabethan witch-speak resembled the clowning style of Richard Tarlton, the great comic actor of the 1570s and 1580s, whose jests were so popular that they proved worthy the cost of copyright protection and were anthologized some sixty years later. As in his signature jests in which he took on the persona of a resourceful rustic simpleton, witches initially "found themselves" in a humiliating situation and were apparently outwitted and shamed. Their Tarlton-like comic skill lay in judging carefully the timing of the reply, as they offered a throwaway insult and threat in place of cleverness: "Yea and that a singer"; "All too deare a paper, ... keepe [it] for me till the next time." Like the popular comic entertainer, some witches were apparently quite capable of shifting their audience's moral allegiances and making an audience laughing *at* them laugh *with* them.

Resistant witch-speak surfaced even in the writings of a group of ministers who, between the 1590s and the second decade of the seventeenth century, attempted "to translate into practical, pastoral terms the Calvinism of Elizabethan Cambridge." Stuart Clark has noted that this particular discourse of witchcraft, part of a wider campaign against popular irreligion, sometimes attempted "to capture the sort of conversation that would have occurred when peasant villagers debated magic and witchcraft with their clerical mentors."[72] These conversations would have included quotes and paraphrases of witch-speak. Among such early modern "anthropologists" were Lambert Daneau, whose *Dialogus de veneficiis* (1574) was promptly translated into English in the following year as *A Dialogue of Witches*; Robert Holland, a minister in Wales and the author of *Tudor and Gronow* (ca. 1595); the Oxford graduate Thomas Cooper, author of

The Mystery of Witchcraft (1617); and the Nonconformist preacher from Essex George Gifford, author of *A discourse of the subtill practices of devilles by witches and sorcerers* (1587) and *A Dialogue Concerning Witches and Witchcrafts* (1593).

The pastor-demonologists set out to correct superstitious misapprehensions that blamed everyday misfortunes on the ill will of witches and sought to undo afflictions through beneficent witchcraft. The message of the clergymen, hammered out again and again for the superstitious populace, cast maleficium as a test of whether one was indeed worthy of divine favor. By subsuming maleficium under the rubric of divine will, the reformers aimed to do away, once and for all, with witch-speak and its users' unsettling exercise of verbal power. Witches, the pastors insisted, had no hand in bringing about destruction, suffering, or death, however evil their intent. They were socially impotent, even though, as "most filthie drudges to the Divell," they undoubtedly deserved human and divine punishment.[73]

As evidenced by the very writings of the pastor-demonologists, such abstract thinking had trouble taking root, at least among the women from the village and small-town communities of early modern England. Perversely arguments against the material power of witch-speak provoked the locals to resort to this power, even when they claimed to abhor witches and referred to them as "old filth." In Gifford's *Dialogue Concerning Witches and Witchcrafts*, the "Scripture man" Daniel makes a sustained effort to dispel his interlocutors' belief in witchcraft. At the end of his extensive argument, his male interlocutors, the schoolmaster M. B. and the countryman Samuel, appear to have been swayed to the minister's side. Samuel's wife, however, remains silently resistant, and, when the goodwife R. stops by the house, she gets her to challenge Samuel's and M. B.'s conversion. Eager to display his newly acquired knowledge, the schoolmaster M. B. argues that witches have no power. Provoked beyond measure, the goodwife R. explodes with an elaborate threat, reminiscent of the surges of witch-speak in legal documents and pamphlets:

> *The goodwife R.* Is your husband turned to? I would you might lose all your hens one after an other, and then I would she would let her spirite upon your duckes and your geese, and leave you not one alive. Will you come to defend witches?
> *[The schoolmaster] M. B.* We doe not defend witches.

The goodwife R. Yes, yes, there be too many that take their part, I would they might witch some of them even into hell, to teach others to defend them. And you, M. B., I would your nagge might hault a little one of these daies: see whether you would not be glad to seeke helpe.[74]

The goodwife R. treads dangerous ground in her heated attack on the new doctrine of the impotent witch, as she curses her opponent, wishing him misfortune and destruction. As Willis has argued, Gifford clearly invites his readers "to dismiss the goodwife as another Eve-like victim of the devil's subtlety."[75] However, her impassioned and practical reasoning must have held some appeal for resistant early modern readers. Besides, she is the winner in the rhetorical exchange with the tentative, ironic schoolmaster. He backs out of the argument, allegedly exasperated with her willfulness, but also, I suspect, awed by the ventriloquized witch-speak in her verbal attack.

The wide circulation of witchcraft narratives through the popular pamphlets of the late Elizabethan era was immediately relevant to the conceptualization of the new national monarchy and its reformed subject. The pamphleteers' patterning of witch-speak contributed to the creation of a political technology of public speech and comportment. Using the negative example of the witches, the pamphlets marked the social limits within which violent speech, expression, and body movement were to be circumscribed; they also indicated the kinds of people that a good subject should refrain from associating with.[76] In corollary this delimitation enhanced a general suspiciousness of female speech and a low tolerance for the public expression of discontent or attacks of social superiors by disenfranchised women.

As Elizabethan witch pamphlets set clear-cut limits on acceptable public speech and comportment, they promoted a psychic economy marked by growing self-control and fear of the other. In the systematic manner of the records of assize court cases, which most pamphleteers followed closely, the press cast the witch as a clear and present danger. Whether the emphasis was on her sinfulness, "malevolent nurture," or rebellion against God's good order and the state, portrayals of the witch usually pitted her *against* her reading public.[77] However, throughout the Elizabethan period, the witch remained both an outsider *and* an authority figure. Among the reasons for this situation was the pamphleteers' failure to divest the witches' fighting words of their appeal to "unredeemed" readers.

Witch-speak resisted orchestration by the regimenting efforts of the pamphleteers. It intrigued live and reading audiences by the illusive character of the supernatural and provoked laughter at the witches' practical jokes. Each time readers laughed *along with* a witch, they breached the stark dividing line between her and the godly subject of the queen. In those moments witchcraft witnesses and pamphlet readers found themselves passing judgment upon the witches' "victims" and deriving pleasure from the ridicule of social superiors. The attempts of the pastor-demonologists to deny the power of the witches to inflict suffering proved too radical for the popular mentality. Keeping the witch in the public eye as a negative example of the reformed civil subject testified to her ambiguous position in relation to power. It also amounted to feeding simultaneously public repulsion *and* public fascination with witches and with witch-speak. Last but not least, it blurred a gender binary that rendered impossible or reprehensible the access to social power of women with a penchant for stupefying violent speech.

5

Courtly Witch-Speak on the Jacobean Stage

With increasing frequency, witches and witch-speak took center stage in theater productions of the Jacobean era. For the most part, these dramatizations of malevolent speech catered to popular entertainment rather than moral reform. In this respect representations of witchcraft in Jacobean drama were not unlike those in the "triviall" (i.e., witty and sensational) pamphlets of the era, which, as Gibson has argued, gained in popularity over their "necessary" (i.e., truthful and moralizing) Elizabethan predecessors.[1] Yet unlike most protagonists of the pamphlets, in Jacobean drama the practitioners of the malevolent art tended to come from privileged social strata. From Middleton's Duchess of Ravenna, who visits a witches' coven to dispose of a hired assassin, through Marston's demonic Lybian king Syphax, who conjures the arch-witch Erictho to arouse the sexual desire of the Carthaginian noblewomen Sophonisba, to Shakespeare's Macbeth and his queen, who resort to demonic rhetoric to obtain the Scottish throne, histrionic nobles and royalty were portrayed as acting quite similarly to what we know of historic witches. Specifically the rhetoric of these characters was clearly indebted to the violent speech of low-born women accused of being witches. In the booming artistic medium of the Jacobean theater, witch-speak came to be portrayed as an instrument of political power in the traditional narrow sense of the term.

The Makings of Theatrical Witch-Speak

Whether at Blackfriars Theatre or the Great Hall of Whitehall Palace, performances of witchcraft in general and of witch-speak in particular were stylized, with swiftly flowing action embellished by the portrayal of spirits flying above the stage, by fire and lightning, earthquakes and sea storms, enchanting music, and kaleidoscopic dance. Such aestheticization was hardly unique to the theaters. Gibson notes that for the entire duration of their publication history, witchcraft pamphlets were similarly marked by "the desire to entertain" their readers, mixing readily "the pleasure of rhetoric, the pleasure of moral righteousness with a spice of 'learned' Latin, and finally a good laugh."[2] When in the Jacobean era witches became a regular stage presence, some pamphleteers labeled their own propensity to lighten the tone of their witchcraft publications as inherently theatrical. Thus the author of the anonymous 1613 pamphlet *Witches Apprehended, Examined and Executed* compared "the Devill and the Witch" who allegedly caused a team of cart-drawing horses to bolt madly to a playwright-and-performers team in a "Tragicke Comedie."[3] Obviously this pamphleteer was interested in demonstrating his familiarity with Renaissance dramatic genres, just as the prefacer of the 1619 edition of Thomas Potts's pamphlet *The Wonderfull Discoverie of Witches in the Countie of Lancaster* was keen to flaunt his knowledge of early seventeenth-century demonological treatises, quoting and summarizing no fewer than seven of them.[4] While intertextual borrowing in multiple directions was endemic to the representations of witchcraft in general, it is worth noting that in Jacobean England borrowings from theatrical representations were becoming more fashionable. Through such complex intertextuality the improvisational theatrics and discursive violence of historical witches were more and more frequently reframed, edited, and aestheticized as the regal injurious performatives of Shakespeare's, Ford's, and Middleton's characters. Considering the cultural significance of the theater in Jacobean England, what historical witch-speak may have lost in authenticity in the process of such a creative translation was regained multiple times in performative force.[5]

Like the injurious speech of scolds and historical witches discussed in the previous chapters, aristocratic witch-speak on the Jacobean stage was an enargaic discourse that dissolved the divide between metaphor and literalness, acting and action. It created overpowering illusions of alternative realities through viscerally threatening, if not readily comprehensible vocal patterns of increasing fortitude. As was the case of witch-speak in the pamphlets, its force drew from the bodies of frequently eroticized female speakers. Stage witches shamed and taunted their addressees with assaults on the ego that sometimes escalated into animatives of physical aggression. The ultimate effect was overpowering the will of the theatrical witch's addressee, albeit temporarily, as victory was typically followed by the destruction of the witch.

At the same time, whether grumbled on the commons of a Yorkshire village or in a royal court scene on the Blackfriars stage, witch-speak had the uncanny power to *connect* witches and bewitched in a bond described by Kenneth Gross as almost erotic.[6] The parties drawn together by this injurious speech not only "coauthored" the witchcraft story; they fed off each other's fears and deep-seated desires, undermined and bolstered each other's power, and recklessly broke restrictions and taboos, transforming themselves as they exchanged the roles of accuser and accused, man and woman, the cursing one and the one cursed.[7] Paradoxically, I will argue, in the world of the plays the witch-speak of Jacobean theatrical nobility and royalty provides the kind of discursive bond that holds a kingdom together.

As royal censors and religious radicals alike were only too aware, stage entertainment was not innocent business. Dramatizing witchcraft in this fashion transferred the authority to pass judgment on it from the magistrates responsible for the functioning of the legal system to socially diverse audiences, which included women, apprentices, students, and assorted "rude mechanicals." While the Jacobean theatrical performances of witchcraft were far from treasonous, their hybridization of low-born witch-speak with the political rhetoric of theatrical nobles and royalty tarnished the ideological narratives of the marvelous monarchy.

"The Future in the Instant": Theatrical Witch-Speak and Political Rhetoric

It is not the titular monarchs who drive political history in Shakespeare's *Cymbeline* and *Macbeth* or in John Ford's *The Broken Heart*. In Shakespeare's plays two nameless queens whip their husbands into violent action with their fighting words. The effect? Lady Macbeth sets her husband on the Scottish throne and buys Scotland a much needed reprieve from the plotting of the fractional thanes and their foreign allies. Cymbeline's "wicked queen" earns the Celtic kingdom its sovereignty from the Roman Empire, however briefly. In Ford's play a noblewoman uses ritual cursing, musical lamentation, and the haunting display of her emaciated body to procure her brother's politically advantageous marriage to the heir apparent of Sparta's throne. Through their witch-speaking performatives these women shape the fates of dynasties and nations before they themselves collapse in madness or melancholy. Their power, brief though it may be, is wielded through enargaic speech that channels the attention of spectators and interlocutors to their bodies, even as these bodies are drained of female fluids and harden into metatheatrical references to the bodies of the boy actors performing the noble women's parts. Their rhetoric, commanding the mind and the senses, brings the direct addressees of courtly witch-speak, men and women alike, into a state of erotic rapture.

From his first entrance on stage, Macbeth displays an affinity for witch-speak. His comment on the day's events, "So foul and fair a day I have not seen" (1.3.36), echoes closely the alliterating chant of the weird sisters in the play's opening scene: "Fair is foul, and foul is fair, / Hover through the fog and filthy air" (1.1.10–11). Yet at this point of the dramatic action the valiant thane can hardly be called a master of witch-speak; his words may diagnose Scotland's volatile political climate precisely, but they do not affect events. Not so with the rhetorical performance of Lady Macbeth. At a pivotal point in the play, when her husband decides to put a stop to the plans for Duncan's assassination, she lashes out in a diatribe, which, in Macbeth's own words, does "bend up / Each corporal agent to this terrible feat" (1.7.79–80). To make her husband's will her own, his body an extension of hers, Lady Macbeth resorts to the rhetorical strategy of shaming: "Art thou affeard / To be the same in thine own act and valour / As thou art in desire?" (39–41). Her charge is clear: going back on the assassination plans would prove Macbeth not only a coward but also an impotent drunken braggart whose "act and valour" fail to match his desire. This suggestion stings the Scottish warrior to the heart, and he promptly asserts his manhood, declaring, "I dare do all that may become a man" (46).

At this point Lady Macbeth employs a rhetorical tactic favored by historical witches: overspeaking, using powerful insinuation to get the upper hand in a verbal strife with her superior in the gender and social hierarchy. Cases of overspeaking abound in witchcraft docufiction. For instance, in a 1579 pamphlet on the notorious Chelmsford witches, Mother Nokes was said to have come to the aid of her daughter when her gloves were snatched by a yeoman prankster. After the young man refused to heed her demand to return the stolen gloves, Mother Nokes told her daughter, apparently loudly enough for the departing yeoman to hear, "'Let him alone, I will bounce him well enough'; at which time he, being suddenly taken and reft of his limbs, fell down." The effect of the old woman's words was supposed to have lasted for at least eight days, during which time the prankster remained bedridden.[8] In a similar fashion Joan Harrison from Royston in Herford County allegedly bested a neighbor who called her "old hag" in a falling-out, firing back, "I will say little to thee, but thou shalt feel more from me hereafter," a response that half an hour later supposedly made her opponent feel "as if he has been set into your Scotch-boot; or Spanish strappado or your Morbus Gallicus was nothing to it—sometimes in a pestiferous heat, at others a chill cold, but at all times in continual aches and racking of his limbs as if the Devil had set him on his tenters to make broadcloth of him."[9]

Compared to these tersely spoken early modern witches, Lady Macbeth's overspeaking of her husband is much more elaborate, but its effects are similarly long-lasting. She asserts her own concept of manhood, which transcends social conventions and historical constraints: "When you durst do it, then you were a man . . . / . . . Nor time nor place / Did then adhere, and yet you would make both" (1.7.49–52). A man, the future queen asserts, is a maker of space and history. Neither social nor physical bonds can withstand manly determination, she continues, rendering her point with an metaphor of uniquely female experience:

> I have given suck, and know
> How tender 'tis to love the babe that milks me.
> I would, while it was smiling in my face,
> Have plucked my nipple from his boneless gums
> And dashed the brains out, had I sworn
> As you have done to this. (1.7.54–59)

This image of manliness as a disrobed and violent female body stuns Macbeth and stalls his peacemaking plans. Its vicious and complex eroticism, which subdues Macbeth, must have been even more provocative for the scene's early modern spectators, for whom Lady Macbeth is likely to have been embodied by a pubescent actor, one caught between childhood and adulthood, masculinity and femininity. In this act of discursive violence Lady Macbeth's ambiguously gendered, protean body, whose maternal generative power is heavily underscored in the text, also acquires a power as destructive as the divine wrath described by the biblical poet: "O daughter of Babylon, who art to be destroyed; happy shall he be, that rewardeth thee as thou hast served us. / Happy shall he be, that taketh and dasheth thy little ones against the stones."[10]

In the outcome of this speech queenly witch-speak achieves its goal: Macbeth's will yields to Lady Macbeth's. If there is any remnant of the royal "we" in his hesitant agreement, "If we should fail?," Lady Macbeth is quick to reword "we" as plural: "We fail! / But screw your courage to the sticking place / And we'll not fail" (1.7.59–61). The witchy noblewoman and the bewitched thane become one as a result of this masterful display of enargaic overspeaking. And Macbeth is quick to bring out the erotic dimension of such conjoining of violent wills. "Bring forth men-children only," he gasps before laying out the specifics of Duncan's assassination (72).

Witch-speak is also audible in the strong cadences, vivid metaphors, and beguiling insinuations of Cymbeline's beloved Queen. At a crucial moment in the history of Cymbeline's kingdom, when the Roman ambassador Caius Lucius has come to court to demand the tribute owed to Britain's Roman conquerors, it is the Queen who announces her state's claim to sovereignty. Her speech, targeting both the Roman and her royal husband, is a masterpiece of shaming. She begins by reminding Cymbeline that he has yet to live up to the valiance of his ancestors or indeed to "the natural bravery of [the] isle" over which he reigns (3.1.18). She then goes on to taunt Lucius with an image of Julius Caesar's double defeat at sea during his attempted conquest of Britain. Her sarcasm culminates in a vision of the Roman ships crushed not by human but by supernatural powers:

His shipping,
Poor ignorant baubles, on our terrible seas
Like eggshells moved upon their surges, cracked
As easily 'gainst our rocks. (3.1.26–29)

Like Lady Macbeth, the Queen in *Cymbeline* suggests that she partakes of a power unconfined to time or place. If the Romans' ships "cracked" "like eggshells" during the reign of "the famed Cassibelan," they can certainly be "cracked" again during Cymbeline's reign. Time stands still in the tableau the Queen draws of the imperial defeat, where nature's violence is rendered strangely domestic through similes belonging to a goodwife's kitchen. This mishmash of apocalyptic and domestic imagery, coupled with the majestic rhythm of her speech, blends together a potent potion of nationalism and ridicule. Cymbeline (though perhaps not the Roman envoy) is struck with awe but eventually finds his voice and declares Britain's independence from Rome. He motivates this huge political risk by recalling his ancestor's law-making and ridiculing "Caesar's ambition, / Which swelled so much that it did almost stretch / The sides o'th'world" (3.1.46–48). In this vivid conceit Cymbeline attempts to reenvision the military conquest of the Roman Empire as some kind of Gargantuan gorging, which threatens the integrity of the planetary body. This is Cymbeline's first attempt at witch-speak, echoing the Queen's discursive stabs, though delivered less poignantly.

For Cymbeline, the Queen's witch-speak is apparently rendered irresistible by her histrionic eroticism. When told that on her deathbed she confessed to plotting his murder and using him in order to install her son on the British throne, the king exclaims weakly, "Mine eyes / Were not at fault, for she was beautiful.... / It had been vicious / To have mistrusted her" (5.6.62–66). In his helplessness against the Queen's charms Cymbeline resembles a victim of love magic from the popular witchcraft docufiction. Like Thomas Simpson, the bewitched lover of the Jacobean witch Philippa Flower, who "was, as he supposed, marvellously altered both in mind and body since her acquainted company," the king also undergoes a radical alteration of his political persona, which he readily attributes to his Queen.[11]

Unlike Cymbeline's and Macbeth's "fiendish" queens, the character in Ford's *The Broken Heart* who best wields the power of witch-speak is justly venerated by the entire court of Sparta. There is hardly anything malevolent about the noble Penthea, who chooses to starve herself to death as self-punishment for having broken faith with her beloved—which is how she views her yielding to the sexual advances of the husband forced upon her by her own brother. Yet when Ithocles (Penthea's twin brother and the most revered courtier in Sparta) repents for having crushed her will, his living martyr of a sister overspeaks his contrition in a manner not all that different from the violent speech of Macbeth's and Cymbeline's "fiendish" queens. To Ithocles' claim that his heart is breaking at the sight of his sister's melancholy, Penthea returns a ritual curse:

> Not yet, heaven,
> I do beseech thee. First let some wild fires
> Scorch, not consume it; may the heat be cherished
> With desires infinite, but hopes impossible. (3.2.46–49)

Like Lady Macbeth and Cymbeline's Queen, Penthea brings time to a standstill in her violent speech. For, as we are about to find out, Ithocles' heart is indeed being consumed by love for the Spartan princess Calantha, whom he has no hope of marrying since he is not a prince himself. Languishing for Calantha, the heroic courtier gains emotional understanding of the daily hell in which he has plunged his sister when he forced an unwanted marriage upon her. There may well be yet another corrosive passion consuming Ithocles' heart: an unacknowledged incestuous desire for Penthea, who, in her selflessness and stoic nobility, doubles Calantha in the play. The dramatic action raises then rejects this possibility, but at least one of the characters, Penthea's jealous husband, reads Ithocles' body language when he is with his sister as undoubtedly incestuous.

The potency of Penthea's language is enhanced by the pitiful figure she strikes in her brother's eyes. Upon his return from the wars, instead of a young bride perhaps soon to bear a new life he is confronted by a living corpse, listless and destitute. It is as if Penthea's body has bled into her words, imparting its life force to them. The noble woman's emaciated body—likely signified on stage by the bony body of an adolescent actor—is carefully showcased to enhance her next bout of potent rhetoric. Having arranged for a private audience with Princess Calantha, Penthea begins by underscoring the contrast between her own recent indulgence in the pleasures of courtly life and her current rejection of "every sensuality" (3.5.20). Moved to tears, Calantha agrees to execute Penthea's will. The dying noblewoman first proceeds to bestow her youth "to virgin wives" (52), then confers her fame on "Time's old daughter, Truth" (62). After a well-timed pause, Penthea culminates her arresting performance by bequeathing her brother Ithocles to the princess "in holiest rites of love" (77). At this point in the scene the political future of Sparta is dictated to the heir apparent by a manipulative dying woman who has managed to breathe into her words remarkable enargeia. Penthea has involved Calantha in a ritual that the princess cannot undo. Mesmerized by the haunting poetry of Penthea's dying words, Calantha tries but cannot resist them. In the play's final scene the new queen of Sparta completes the ritual initiated by Penthea and dies after performing a ghastly marriage ceremony with Ithocles' corpse. Not just the executrix of Penthea's will, in this scene the Princess Calantha—a virgin wife like those on whom Penthea bestowed her youth—embodies Penthea's will *and* her memory.

On the Jacobean stage, as in real life, performances of witch-speak required a concerted effort of the body, calling for physically intensified language. No wonder, then, that music and especially songs, "airs," whose affective power the early moderns attributed to the mingling of the body's soul into the performer's breath, were often used in theatrical performances of magic and witchcraft. Examples abound in plays such as Middleton's *The Witch* and Shakespeare's *Macbeth* and *The Tempest*, but perhaps the most sustained association of music and witchcraft is the representation of the arch-witch Erictho in John Marston's play *The Wonder of Women or The Tragedy of Sophonisba*. Each of Erictho's stage entries is accompanied by soft "infernal music" played by "a treble viol, and a bass lute," instruments traditionally played by women.[12] When the dishonorable Libyan king Syphax courts Erictho's necrophiliac witchcraft, he refers to it as "high mysterious science" (4.1.139–40), but she herself insists it is "art" (170), namely, aural, sonorous art. The charm that the arch-witch promises to raise for the benefit of her supplicant is one "which Jove dare not hear twice" (168) and "whose potent sound will force ourself to fear" (181). To make this charm work Erictho compresses the elements, forcing "the air to music," as a trained vocalist or wind instrumentalist would (178). The immediate musical performance context adds considerably to the potency of her artistic witchcraft; its effect is enhanced by the witch's comments that its "sweet sounds" derived their harmony from "the shades of night," the time of the scene's action (179–80).

Music is also associated with the witch-speak performatives of Penthea from Ford's *The Broken Heart*. Although she herself never sings, her haunting commands are either preceded by disembodied songs or are perceived by their addressees as "sounds celestial" (3.2.174). Shakespeare's Lady Macbeth too does not take long to abandon the blank verse of nobility for the sing-song of the weird sisters. Shortly before Macbeth's coronation banquet, we find her chanting to herself:

> Naught's had, all's spent,
> Where our desire is got without content.
> 'Tis safer to be that which we destroy
> Than by destruction dwell in doubtful joy. (3.2.6–9)

There is too much pattern, too many internal rhymes and alliterations in this incantation for a simple expression of rancor that no son of hers has been prophesied to inherit the Scottish throne. As soon as Macbeth comes on stage, the queen interrupts her deadly alliteration of the very same sounds that the weird sisters incant in their infamous "double, double, toil and trouble" (4.1.10). But it seems that the queen's spirits, along with her words, have already entered Macbeth's ear. By the end of their exchange in this scene, the king pledges that "a deed of dreadful note" will be suffered by Banquo and his son. He does not specify how, but bats, beetles, and crows—all of which are traditionally associated with the "familiar spirits" of early modern English witches—figure prominently in his description of that dark "deed" (3.2.41, 43, 51).

If Lady Macbeth's magical incantation in this scene resonates with the aural patterns of the witches' sing-song, in Macbeth's case witch-speak is permeated with musical imagery as he devises plans for Banquo's and Fleance's murders: "Ere to black Hecate's summons / The shard-borne beetle with his drowsy hums / Hath rung night's yawning peal, there shall be done / A deed of dreadful note" (3.2.41–44). The "drowsy hums" of the "familiar" beetle, which Macbeth seems to have borrowed from the night queen Hecate, turn out to be indistinguishable from the "night's yawning peal" of church bells. With this demonized "yawning peal," Macbeth literally sounds Banquo's death knell. The ominous pun on "note" at the end of this passage brings together musical notation, allusions to the night calls of the familiar spirits summoned to carry out the dark deed, and the notable political advantage of Banquo's murder for Macbeth's dynasty.

Incapable of containing himself in this malevolent outpouring, Macbeth proceeds to evoke the circumstances of the projected murder as if unfolding in the present:

> Light thickens, and the crow
> Makes wing to th'rooky wood.
> Good things of day begin to droop and drowse,

> Whiles night's black agents to their preys do rouse.
> Thou marvell'st at my words; but hold thee still.
> Things bad begun make strong themselves by ill.
> So prithee go with me. (3.2.51–57)

Whose brain, whose body conceived of this invocation? Light in Macbeth's enargaic and energeic image thickens like his demonic queen's blood in the outcome of her unforgettable prayer to the "murdering ministers." The deadly *d*'s from Lady Macbeth's witch-song reverberate in Macbeth's pledge, made even more ominous by the rumbling of those strong Scottish *r*'s. The noble blank verse from the opening of Macbeth's murderous pledge eventually yields to foreboding rhyme: drowse—rouse, still—ill, prithee—me. The apprehensive entreaty "hold thee still" may be addressed as easily internally, to the beleaguered speaker of this witch-speak incantation, as to the allegedly frail queen. In these lines queen and king, witch and bewitched, are one being, breathing life into a single supernatural discourse of political violence.

"My Spell Is Lawful": Theatrical Witch-Speak and Political Redemption

If Macbeth's downfall is dramatized as largely due to his receptivity to women's witch-speaking performatives, the opening of *The Winter's Tale* portrays Leontes' *resistance* to the "potent" speech of his queen as the cause of a crisis in the polity and the royal family. In an uncontrolled eruption of jealousy triggered by the sight and rhetoric of his queen, the Sicilian king accuses Hermione of high treason and contemplates burning her at the stake, calls for the murder of the king of Bohemia, annihilates the age-long alliance between the two kingdoms, orders his newborn daughter to be abandoned in the wilderness, and causes the deaths of his son and a devoted counselor. As a result Sicily is left in international isolation and on the brink of a succession crisis. The king's counselors are alienated or exiled, while the king himself, awakening to the enormity of his actions, succumbs to a sixteen-year-long depression. The reason for this rampant desolation wrought by verbal violence is Leontes' horrified realization that his status in the international arena as well as the continuity of the royal bloodline hang on the "potent" words of his queen—enargaic words of erotic charge and performative power, two important components of witch-speak.

There is no mistaking the erotic charge of Hermione's speech. Uttered by a female character whose advanced pregnancy is an overdetermined signifier of maternal fecundity and erotic activity,[13] her words alternate sexual taunts and teases. Hermione parodies Polyxenes' professed desire to be reunited with his family as "limber vows," that is, "limp, flaccid, flabby" (1.2.48).[14] Shortly after shaming the Bohemian king into a predetermined choice ("My prisoner? or my guest?"), the queen urges a reward from her husband in no bashful terms: "Cram's with praise, and make's / As fat as tame things" (56, 93–94). A Cleopatra in her sexual openness, as Katherine Eggert calls her, Hermione then hastens to suggest to her husband, "You may ride's / With one soft kiss a thousand furlongs ere / With spur we heat an acre" (96–98).[15] On the early modern stage this bawdy double entendre may have acquired an additional homoerotic twist when delivered by a sprightly adolescent actor to an adult member of the troupe.

As several critics have argued, Hermione's "potent" words are sorely needed for the perpetuation of Leontes' political power, for what else can guarantee the legitimacy of the royal offspring?[16] It turns out that the queen's powerful rhetoric and the "boundless tongue" of her lady-in-waiting and chief defender, Paulina, are also indispensable for Sicilia's political redemption and the restoration of the state's political future. The two women prove to be tough "court physicians." They start out by shaming Leontes and delivering bitter public diagnoses of his attempt to eradicate the feminine from the polity. Accused of witchcraft and heresy, Paulina storms back:

> I'll not call you tyrant;
> But this most cruel usage of your queen—
> Not able to produce more accusation
> Than your own weak-hinged fancy—something savours
> Of tyranny, and will ignoble make you,
> Yea, scandalous to the world. (2.3.116–21)

After Paulina labels Leontes' disastrous fear of female sexual and verbal potency "scandalous" and in dire need of reform, she proceeds to instruct the king's attendants that diplomacy would be of no avail in restoring Sicily's reputation.

In her self-defense Hermione reiterates Paulina's charge against Leontes' tyranny and prophesies that "powers divine ... shall make / False accusation blush, and tyranny / Tremble at patience" (3.2.26–30). This prophesy (or is it a formal curse?) comes true as soon as the message of Apollo's oracle has been read: "Hermione is chaste, Polixenes blameless, Camillo a true subject, Leontes a jealous tyrant, his innocent babe truly begotten, and the King shall live without an heir if that which is lost be not found" (131–33). In Michael Bogdanov's 2003 production of this scene at Chicago Shakespeare Theatre, the royal court literally shook at this moment, as a giant statue collapsed with a deafening crash at the pronouncement of Hermione's moral victory over Leontes. The early modern stage was likely less emphatic in showcasing the powerful words of the queen and her lady-in-waiting, but even the spontaneous response of the assembled nobles, "Now blessed be the great Apollo!" (134), testifies that the witch-speak of noblewomen has already united them against Leontes' tyranny.

What remains to be done is to reconcile the king to the overdetermined signification of the female body and teach him receptivity to the excessive materiality of Hermione's and Paulina's potent prophesying and witch-speak. Both goals are accomplished in the last scene of *The Winter's Tale*, in which Paulina repeatedly challenges the royal party not to brand her "resurrection" of Hermione's "statue" as the "unlawful business" of witchcraft. Significantly these challenges arise only after Paulina has already enticed Leontes to engage in a series of discursive performatives typical of witch-speak. As the visitors to her chapel stare dumbfounded at the "statue," Paulina urges Leontes to voice his "wonder." His prompted response, "Chide me, dear stone, that I may say indeed / Thou art Hermione" (5.3.24–25), begins to permeate the "statue" with a life of its own. Skillfully guided along by Paulina's suggestion, "No longer shall you gaze on't, lest your fancy / May think anon it moves," the king proceeds to speak the "statue" into movement with a classic Austinian performative utterance: "Let be, let be!" (60–61).

At this moment Leontes bears some resemblance to historical examiners of suspected witches, who sometimes experimented with unlawful methods of inquiry to get to the desired outcome. One such examiner was

Gilbert Pickering from Northampton, who, along with his brother Henry, participated actively in the investigation of the alleged bewitchment of their nieces in the Throckmorton family and who contributed significant segments of the 1593 pamphlet on the Warboys witches discussed in the previous chapter. Gibson describes how Pickering encouraged one of the supposedly bewitched children to scratch the accused witch. The gentleman even held her hand forcibly as this was happening, even though he was advised that this folk method of identifying a witch was unlawful or, worse, a "trumpetry" of the devil, to use the words of a seventeenth-century divine.[17] But the eager investigator claimed that he did not want to miss an opportunity offered by the possessed child—a choice, Gibson explains, that amounts to a rejection of "divine authority in favour of deductive observation, though rigidly based on given beliefs."[18] Prompted by desire, Shakespeare's Leontes also proves willing to reject divine and legal prohibitions against witchcraft and participate in an unprecedented empirical experiment with words and bodies.

This is not Leontes' first experience in wringing reality out of words. As Carol Thomas Neely suggests, it was the king's language in the play's first act that reduced Hermione from a unique "she" to a grotesque "it," composed of the basest elements: "mingling bloods," "paddling palms," "pinching fingers."[19] But there is a difference between the "experiment" in the statue scene and Leontes' destructive rhetoric from the opening scenes of the play or the intrusive empirical curiosity displayed by an investigator with a penchant for physical violence like Gilbert Pickering. Whereas the latter two injurious performatives follow scripts of inevitable outcomes, authored and staged by men of power and authority, the performatives that Leontes utters in Paulina's chapel are communal and open-ended. In the opening of the play the king, in his capacity as supreme legal authority in the realm, wields autonomous injurious speech: "Away with her to prison"; "Thou art here accused and arraigned of high treason" (2.1.105, 3.2.13). In the final scene, under Paulina's direction and with the support of the rest of Hermione's enchanted spectators, Leontes engages in a performative act authored by a collective speaking subject. Like historical witch-speak, his power to imbue the "statue" with life now rests not with himself as an individual office holder but rather with an unfolding history of invocations able to grant or take away life.[20] When, having evoked this history, Paulina announces to her on-stage audience the imminent miracle of Hermione's resurrection, Leontes not only acquiesces to Paulina's supernatural art but virtually acts as her apprentice.

As is the wont of witch-speak, Hermione's and Paulina's rhetorical strategies are underscored by the power of their strategically displayed bodies. If Hermione's "statue" was indeed done in Julio Romano's mannerist style, as suggested by the gentlemen at Leontes' court (5.1.104–5), then the posture struck by the early modern actor would have been dramatically exaggerated and perhaps somewhat contorted. The king comments on the emotional impact of Hermione's posture: "O, thus she stood, / Even with such life of majesty—warm life, / As now it coldly stands—when first I wooed her" (5.3.34–36). Perdita yearns to kiss Hermione's hand, Polixenes lovingly muses on the apparent warmth of her lips, while Leontes, after gazing at the blood-pulsing veins of his queen, is stirred by the "air [that] comes from her" and moves to kiss her. In this extraordinary communal celebration of the female body, the king is cast in the lead role, but it is Hermione who is praised as lover, ruler, mother, Holy Mother, a woman brimful of life.

In the statue scene the corporal and discursive components of witch-speak are divided between Hermione's enchanting postures and Paulina's verbal performatives. Yet this division does not signal a weakening or silencing of queenly witch-speak now that it has fulfilled its function of healing the polity.[21] Hermione's silence in this scene is no less powerful than her verbal battle against Leontes' deathly legalese. For, as Janet S. Wolf has argued, in their fury and in their benevolence Hermione and Paulina overlap as much as Demeter and Hecate do in the Persephone myth.[22] The two of them nurse Perdita, publicly denounce tyranny, haunt the conscience of the guilty, and bring light to the truth. Arguably the performative witchery of the statue scene is also the product of their *collective* authorship, directing, and acting. At the end of the play Leontes, for one, is left thirsting for more of these women's "potent" words. As the royal party exits the stage, he charges Paulina with the task of orchestrating the healing myth-making of his "dissevered" polity and family:

Good Paulina,
Lead us from hence, where we may leisurely
Each one demand and answer to his part
Performed in this wide gap of time since first
We were dissevered. Hastily lead away. (5.3.152–56)

"Thou Shame of Greatness": Theatrical Witch-Speak and Political Frailty

The Winter's Tale is unique in Jacobean drama for its endorsement of women's "potent" witch-speak as politically revitalizing art, one as "lawful as eating" (5.3.11). Other Jacobean plays foreground the ubiquity of this traditionally female discourse, including its echoes in the deeds and the majestic meter of theater monarchs, but their portrayal of witchcraft in high places typically casts a shadow on the popular image of the dazzling court. Thus the Lybian king Syphax in Marston's *Tragedy of Sophonisba* degenerates from committing treason to conjuring evil spirits to having intercourse with a succubus; at the court of Ravenna in Middleton's tragicomedy *The Witch* witchcraft is the courtiers' tool of choice in carrying out ruthless plots of assassination, whoredom, and adultery, with little regard for state affairs; in Shakespeare's *Tempest*, the exiled Duke of Milan combines his mastery of witch-speak with a penchant for mental and physical torture in an arguably unsuccessful attempt to secure the political control over his island kingdom and his former dukedom. In all these plays witch-speak at court is the symptom of moral depravity and political impotence.

From the very opening of Marston's play, Syphax is portrayed as driven by a relentless ambition to be the first among the seventeen feodars (confederate lords) of Carthage. When the Carthaginian beauty Sophonisba chooses his rival Massinissa for her spouse, Syphax takes this as a devastating blow to his royal reputation. He may well have a point: an alliance through marriage with Sophonisba's influential father would secure her spouse the seat of honor among Carthage's feodars. As it is, Syphax's frustrated political and amorous ambition rapidly turns destructive. He starts by betraying the Carthaginian alliance and switching sides to the Romans as their legions converge upon the famed city. After the African senators decide to buy back his military force by handing over to him the reluctant Sophonisba, Syphax threatens to rape her and remains unmoved when she threatens to plunge a knife into her own heart rather than yield to him. Callously he warns her:

> Do, strike thy breast. Know, being dead, I'll use
> With highest lust of sense thy senseless flesh,
> And even then thy vexed soul shall see,

Without resistance, thy trunk prostitute
Unto our appetite. (4.1.58–62)

There is a close resemblance between Syphax's sadistic visualization of raping Sophonisba's still warm corpse and his description of the necrophiliac rites of the arch-witch Erictho. In a passage closely echoing Marston's source, book 6 of Lucan's *Pharsalia*, the king draws a ghastly scene of Erictho as a sexual predator upon fresh corpses:

But if she find some life
Yet lurking close, she bites his gelid lips,
And sticking her black tongue in his dry throat,
She breathes dire murmurs which enforce him bear
Her baneful secrets to the spirits of horror.[23] (4.1.118–22)

The necrophiliac gluttony of this unambiguously classical witch was attributed to early modern witches as well, as evidenced by the language of the prohibition in the 1604 Act against Conjuration, Witchcraft and dealing with evil and wicked Spirits. Among other things, the Act prohibited on "pains of deathe as a Felon" the taking up of "any dead man woman or child out of his her or theire grave, or any other place where the dead bodie resteth, or the skin bone or any other parte of any dead person, to be imployed or used in any manner of Witchcrafte Sorcerie Charme or Inchantment."[24] Prohibited too was the intertwining of physical and verbal transgression, characteristic of Erictho's and Syphax's demonic acts.

Syphax's description of Erictho's ghastly actions is actually the culmination of his invocation of demonic spirits. He turns to them for assistance with love magic upon realizing that the "forced use" of Sophonisba is unlikely to be enjoyable, at least not in the long term (4.1.70–72). Within a couple of lines the arch-witch Erictho shows herself to the king. Yet even before Syphax renders audible the "dire murmurs" he has learned from Erictho, he has begun to condense his own speech into rumbling alliterations of the kind that also characterizes the witch-speak of the Macbeths: "Here, in this desert, the great soul of charms, / Dreadful Erictho lives, whose dismal brow / Contemns all roofs of civil coverture" (97–99). The drumming *d*'s and *t*'s and the thundering *r*'s in the king's invocation of an alternative reality—a demonic and uncivil one—quickly coalesce into "infernal music," called for in a stage direction in the 1606 quarto of the play. Next Erictho enters, conjured by Syphax's enargaic speech.

From this point on, until Erictho restores her youth with Syphax's "proud heat" and abandons her disguise as Sophonisba, king and witch are hardly distinguishable (5.1.19). They both force "the air to music," punctuating each other's lines as if in an operatic duet (4.1.178). Even Erictho's devastating blow when she reveals that the love magic she promised the king was nothing more than a bed trick fails to sever Syphax's links to the demonic. Kneeling, and possibly shaking a fist at heaven, he cements his alliance with the dark powers with a ritual curse:

> He whose life's loathed, and he who breathes to curse
> His very being, let him thus with me
> Fall 'fore an altar sacred to black powers
> And thus dare heavens! (5.1.25–28)

The alliance of the abject, which Syphax calls into being through this ritual curse, is not a hypothetical one. The king's rebellious witch-speak conjures the ghost of a fellow political antisubject, the royal Carthaginian traitor Asdrubal, who had courted Syphax's military might by offering him his daughter Sophonisba, then just married to Syphax's rival Massinissa. But there are other good candidates for the demonic alliance: the feodars of Carthage Carthalo and Bytheas, the captain Hanno Magnus, and perhaps even that master of realpolitik, the Roman general Scipio. The only three characters morally distinguished from the demonic in this play are the royal lovers Massinissa and Sophonisba and the senator Gelosso. At the end of the play Gelosso and Sophonisba are dead. Massinissa, the Lybian king who wins Carthage for Scipio, gets neither a crown nor a laurel wreath. Instead it is Sophonisba's corpse that Scipio adorns with the regalia of the victor—an honorable gesture of no political consequence.

Similarly to the Carthaginian court in *Sophonisba*, demonic alliances among the nobles are endemic to the court of Ravenna in Middleton's satiric play, *The Witch*. Upon returning from the wars, the courtier Sebastian, seeking retribution against the man who has married his fiancée, does not think twice about visiting Queen Hecate's coven for help. Once there he commands "the chief witch" as he would a bumbling servant to "up and laze not" in satisfying his demands for a potion that would render his rival Antonio impotent (1.2.121).²⁵ Hecate submits in a comically exaggerated manner: "Thy boldness takes me bravely. We're all sworn / To sweat for such a spirit" (127–28).

Like Sebastian, the Duchess of Ravenna also rushes to Hecate for supernatural help in killing her alleged lover, Almachildes, once she is convinced that he has fulfilled her orders to murder her sadistic husband. (In fact Almachildes has not; 5.2.1–45). While the duchess's curt commands initially provoke Hecate's irritation—"They make me mad," the arch-witch exclaims (17)—the two finish each other's lines with an ease that seems to justify Hecate's address to the duchess as "daughter" (25) and the duchess's eager-to-please reply, "I did not doubt you, mother" (33).

It is both language and deeds that render the Ravenna nobles witch-like, but Middleton's play text also calls for terror-striking supernatural stage action involving nobility. The lustful Antonio, this "devil in a sheep-skin," is reported to have died falling through a trap door "into a depth / [that] Exceeds a temple's height, which takes into it / Part of the dungeon that falls threescore fathom / Under the castle" (5.3.30–33). The governor interprets his end as divine retribution for Antonio's wrongdoings, but the architectural symbolism of the Jacobean stage, where the area to which Antonio would have descended was also known as "hell," may well indicate that his was an evil spirit who returned to where he originally came from. In an earlier, more frivolous scene, Almachildes, as bawdy and tongue-loose as any witch, shows off to Hecate and her coven his talents at figure casting and fiddles carelessly with love magic (1.2.194–231).

As Anne Lancashire has pointed out, "'The witch' is not only Hecate but also the various characters in all plots who sexually enchant one another by fair means or foul; and the play deals with the witch motif, literally through the three so-called witch scenes and metaphorically throughout."²⁶ While the trafficking between Hecate and the Ravenna courtiers is comically exaggerated, the ease with which the vogue for witchcraft spreads throughout the court provokes anxiety about its contaminating power. Not so much a witch as "the embodiment of witchcraft," in Purkiss's words, Hecate functions as the source of hellish corruption but also as the terrifying representation of a demonic alliance of nobles and commoners whose supernatural practices are neither qualitatively nor ethically different.²⁷

As early as 1937 critics have commented on the real-life parallels between the play and the Essex divorce hearings and subsequent Overbury poisoning trial. Attention has focused mainly on the impotence-causing witchcraft in the Isabella-Sebastian-Antonio plot and its relationship with the 1613 annulment, on the grounds of nonconsummation, of the marriage between Frances Howard and Robert, Earl of Essex. As the 1615–16 state trials for the murder of Overbury disclosed, Howard had apparently employed witchcraft to repel her husband and attract James's favorite Robert Carr, soon to be earl of Somerset, whom she married shortly after the annulment of her first marriage.[28] In addition to the male conjurers Simon Forman and Dr. Savory, Howard's conspiratorial network involved a host of cunning women, among them her ambitious confidante, Anne Turner, as well as the apparently low-born swindler Mary Woods, "said to have cozened Frances Howard of a jewel of great value in exchange for poison."[29] There were speculations that the network reached as high as the monarch. James's removal in late 1615 of Sir Edward Coke as chief prosecutor in the Overbury trials started rumors in London that the chief justice had come too close to private concerns of the king, who could be seen as concealing real traffickers with the supernatural.[30] Whatever the exact relationship between the legal trials and Middleton's play, both the legal texts and the play triggered by Howard's case display the same apprehensiveness about the entanglement of high and low witchcraft.

The diffusion of witchcraft across social strata is also portrayed in Shakespeare's *Tempest*, performed, like Middleton's *The Witch*, at Blackfriars Theatre and at court. In this play too the magical incantations and theatrics of the monarch—the chief means through which Duke Prospero wields power over the island's inhabitants—have all the distinctive features of witch-speak. As various critics have noted, Prospero's learned Neoplatonic magic bears disturbing parallels to the "mischiefs manifold, and sorceries terrible" of the witch Sycorax, the island's previous ruler (1.2.264).[31] She is dead before the play begins, and our only source about her history is Prospero. In his self-interested narrative, Sycorax's malevolent powers are described as combining rhetorical enargeia and animative power, typical of the portrayal of demonic courtly characters in Jacobean drama as well as of historical witches from the pamphlet literature. Prospero too bears a distinct resemblance to the low-born witches featured in popular Elizabethan docufiction in his predilection for inflicting physical and mental suffering. His spirits pinch, goad, and cramp Caliban, Stephano, and Trinculo, madden the Neapolitan party, paralyze Ferdinand and the "three men of sin," confine, imprison, and confuse the senses. He torments Caliban with apes, hedgehogs, and adders and later releases his spirits in the shape of dogs upon the clownish conspirators.

The extent of Prospero's indebtedness to low-born witch-speak is revealed in his exchange of malicious retorts with Caliban. When he first bursts onto the stage, Prospero's slave hisses out an elaborate curse apparently inspired by the memory of his mother's witchcraft and complete with the acoustic suggestiveness of this enargaic speech:

> As wicked dew as e'er my mother brushed
> With raven's feather from unwholesome fen
> Drop on you both. A southwest blow on you
> And blister you all o'er. (1.2.321–24)

Caliban's attempt to alter the conditions of power on the island through an exercise of discursive power fails. Like Hamlet, he has confused incidental rhetorical violence with violent action.[32] Instead of unleashing the kind of injurious speech capable of unbalancing the world of its addressee, Caliban does not even dare breach the spatial and hierarchical boundaries between himself and his master. The question arises, however, how Caliban knows about enargeia. He cannot possibly remember Sycorax's injurious speech. If we are to believe Miranda, at the time of her arrival on the island Caliban had no words with which to make known his "purposes" (1.2.356). He learned language from her and Prospero, as his mastery of blank verse testifies. It is likely, then, that malevolent speech is also something he learned from the duke. Indeed in his response to Caliban's curse, Prospero comes across as a master of overspeaking:

> For this, be sure tonight thou shalt have cramps,
> Side-stitches that shall pen thy breath up. Urchins
> Shall [forth at] vast of night that they may work
> All exercise on thee. Thou shalt be pinched
> As thick as honeycomb, each pinch more stinging
> Than bees that made 'em. (325–30)

Not content to simply redirect the curse, substituting Caliban's name for his own as the object of physical suffering, Prospero unleashes a series of fairly localized physical threats, which gather momentum to a point where they threaten to turn his slave's already deformed body into a shapeless mass, "as thick as honeycomb." Judging from Caliban's fearful reaction, he must be familiar with the effectiveness of Prospero's words. Perhaps the slave's deformed body is the physical record of the duke's injurious speech. Prospero is indeed a master of "bad-tongue" improvisation, effectively paralyzing both verbal and physical response and arresting his verbal opponent into an abject social position.

Just as Prospero overpowers Caliban's malevolent speech, so did he, in all likelihood, excel over Sycorax in using the supernatural to political ends. Exiled to the island, Sycorax must have ruled with an iron fist, judging from her punishment for Ariel's insubordination: imprisonment in "a cloven pine" (1.2.277). So does the usurper of her title. Prospero threatens to use his "art" to enact the same form of punishment on Ariel for resisting his commands: "I will rend an oak / And peg thee in his knotty entrails" (294–95). This is not simply an attempt to outdo Sycorax by choosing a tighter, more claustrophobic site of imprisonment for the insubordinate subject. As Mary Ellen Lamb has perceptively argued, if Sycorax's imprisonment of Ariel in a tree trunk "cloven" like a vagina suggests a forced return to the womb, Prospero's description of the oak's entrails as "his" implies that Prospero's trunk has a womb-like interior.[33] Entrapment in this securely knotted male womb would be eternal. It appears that the duke's control over his subjects on the island relies not only on Sycorax's intimidating rhetoric but also on his appropriation of female gestational powers.

Even as Prospero renounces his "rough magic," he delivers a speech that both performs and commemorates his "so potent art" (5.1.59, 50). Summoning the very elves and demi-puppets with whose help he "bedimmed / The noontide sun, called forth the mutinous winds," shook "the strong-based promontory," "plucked up / The pine and cedar," and awakened the dead (5.1.41–42, 46, 47–48), Prospero intensifies verbal effect by ritual action performed under the accompaniment of "solemn music." He draws a circle on the ground, waves his staff and perhaps breaks it, thus adding bodily expression and force to his enargaic supernatural discourse.

Numerous critics have noted that the duke's speech echoes the words of the witch Medea as rendered in Ovid's *Metamorphoses*.[34] The passage must have been popular with theatricals and theatergoers of the early modern era, for a few years after *The Tempest* was produced for the first time, Ovid's rendition of Medea's cosmic magic would be uttered again, this time in the original Latin, by Middleton's Hecate in *The Witch* (5.2.18–25). At about the same time, Robert Armin, the actor who played Caliban in the original production of *The Tempest*, gave a rough approximation of Medea's speech to the Witch in his play *The Valiant Welshman*.[35] What has escaped critical attention is the number of similarities between Medea and the two royal women in *The Tempest*: Sycorax, the island's original ruler, and Miranda, the future queen of Naples and Milan. Medea was the only surviving child of the rightful king of Corinth, Aeëtes. Like Miranda, she emigrated with her father to Colchis after the usurpation of the Corinthian throne by Corinthus. Like Miranda again, she effectively reclaimed her father's throne when the Corinthians accepted her husband, Jason, as their king. Like Sycorax, Medea could not secure the throne for her children once Jason proposed to divorce her and enhance his power by marrying Glauce the Theban. In this context Ferdinand's "false" playing in the game of chess seems to be a sinister omen for the future of his marriage with Miranda. In some myths Medea's sons are subsequently stoned to death by the Corinthians, enraged at Medea's revenge on Glauce and her father—a fate arguably spared to Sycorax's son only because Caliban's knowledge of the island was indispensable to Prospero.[36]

Sycorax, the old witching queen, may be dead, but her potent words prove indispensable to Prospero in ruling over his island kingdom. However, even as ventriloquized witch-speak defines Prospero's marvelous monarchy, it undermines his moral right to rule and dooms the future of his dynasty. Perhaps with this realization he rejects his magic at the end of the play, which leaves him no choice but to retire to Milan, relinquish the political entity of his dukedom to the future king of Naples, and cast "every third thought" on his grave (5.1.311).

Of course, when Prospero's kingcraft, contaminated as it was by witch-speak, was viewed in the context of the Platonic-Pythagorean "frozen magic" of Whitehall Palace's Banqueting House, it could be framed as an intricate compliment to the play's most privileged spectator, King James.[37] Orazio Busino, almoner to the Venetian ambassador, who had attended a masque there on January 6, 1617 or 1618, described this performance space in the following terms:

A large hall is fitted up like a theatre, with well secured boxes all round. The stage is at one end, and his Majesty's chair in front under an ample canopy.... Whilst waiting for the king we amused ourselves by admiring the decorations and beauty of the house, with its two orders of columns, one above the other, their distance from the wall equalling the breadth of the passage, that of the second row being upheld by Doric pillars, while above these rise Ionic columns supporting the roof. The whole is of wood, including even the shafts, which are carved and gilt with much skill. From the roof of these hang festoons and angels in relief, with two rows of lights.[38]

In this performance space the courtiers and foreign dignitaries in the boxes flanking the rectangular hall were actually following two concurrent spectacles: the on-stage courtly action of *The Tempest* and, in front of it, the imposing tableau of the luminous monarch, positioned, as John Orrell explains, "where no member of the audience would have their backs to it." Since a political theology, the goal of Jacobean state ideology, allowed for only one master of political and supernatural narratives, Prospero's failure as a ruler and his moral dubiousness as a magician would have underscored the political and moral triumph of his counterpart in the privileged locus of the complex royal spectacle. After all, when the play was performed at court, the duke abjured his magic under the discerning gaze of a monarch who took pride in his ability to distinguish between witchcraft and its simulation. This ability, the demonologist Thomas Cooper asserts, was a divinely afforded "blessing of Governement"; it "very mercifully" curtailed the effects of witchcraft. Uttered in the same hall where flamboyant Epiphany masques celebrated the presence of divinity in the person of the king, the Epilogue in which Prospero acknowledges that his "charms are all o'erthrown" as he comes out of character would have testified not so much to the corruptibility of James's kingcraft as to the mystical omnipotence of the royal spectator.[39]

In the commercial theaters of early modern London, however, Prospero's performance would have resonated quite differently. Without the physical presence of the harmony-restoring royal spectator, the witch-speak in the duke's "art" would have marked his kingcraft as corruptible and untrustworthy. Moreover, addressed to the mixed audiences at Blackfriars, which included fellows berated by Ben Jonson as "sinfull sixe-penny

Mechanicks," Prospero's acknowledgment, "I must be here confined by you, / Or sent to Naples" (Epilogue 4–5), acquires considerable seditious power.[40] Not only does it explicitly raze the social differential between the on-stage monarch and the off-stage subjects; it casts the spectators as figures of legal authority, comparable to the magistrates who "examined" early modern witches and their accusers to determine the feasibility of legal action. In the case of legal narratives of witchcraft, Gibson claims, deposers, witnesses, and accused witches fashioned each stage of the development of their stories to meet the expectations of "the learned person, who will expect certain features, ask searching questions, then act."[41] Theater professionals likewise tailored their witch-speaking spectacles in view of the expectations and knowledge of their spectators. In the process, I suggest, they endowed these audiences with considerable social authority: the authority to "ask searching questions" of the representations of nobles and royalty and "then act."

Resounding in the commercial theater halls, the Jacobean dramatizations of witch-speak bridged the moral gap between the mystical court of the male monarch and low-born witches from the English countryside. Were the theater professionals intentionally politically subversive in these representations? Hardly. Yet neither were these socially engaged opportunists overly deferential to political authority. As they imbued with witch-speak the speech and actions of aristocratic characters, the mystical allure of the court began to lose its luster. As early as the turn of the sixteenth century, when the old King Hamlet was portrayed as "a goblin damned" (1.4.40), the theaters began preparing a change in political mentality that by the midcentury would make it conceivable for the Puritan revolutionaries to put on trial and execute—like a low-born witch—God's lieutenant upon earth, King Charles I.

6

Gender and Politics in Early Quaker Women's Prophetic "Cries"

If Jacobean theater had a penchant for aristocratic and even royal feminine witch-speak, by the middle of the seventeenth century violent speech wielded by women at court was no longer a matter of stage representation only. Almost 375 Quaker women prophesied publicly in the second half of the seventeenth century.[1] They threatened divine wrath against ministers and church congregations, mayors and magistrates, judges and courts of law. A good number of these prophets unleashed their verbal onslaughts against men like Oliver Cromwell and King Charles II, men positioned at the very pinnacle of political power. Curiously these state leaders were hesitant to fend off the attacks.

Among the assailants from the emerging Society of Friends was Mary Howgill, a Quaker minister who, at "about ten a clock at night" on July 7, 1656, in Whitehall Palace issued this prophetic warning to the Lord Protector of England, Oliver Cromwell:

> But thou, where thou standest, thy reign shall be for a time, for misery and great condemnation shall be thy portion, and all them who have forgotten the Lord our God; for we have the Lord to be our strength, and thou who acts against him, the time is come that we are justified, and with him that justifies us shall thou be condemned, and thou shall know that thou hadst better thy tongue had been cloven to the roof of thy mouth, ere these things had been acted in thy name (we are kept in perfect peace).

Howgill was not the first Child of Light to assail Cromwell's ear; several of the traveling ministers known as the First Publishers of the Truth had paid him visits in Whitehall earlier. Yet something about Howgill's speech must have "pierced" the Protector's conscience to allow for "much discourse" with her in spite of the late hour.[2] Before departing she left a copy of her scathing call for repentance in Cromwell's hands, as was the custom with petitioners.

There is little in the content and discursive structure of Howgill's letter to account for the earnest consideration of her message on the part of the Lord Protector, who only a few weeks later would declare in a speech to Parliament, "It shall be found to be the Civil Magistrate's real endeavour to keep all professing Christians in this relation to one another; not suffering any to say or do what will justly provoke the others;—I think he that will have more liberty than this, is not worthy of any."[3] She asks for nothing. Her tone is harsh. Like other Quaker petitioners, she charges Cromwell directly with condoning the persecution of Friends and worse: with worldly corruption and with having "crucified the Lamb of God." Furthermore she draws a clear line between "we [who] know our being and our habitation with the Lord" and "thou" who are "one with all them that are in the evil."[4] As a cry of woe for the spiritual fall of the Protector, signed "by a lover of thy soul" and utilizing throughout the socially leveling "thou" characteristic of Quaker speech, it strikes an intensely (and inappropriately) personal note. Yet the speaking subject of the *Remarkable Letter* positions herself at a considerable distance from both her addressee and the immediate discursive context. She refers to herself as one "grafted" into God and immersed into an everlasting divine time transcending distinctions of past, present, and future. Why, then, in spite of the antagonizing content of the address, its disregard of social decorum, and the discursive distance the speaker maintained from her addressee, did it procure Howgill a lengthy conversation with the most powerful man in England so late at night?

Clearly Howgill's address derives its style from the symbolism of Old Testament prophesy, as is evident from the harshness of its tone, the spiritual distance between speaker and addressee, and the alignment of the speaker with the divine. In a deeply religious culture such prophesying was bound to deliver a powerful punch to the addressee, putting him—at least momentarily—out of control of the immediate rhetorical context. Such unexpected perplexity, the "cornering" of the addressee by precluding a comeback, was singled out by Žižek as the signature effect of injurious speech.⁵ The disorienting interpellation of Howgill's address renders it injurious speech, something that the Lord Protector apparently realized by the time he delivered his Parliament speech. If in the case of scolding the disorientation was a matter of the contentious speaker's upending of the social hierarchy, the woman prophet delivered her rhetorical blow by refiguring the temporal frame of the discourse. As Butler explains, "To be addressed injuriously is not only to be open to an unknown future, but not to know the time and place of injury, and to suffer the disorientation of one's situation as the effect of such speech. Exposed at the moment of such a shattering is precisely the volatility of one's place within the community of speakers."⁶

To establish the immediate cause for the efficacy of Quaker women's prophesies, however, we need to look beyond their stylistic resemblances to Old Testament rhetorical models. As was the case of scolding and witch-speak, the effect of Howgill's and other spoken addresses by Quaker women to men in high places had more to do with performative rhetoric, that is, with style as embodied in vocal and gestural delivery.⁷ Their impact was due neither exclusively to the exhortative content of the messages nor to their distinctive style but rather to the discursive performance by women of a message that appeared to have been authored by a godly community ("we [who] have the Lord to be our strength"). An inalienable—and entrancingly dynamic—element of this performance was the gender of the speaker. It is the performative process of gendering the militant style of the early Quakers by women ministers that constitutes the focus of my inquiry in this chapter. Such agile refashioning of deeply ingrained gender identities and hierarchies, accomplished with sensitivity to the human participants and the architectural conditions of oral performance, entailed the potential to upset other social identities and relations of power as well. Attentively, relentlessly, and often collectively Quaker women prophets enacted a relation of spiritual domination over their addressees that injured the prestige of political leaders in sites symbolizing state power.

The case studies below present contentious and downright injurious speech acts carried out by speakers lacking the social authority to perform and reform symbolic action in locations associated with state symbolism. An immediate effect was the prophesying women's unsettling of their gender roles, roles habituated as what Bourdieu calls "embodied history" or the internalized set of behaviors that renders cultural roles and relationships second nature.[8] Quite apart from the psychological challenges and personal risks undertaken by these women, theirs was no easy act. The discursive insurrection of female prophetic speech and its associated principle of silence took place within a dynamic field of social relationships, actions, and meanings. Quaker women ministers were by no means capable of fully controlling the signification of the cultural symbol of their prophesying. But they made concerted efforts to offset symbolic action to their best advantage, to exert control over the discursive field and, by extension, over the conduct of social life. Often they succeeded. Essential to these efforts, I argue, was the dynamic gendering of prophetic speech.[9] To reflect on the rhetorical effects of the injurious speech of Quaker women at Whitehall Palace, the seat of state power in the mid-seventeenth century, I analyze its stylistic patterns and attempt to reconstruct vocal and physical delivery from clues in the written documents. Whenever possible I attend to the soundscape in which this discourse was embedded, or what Bruce Smith describes as the "interaction between speech communities and their acoustic environment."[10]

Gender, Writing, and the Sound of the Word

While no government record of the late-night exchange between Howgill and Cromwell survives, we learn how it came about from Howgill's *Remarkable Letter*, which was published in the following year, with handwritten copies possibly circulating shortly after her visit to Cromwell's palace. It is from such publications that we can extract clues about the delivery of the early Quaker women's injurious words. It is important therefore clarify the relationship between letter and sound in them.

Like many petitions and proclamations published by early Friends, Howgill's letter was likely composed as the next best substitute for a direct address in the event that she were not able to deliver her message or as a reminder for action to be taken by the addressee. Even though it is a written text, it was meant to be urgently sounded, not consumed privately in the silence of the page. Howgill refers to this and several earlier prophetic addresses to Cromwell as a "cry" against which the Lord Protector had hardened his heart.[11] The urgent sound of such prophesying cries must have been inalienable from their content, for early Quakers refer to the aural qualities of their messages even when discussing written texts. Thus in a 1656 address George Fox charges, "Let all nations hear the word by sound of writing. Spare no place, spare not tongue nor pen, but be obedient to the Lord God and go through the work and be valiant for the Truth upon earth."[12] Literally animated by what early Friends imagined as a tremulous soul bearing the divine Word, Quaker writing was conceived of as an acoustic phenomenon. Its rhetorical power was attributed to the power of the prophet's voice to affect the harmonics of the human body and the soul residing within it, unless, of course, listeners had hardened their hearts.[13]

For early Quakers, the aural qualities of prophesy preceded the acts of composition and enunciation. Like many Quaker proclamations, the *Remarkable Letter* was a text whose main goal was to voice the Word of God dwelling inwardly.[14] For Howgill and other "Children of Light," prophesying, or releasing the Word into the world through their bodies, was an act of spiritual obedience. It started by opening the ear—the organ that the early moderns believed was the gateway to the heart and by extension to the soul—to the divine call. Thus Dorothy White, the most prolific early Quaker woman writer next to Margaret Fell, relates that her 1659 tract, *A Diligent Search Amongst Rulers, Priests, Professors, and People*, was conceived only when she actively heeded to the sound of the Word: "Upon the 25th day of the second moneth, [16]59. as I was passing along the street, I heard a cry in me; again on the 26th day of the same Moneth, the same cry was in me; againe on the 27th day, the same cry was in me, and as I was waiting upon the Lord in silence, the word of the Lord came unto me."[15] White's experience suggests that sounding was an important aspect of early Quaker prophetic tracts, to a degree that can probably be matched only by the dramatic literature of the early modern era. These were texts that started with the aural perception of the Word in the soul of the believer, that were composed either as blueprints for aural delivery or as recording the memory of such delivery, and that sought their fullness in the immediacy of vocal, polythetic performance.

In one respect at least, this ecstatic conception of Quaker prophecy resembles the calls for willful acceptance of the divine word recurring in early seventeenth-century Protestant sermons: in both the hearer is portrayed as the receptor of the Word of God. As Wes Folkerth points out in his study of the cultural practice of listening in early modern England, Protestant preachers described hearing as a feminized faculty and underscored its agricultural and reproductive associations, typically resorting to the gospel parable of the sower. According to the parable, just as it takes good soil for a seed to grow and yield harvest, it takes honesty, open-mindedness, attentiveness, and perseverance to accept God's Word and cultivate it in the world.[16] The sermons, Folkerth explains, interpret the Word "as seed, the ear [as] either the vaginal gateway through which the seed must travel on its way to the earth/heart/womb, or . . . the womb itself."[17] The underlying assumption in these interpretations is that the minister is the one performing the masculine task of spiritual planting or impregnation, while attentive churchgoers are cast in a feminine role as obediently penetrable and spiritually fertile. Similar images of penetration and impregnation were used by early Friends as well. Elizabeth Stirredge, for example, recalls the powerful ministry of two of the first Publishers of the Truth thus: "I was in the Nineteenth Year of my Age, when J. Camm and John Audland came first to Bristol, in the Dread and Power of the great God of Heaven and Earth; and I am a living Witness that his powerful Presence was with them, and made their Ministry so dreadful, that it *pierced* the Hearts of Thousands."[18]

Yet the gendered imagery of speaker and listener in Quaker religious discourse deviates in interesting ways from that in the Protestant ministers' sermons. As Stirredge continues her recollection of the impact of Camm's and Audland's speech, she draws on another Scriptural narrative: "But before the Meeting was over, *the Spirit of the Lord moved in my Heart*, and in the Light I came to see my woful and deplorable State, which made me to cry to God for Mercy; a Day never to be forgotten by me."[19] To the imagery of overpowering and piercing, evocative of the Annunciation story, wherein Mary is said to have conceived her son as God's message entered her ear, this Quaker adds a reference to the "quickening" of the divine spirit within her heart or womb. The latter reference recalls the story in Luke's gospel of the first stirring of Elizabeth's baby when the pregnant Mary greeted her, followed by Elizabeth's prophetic blessing on Mary and the fruit of her womb: "God's blessing is on you above all women, and his blessing is on the fruit of your womb. Who am I, that the mother of my Lord should visit me? I tell you, when your greeting sounded in my ears, the baby in my womb leapt for joy. Happy is she who has faith that the Lord's promise to her would be fulfilled."[20] In her "Christian Testimony" Stirredge portrays the spiritually fertile listener as somewhat akin to the conceiving Mary, but more so to the sanctifying Elizabeth. By implication the bearers of the Word in her narrative are somewhat masculine, like the angel Gabriel bearing the message of the Holy Spirit, but also feminine, like the pregnant Mary.

Such dynamic transgendering of speaker and listener recurs in both female and male Quaker discourse, and the gender emphasis can go either way. In an address to the Parliamentarian Army, the famous Quaker minister Richard Hubberthorn refers repeatedly to his and other Friends' "tender conscience," "susceptible to moral and spiritual influence, impressionable, sympathetic, sensitive to pious emotions," qualities traditionally gendered feminine.[21] He signed the same address in unmistakably masculine terms, as "a member of his Army, who makes War with the sword of his mouth."[22] Likewise, in commemorating Stirredge's ministry, her neighbor John Thornton says of the woman who portrayed her convincement in terms of the quickening of the divine within her heart and womb, "She commonly had a sharp and piercing Testimony against such that the great Enemy had so misled." According to her own account of her life, Stirredge's prophetic speech—and her silence—could be not only unsettling and injurious but downright deadly. On one occasion, after staring silently for some forty-five minutes upon justices of the peace and assorted officers who had gathered to assess confiscated Quaker goods, she felt called to deliver a "dreadful Warning" to the men and prophesied their sudden "destruction." She reports, "The Lord was pleased in a very short Time to fulfill that Testimony on them. For in a few Weeks, as they were making Merry at a Feast, Two of them died on a sudden after Dinner, and the Rest very hardly escaped, about the Year, 1674." Silent and pregnant with the Word, with an ambiguously gendered spirit that was "greatly enlarged by the mighty Power of the Lord," when called upon Stirredge was apparently also adept at piercing ears and hearts in a masculine manner and capable of sounding the destructive power of divine wrath.[23]

Conceptually and pragmatically there was supposed to be little difference between the acoustic makeup of male and female Quaker prophetic discourse. Once the Word entered its witnessing bearers' bodies and souls (the latter believed to be seated in the heart), it dynamized their voices. Prophets were speaking agents insofar as they lent their breath to the Word within, but the resulting "cry" was beyond their control.[24] This cry in turn either "pierced" those who opened an eager ear to it and retuned the harmonics of their souls or overpowered and destroyed "hardened" listeners. It was the "audible," or enargaic, qualities of the volatile "cry" rather than the semantic content of prophetic speech that Quakers credited with the power to convince or, alternatively, to destroy. Thus Alice Curwen rendered her deathbed testimony of God's imminent conquest of the world "with a Heavenly Melody." Though she requested that someone record her words, there was apparently little that could be recorded in writing, for, as the witness Anne Martindell recalls, Alice "spoke a long time, but I do remember very few of her words." Still, all gathered at her bedside were "broken into Tenderness" by her melodious prophecy.[25]

Yet in spite of the shared origins, spontaneous transmission mechanism, and reported effect of male and female prophesies, those uttered by Quaker women were much more resented and feared. Misgivings about them surface in the writings of male Friends as well. In 1653, some six years after the Quaker leader George Fox first began "declaring truth" publicly, he wrote to "Friends in the Ministry," urging them to "quench not your prophecy, neither heed them that despise it, but in that stand that brings you through to the end." However, when Fox specifically addresses women ministers in the same epistle, he is markedly cautious: "And ye daughters, to whom it is given to prophesy, keep within your own measure, seeing over that which is without. . . . Neither be lifted up in your openings and prophecies, lest ye depart from that which opened."[26] There is a palpable concern here about the women prophets' ability to speak the "plain" language of the Inner Light without adulterating it with the materiality and dynamics "of carnal talk and talkers."[27] The epistle suggests that when these women added their voices to the Word within, they were prone to lift themselves up above their listeners, depart "from that which opened" within, and get mired in the immediate social context of their utterance ("that which is without").

Predictably Fox's contemporaries from other religious persuasions were downright hostile to the insurrectionary speech of early Quaker women. They consistently portrayed Quaker women prophets as analogous to such notorious disruptors of the social order as scolds and witches. Thus the sectarian Lodowick Muggleton noted the rhetorical "excess" of Elizabeth Hooton's preaching in Nottinghamshire, before calling her "an old she serpent" who "hath shot forth her poisonous arrows at me in blasphemy, curses, and words, thinking herself stronger than her brethren." He pronounced her "cursed and damned . . . to eternity." The mayor of Carlyle chose to criminalize Dorothy Waugh's speaking "against all deceit and ungodly practices" at the marketplace in the town and had her hauled away and paraded through the streets fitted with a scold's bridle of "a stone weight." New England Puritans routinely leveled witchcraft accusations against female Quaker ministers who challenged their theocracy.[28] While male Quaker ministers were also imprisoned, publicly whipped, and called witches, the severity of the reaction and the punishments of women suggests that female prophesying posed unique challenges to cultural norms and social relationships.

Such cultural anxiety was not simply a function of the profoundly unsettling cultural symbol of the outspoken and disorderly woman in a world that in the mid-seventeenth century was being turned upside down in a fashion having little to do with the temporary rejection of social order during carnival nor with stage dramatizations of upheavals, reversals, and parodies of cultural norms. Male figures of authority, from leaders of Civil War radical religious groups to civic magistrates, responded to a set of recurrent rhetorical qualities of female prophetic speech. As injurious speech, women's prophesies resembled the rhetorical eruptions of early modern scolds and witches. But unlike the exclusively improvisational witch-speak and scolding, the prophecies of women Friends were more likely to incorporate familiar and influential biblical motifs within their rhetorical contour. With male Publishers of the Truth prophesying women shared a haunting style, which Jackson Cope describes in a programmatic essay as marked by enargaic "incantatory" rhythms, repetitive word clusters, and slippages between literalness and metaphor.[29] Both men and women attended to the experience of the Word of God opening within and reportedly harmonized their breath with the divine message. But, as perhaps Fox was too well aware, Quaker women prophets did not restrict themselves to adding voice to Vox. As the case studies below illustrate, they made creative use of the acoustic and visual impact of the ecstatic speaker's female body, whose difference from the costuming, gesture, and sound of high society they strategically underscored and whose gender they resignified as needed. They entered domains of political and ecclesiastical power in which low-born women had never before set foot, tuned in to their architecture and acoustics, and devised performative ways to deliver the heaviest rhetorical punch in the given setting.

"So Did This Oppression Ring over All the Court"

In numerous petitions to Parliament and king, Quaker women issued stern warnings of divine wrath to men in power.[30] Testifying in person at Whitehall, however, was a more daunting speech act, one that could result in imprisonment or worse. It was not an act that many women Friends were eager to engage in. Even a prophet with a reputation for "sharp and piercing Testimony," such as Elizabeth Stirredge, resisted for a long time the divine "opening" within that called her to prophesy at court:

> Knowing my self to be of such a weak Capacity, I did not think that the Lord would make choice of such a contemptible Instrument as I, to leave my Habitation, and tender Children, that were young and tender, to go to King Charles, which was an Hundred Miles from my Habitation, and with such a plain Testimony as the Lord did require of me; which made me go bowed down many months under the Exercise of it, and often times strove against it; but I could get no Rest, but in giving up to obey the Lord in all Things that he required of me.

In spite of these misgivings, Stirredge not only successfully delivered into the hands of Charles II her written warning about the consequences of the persecution of the righteous but also unleashed her pent-up prophetic voice in front of him: "Hear Oh! King, and fear the Lord God of Heaven and Earth." It is not that surprising that Stirredge was able to obtain access to the monarch; Charles II was an inveterate walker who cultivated a reputation of accessibility to all his subjects. What is startling is the king's response to a petition that was neither structured in the customary manner (an explication of the situation that needed to be rectified and a succinct summary of the exact nature of the petition) nor declared the petitioner's devotion and humility in its opening and ending.[31] In spite of this, Charles was deeply moved. Stirredge reports that "paleness came in his Face, and with a mournful Voice he said, *I thank you, Good Woman.*" As for the manner of delivering the prophecy, she notes that as she spoke, "the Dread of the Most High God... made me tremble, and great Agony was over my Spirit."[32] This trembling voice is perhaps signaled typographically by the Quaker printer with an unusually placed exclamation point calling for a breathless pause within her opening invocation, "Hear Oh!

King." The terse internal rhyme of "hear and fear" echoes throughout the written testimony. But the full effect of Stirredge's short speech on the king was more likely due to the arresting sound of a prophetic message coming out of a female body worn out by travel, trembling, and "bowed down" under the weight of her challenging performative task.

The semantic and rhythmic patterns of Quaker female prophecies are easier to discern in the 1662 *Letter to Charles, King of England* by Anne Gilman of Reading. Her verbal attack upon the monarch's ear is mounted in the incantatory mode that was a staple of Quaker speech. Gilman's epistle opens by doubling the signature Quaker violation of the politeness formula, which proscribed the use of "you" with superiors so as to avoid the impression of "clownishness" or "contempt": "What have we done (O King) that such usage we should receive from thy hands, and by thy orders." The very next sentence increases the force of the verbal attack through precise rhythmic and semantic parallelism: "I say, What have we done that we should be haled, many of us, out of our Meetings, and cast into stinking Prisons on heaps." Similarly to Howgill's address to Cromwell, Gilman concludes with a declaration that thoroughly alters the rhetorical goal of the letter: "And so whether thou wilt hear or forbear, I have cleared my self in the sight of my God concerning thee."[33] At the opening she strove to impact the tremulous soul of her royal addressee, sounding her righteous indignation in mounting waves of aural symmetry. The coda, however, transforms the letter into an act of communion between writer and God, an act in which the king is relegated to a marginal role at best.

Of course verbal and rhythmic patterns by no means guaranteed the effect of Quaker women's prophecy upon their socially elevated audiences. Thus on January 11, 1664, Samuel Pepys recorded that the king humorously parried a young Quaker woman's verbal charge upon her conscience:

> This morning I stood by the King, arguing with a pretty Quaker woman that delivered to him a desire of hers in writing. The King showed her Sir J Minnes, as a man fittest for her quaking religion, saying that his beard was the stiffest thing about him. And again merrily said, looking upon the length of her paper, that if all she desired was of that length, she might lose her desires. She modestly saying nothing till he begun seriously to discourse with her, arguing the truth of his spirit against hers. She replying still with these words, "O King!" and thou'd him all along.[34]

The king's lewd reference to Sir J. Minnes's lack of stiffness ("his beard was the stiffest thing about him") and the length of what the petitioner allegedly desired ("if all she desired was of that length, she might lose her desires") were clearly to demonstrate his own complacent control over the discursive field and to amuse the male attendants whose suggestive snickering would have demonstrated their savvy about relationships at court. Pepys, by all indications an eager member of this discursive community, thus points to one way the socially explosive charge of Quaker injurious words could be diffused.

Courtly laughter, however, does not have the last word in the diarist's record. It is undercut by the young woman's silence. This silence successfully resists the king's parodic gendering of the young woman and parries his deployment of the masculine rhetorical pleasures of the court.[35] Hardly at a loss for words, the young woman chose to curtail what Quakers thought of as the carnal activity of outward speech while physically standing her ground until the king "begun seriously to discourse with her, arguing the truth of his spirit against hers."

For the petitioner this silence may well have been the effect of attentive listening to what the seventeenth-century Quaker Charles Marshall describes as "the small still voice, moving in man Godwards," one of the fundamental ways by which Friends attained a desired spiritual condition.[36] She could have been withdrawing mentally from an outward discursive context dominated by lewd male voices and laughter, seeking a unity with the very object of Quaker faith: God's speech. In the meantime the modest yet resolute stillness of her body would have resignified femininity not as driven, in the terms put forth in the aggressively masculinist courtly discourse, by sexual desire but rather as inwardly contemplative, as befitting the wise virgin Sophia. And while there is no reason to suspect that Pepys or other men at the court recognized the spiritual significance of Quaker silence, they readily acknowledged that the young woman's performative act eventually leveled a discursive field that had been dominated by the king. It was her stillness and silence that led the king to engage in a conversation on spiritual issues with her, a conversation in which, as Pepys records, she repeatedly refused to honor the monarch's social superiority "and thou'd him all along."

While Pepys's diary entry supplies little material to reconstruct the acoustics of Quaker women's prophesies at Whitehall Palace, Elizabeth

Hooton's letter about her "cries" at court, generically addressed to "Friends," provides numerous clues about the acoustics and the effect of her speech. The letter, dated 17. 8 (October), 1662, maps the complex soundscape at Whitehall, Hooton's evolving strategies in acquiring control over it, and the rapt response of her audience.

When Hooton first entered the palace in October 1662, most likely climbing up from the Thames embankment the Whitehall stairs that would take her past the royal chapel, she found herself among a multitude of watermen, citizens, countrymen, palace guards, courtiers, and priests.[37] "Ane old woman above three score yeares," an advanced age for the seventeenth century, she had recently returned from a mission to Barbados and New England, which had involved imprisonment, whipping, starvation during a "neire two dayes journey in the wilderness . . . without any victuals, but a few biskets that we brought with us whicwe soaked in the water," and an enforced passage back to England, which she describes as rough and dangerous.[38] Her body must have been thin and sinewy, her face bearing the marks of malnourishment and long-term exposure to the elements, as well as the labor of the hundred-mile travel to London from her home.[39] Even if she kept silent as she approached through one of the long galleries the open space at the heart of the palace known simply as "The Court," her ascetic look must have drawn curious attention. Hooton was a northerner, and her severe style of rural simplicity must have contrasted starkly not only with the colorful velvets and taffetas of the courtiers but also with the refined fabrics imported from Italy and the Low Countries worn by the status-conscious Londoners who frequented the court.

In the open inner courtyard of the palace, a place designed for declamations, Hooton would have been met by the loud hum of hundreds of people conversing, a veritable Babel of dialects and languages: courtiers exchanging the gossip of the day, loquacious Londoners boasting the importance of their petition to the king, servants running about on their daily business, pages and soldiers clearing a passage for someone important, foreign visitors exchanging their impressions of English sights and customs, watermen hawking their services. In his pioneering study of the acoustic world of early modern England, Bruce Smith draws attention to the sound of people talking as the most prominent feature of the soundscape of preindustrial London. Whitehall's inner court was enclosed by sound-reflecting walls, its ground covered with sand or gravel, material that was less sound-absorbing than the mud on the streets of London. Human speech in this environment, punctuated now and again by the keynote sounds of splashing fountains and birds, would have come across as louder than the constant chatter on the city streets.[40]

The entry into the court of King Charles II, likely announced by the sight and barking of his beloved small spaniels that accompanied him everywhere, would have quieted the noisy rumble of conversations and asserted his control over the acoustic environment.[41] This is probably when Hooton's voice rose in the stillness. She describes it as "ring[ing] over the court," in analogy to the clear sound of church bells that, Schafer reminds us, marked the territory of the early modern parish and was meant to "frighten away evil spirits."[42] "I waite for justice of thee, o King," she thundered before going on to list her personal grievance against magistrates, sheriffs, and bailiffs who had confiscated her horses and "goods contrary to the law." Judging from Hooton's letter, from this point on her cries dominated the soundscape of the court. She relates, "Soe did I open the grievances of our freinds, all over the Nation, the Cry of the Innocent is great, for they have made Lawes to persecute Conscience, and I followed the King wheresoever he went with this Cry, the Cry of the innocent regard, I followed him twice to the Tenace Court, and spoke to him when he went up into his Coach, after he had been at his sport." Coming in one strong, repetitive sound wave after another, Hooton's distinct northern voice would have bounced off the reflective walls, drawing the attention of nobles and visitors in the inner courtyard as well as those standing by the surrounding windows. Her voice was the living embodiment of the social metaphor of the crying innocents, and there was no public space in Whitehall—the royal tennis court included—where her social and religious message could be ignored. Nor did she lower her voice or body in front of the sovereign in the traditional petitioner's humbling pose: "I did not Kneele, but I went along by the King and spoke as I went."[43]

Reception of Hooton's acoustic and spiritual challenge to the monarch was mixed. She reports that a royal guard laughed at her, that "the people murmured" in disapproval of her refusal to kneel in front of the king, that there were those who suggested that her performative bravura "was of the devil." On the other hand, one of the king's coachmen and several unidentified visitors to Whitehall were sufficiently taken by her performance to read aloud her letters to the king, thus joining their voices to hers. Others reproved the guard who laughed and silenced "gainsayers" protesting Hooton's usurpation of social and gender authority. There were even those, she reports, who wished that they had her spirit and who on two occasions she calls her disciples. Hooton's audience was clearly divided on how they interpreted her discursive performance. But in the aftermath of her assured navigation and effective shaping of the soundscape of Whitehall Palace, it was no longer possible to regard the royal addressee of her petition as the summit of uncontested discursive power. As she herself relates, "I had pretty time to speake what the Lord gave me to speake, till a souldier Came and tooke me away, and said, It was the Kings Court, and I might not preach there, but I declared through both Courts as I went along."[44]

This was not the last of Hooton's prophesyings at Whitehall during this particular visit to the palace. As she reports excitedly, "It Came upon me to get a Coat of sackecloath, and it was plaine to me how I should have it, soe we made that Coat, and the next morning I were moved to goe amongst them again in Whitehall in sackecloath and ashes, and the people was much stricken, both great men and women was struken into silence, the witnesse of god was raised in many, and a fine time I had amongst them." This time Hooton's performance seems to have been modeled after the two witnesses of unspecified gender in Revelation 11, who were "to prophesy, dressed in sackcloth, for those twelve hundred and sixty days." Injuring the prophets, as any seventeenth-century reader versed in the Bible knew, was supposed to provoke them into causing a drought, turning water into blood, or afflicting the earth with disease; killing them, once their appointed time had run out, was to bring a violent earthquake and the death of thousands in the city.[45] If on her first day of this visit to Whitehall Hooton gained command over the palace soundscape by emulating the ambiguously gendered trumpeting Angel of Revelation, on the following day she resolutely gendered the characters in the biblical narrative of the earth's last days as she staged it through her weary, penitent female body, bent over with age and hardship.

When the king failed to take action on Hooton's petition for justice for herself and her Friends, she came back again and again—no fewer than seven times. Each subsequent petition culminated in more overtly political and condemning language. Thus early on in her visits Hooton concluded with a general apostolic hope for the spiritual illumination of the king and his council: "Let me not loose my labour . . . that I may go home to my owne Country, and come noe more about this, to the light of Christ in all your consciences which will touch you to God justly I appeald." The later appeals, however, culminate on a decisively militant note: "And if thou suffere company to destroy us and drive us out of the Land, it will fall upon thy owne head. If thou flee thou shalt not scape, therefore in Time hearken, for if thou consider what hath beene formerly done in carrying our friends away, thy ships new wars have not prospered, nor new weapons furnished against Gods people shall ever prosper. And if thou be found a fighter against God thou cannot stand; therefore depart from iniquity." Trumpeting the king's projected military and technological impotence, Hooton synchronizes her voice with a divine warning. Past and present are consolidated into one. Former maritime defeats are rendered contemporaneous with the failure of "new weapons" to be wielded against Quakers. The judgment against Charles's "iniquity" takes place at once in the timeframe of the utterance and in an unspecified future moment. Hooton speaks from within divine time. And she couches her warning both as a cry of deeply felt anguish for the king and as potent judgment of his religious politics: "If those thinges goe on O King! Charles! what will become of thee; If thou wilt not doe Justice, and Judgement to the Innocent, To the widow, and the fatherless, what will become of thee, and the Nation; I cannot but say it before thee least thou perish without Warning once more from Mee; for thou hast had many Warnings, but thou hast not harkened, but has denied thy heart as Pharaoh."[46]

For all their derision of theatrical "idolatry," Quaker women prophesying at Whitehall proved adept at utilizing performative strategies when they struck their elite audiences with amazement. Attentive to the architectural and acoustic setting, they showcased "costumes" and appearances markedly different from those of the fashionable crowd at court, timed their prophetic interruptions of the flow of polite courtly conversation effectively, and delivered their messages in striking tones and cadences. They heeded closely the divergent responses of the closely assembled audience and often succeeded in uniting it in a silent contemplation upon the confluences of present events with biblical history and upon the part that the prophet and her addressee played in both. In the process they dynamized and enriched the significance of feminine gender, at least for the duration of their powerful performative acts. In the insurrectionist speech of Quaker women prophets femininity stood not only for powerful, polymorphous, and morally ambiguous spirituality, as Phyllis Mack has perceptively argued, but also for qualities she ascribes to the political sphere: self-consciousness, self-control, practicality, and toughness.[47] No small feat to accomplish at Whitehall.

Epilogue

*Margaret's Bitter Words and the Voice of
(Divine) Justice, or, Compulsory Listening*

Among the remarkably sharp-tongued women of Shakespeare's first tetralogy—the bewitching and prophetic Joan la Pucelle, the fiery Duchess of Gloucester, the taunting Countess of Auvergne, and the Duchess of York, with her devastating maternal curses— Queen Margaret stands out as a master of rhetorical stratagems. In a single breath she is able to switch from maidenly decorum to coy flirtation, from militant oratory to callous sarcasm, from political counsel to hair-raising prophesy. Her strong speech compels acknowledgment among on-stage auditors. It effortlessly emasculates and belittles her powerful male opponents. At the end of *3rd Henry VI* an exasperated Richard, her toughest adversary on the battlefield, dismisses her as a "Captiv Scold"; however, when he encounters her next in the tetralogy's last play, he is the one acting as a scold, if not a childish prankster, as he attempts to counter Margaret's ritual curse (*3rd Henry VI* l.2879; *Richard III* 1.3.224–43).[1] Small wonder, as cursing is Margaret's forte.

As M. L. Stapleton points out, "curse" and its cognates show up some fifty times in the tetralogy, most often in *Richard III*; ten of these uses are Margaret's.[2] In this epilogue I explore the overpowering quality of Margaret's curses, their capacity to suppress aural resistance and transcend orchestration by the speaker, to engender feminine rhetorical violence among the auditors, and to fashion nature and history in Margaret's own way. While several critics, most notably Phyllis Rackin, have viewed Richard's performance of the feminine discourses of witch-speak and defamation as his appropriating of the transgressive power of female characters, especially Margaret's, I disagree.[3] Rather the uncontained and uncontainable voice of this queen draws out for all to hear the violent voice of the Law, the very voice that constitutes the grounds for its authority and simultaneously bars the Law from authority.

Coprolalia

Like most instances of speech violence, Margaret's cursing is at once deliberate and convulsive, a claim of authority and a demonstration of incapacity. In their study of the poetics of cursing, Kate Brown and Howard Kushner liken it to coprolalia, a frequent accompaniment of the neurological disorder known as Tourette syndrome that entails the disruption of speech at the point of grammatical pauses by curses or other socially inappropriate utterances that are impossible to suppress. In coprolalia the question of the subject of the cursing voice is far from simple. What starts out as an expression of the speaking subject's will (volitional cursing) becomes "something that *happens to* a subject."[4] In other words the curse may be brought out by a volitional act of the speaker, but as it compels its speaker to become its own auditor, it precipitates an uncontainable avalanche of further cursing. The effect: the curse may issue from a particular, circumscribed "here and now," but it transforms it into an expansive present that suspends historical memory and projects it into the future.

While cursing, Margaret is often taken over by forces that seem beyond her control. We first witness her curse on stage in the aftermath of Suffolk's banishment in *2nd Henry VI*, when she calls for revenge on the king and Warwick:

> Mischance and Sorrow goe along with you,
> Hearts Discontent, and sowre Affliction,
> Be play-fellowes to keepe you companie;
> There's two of you, the Devill make a third,
> And three-fold Vengeance tend upon your steps. (ll. 1953–57)

The curse starts out as deliberately articulated, with the long *o* and *a* sounds showcasing the emotional state of the speaker signaled by the First Folio's capitalization of key words, such as "Sorrow," "Discontent," "Affliction." However, the rhythm quickens dangerously with the concentration of plosive and sibilant consonants in the final couplet of the curse: "There's two of you, the Devill make a third, / And three-fold Vengeance tend upon your steps." The enargaic speech conjures up an infernal trinity, binding into a single image—blasphemous and treasonous—her husband, Warwick, and Satan. The voice seems to slip out of the control of the speaker, as both Suffolk and Margaret recognize. Suffolk responds in alarm. The queen's initial reaction to her own curse suggests that she is similarly taken aback. "Fye Coward woman," exclaims she, diagnosing her fearful response to her own utterance and whipping herself into action in the same breath.[5]

By the time Margaret returns (in defiance of the historical record) to the victorious court of the Yorkists in *Richard III*, she has been steeled by loss upon grievous loss. This experience may account for her initial restraint as she observes the squabble among the victors, only muttering sardonic comments for the benefit of the off-stage audience. Margaret's invisibility and inaudibility to the court until she addresses them as "wrangling Pyrates" suggest that at the beginning of the scene she likely performed on the forestage *platea* area. The platea has been described by Robert Weimann as the performance space outside of the upstage *locus* of the mimetic dramatic action, a liminal space from which characters can comment on the dramatic action and engage audiences directly.[6] As appropriate to an outsider, Margaret's first curse in this scene is a commentary on rather than a contribution to the dramatic action proper in the locus. She augments Elizabeth's prayer for a simple life away from the contentious court with a wish that the Yorkist queen's desire is more than fulfilled: "And lesned be that small, God I beseech him / Thy honor, state, and seate, is due to me" (1.3.114–15). As Margaret's curse contracts the distance between the present politics of the court and a historical horizon of doom for the Yorkists, her wit in this repartee allows for alliances across the division between characters and off-stage audience. These alliances are further nourished by the laughter that her hard-hitting sarcasm calls for, when she comments on Richard's complaint that his Civil War "paines are quite forgot":

Out Divell,
I do remember them too well:
Thou killd'st my Husband Henrie in the Tower,
And Edward my poore son, at Tewkesburie. (1.3.121–24)

Epilogue 149

Ultimately, however, Margaret finds it impossible to confine her speech to sarcastic commentary. "I can no longer hold me patient," exclaims she as she moves into the locus to overwhelm her opponents with a barrage of individualized curses (1.3.164). Her words are "quick" and effusive (203). Even Richard's attempt to short-circuit her nineteen-line long curse against him by inserting her name at its climax fails to arrest this verbal deluge. "Oh let me make the Period to my Curse," she calls, not to Richard but to a power beyond the characters on stage, beyond the self (247). The period, however, does not come until sixty-seven lines later.

Tuning Nature and History

Such division of voice from speaker, of curse from curser would suggest a devaluation of Margaret's agency, were it not for congruence between her desires and the effect of her curses. The latter appear to channel a power exceeding natural and even supernatural forces. Thus in the aftermath of Duke Humphrey's death in *2nd Henry VI*, as Margaret attempts to impress upon the king her devotion, she attributes her successful landing on the English shore to her having cursed into submission both the "aukward winde" that twice drove her ship away from England and the god of winds, Aeolus (ll. 1728–36). The "gentle gusts," "he that loos'd them forth their Brazen Caves," the sea itself—they all submit to Margaret's curse. Her voice tunes the elements.

The way her cursing voice controls history is not much different. The dead for whose revenge she calls when invading the Yorkist court in *Richard III*—her son Edward, King Henry VI—are literally summoned on stage in Richard's dream, pre-enacting his demise at the battle of Bosworth. They are joined by those whose death she had prophesied: Rivers, Grey, Vaughn, Hastings, and Buckingham. Margaret is never restored to political power; nonetheless, by the end of the tetralogy's last play the arc of history is bent in the direction of her curses.

Along with the power of Margaret's curses to shape nature and history, they also have the capacity to resound in the cadences of their auditors. This is most prominently the case in the "scene of mothers" in *Richard III*, alternately compared to the ritualized keening of Andromacha, Hecuba, and Helena in Seneca's *Troas* and to a parodic distortion of the Easter liturgy.[7] At the opening of the scene the Duchess of York declares that her voice is faltering with grief even to the point of silence: "So many miseries have craz'd my voice, / That my woe-wearied tongue is still and mute" (4.3.17–19). The soft *m* and *w* sounds in this complaint muddle the rhythm in the falling intonation of the statement. The duchess's flagging voice—and, a bit later, Elizabeth's—are countered by the brisk rhythm and taut parallelisms in the phrasing of Margaret's response: "Plantagenet doth quit Plantagenet, / Edward for Edward, payes a dying debt" (21–22). This is an aside, but as James Hirsh explains in his study of the soliloquy tradition, it could have been overheard by the other characters on stage.[8] The duchess picks up the doubling phrasing and energetic rhythm of Margaret's voice and issues a masterpiece of that "vicious" rhetorical figure Puttenham terms *amphibologia*:[9]

> Dead life, blind sight, poore mortall living ghost,
> Woes Scene, Worlds shame, Graves due, by life usurpt,
> Breefe abstract and record of tedious days,
> Rest thy unrest on Englands lawfull earth,
> Unlawfully made drunke with innocent blood. (26–30)

It is far from clear whether these verses are directed against the speaker herself or against England's blood-soaked land; however, they have the unmistakable semantic and acoustic contour of a curse. Quickly overwhelming the speaker, they transmute the subjective experience of pain in the here and now into an eternal present. Margaret's cursing voice, imbued by the soundscape or overheard by the duchess, has tuned hers.

Once Margaret joins Elizabeth and the duchess on the stage locus, the parallelism of the speech patterns of the women becomes even more prominent. Margaret's own curse of Richard in this exchange is clearly indebted to the staccato phrasing and infernal imagery of the duchess:

> Earth gapes, Hell burnes, Fiends roar, Saints pray,
> To have him sodainly convey'd from hence:
> Cancel his bond of life, deere God I pray,
> That I may live and say, The Dogge is dead. (4.3.75–78)

The duchess in turn is an eager student of Margaret's instruction in "quickening" violent words, as evident from the heavy curse that she casts upon her own son, Richard, a curse that leaves him, for the first time in the tetralogy, speechless.

Women are not the only students of Margaret's cursing. Suffolk is in fact the first to pick it up, when he augments her call for "three-fold Vengeance" upon Henry and Warwick in the scene of his exile in *2nd Henry VI*. The manner of his delivery is worth analyzing:

> Would curses kill, as doth the Mandrakes grone,
> I would invent as bitter searching termes,
> As curst, as harsh, and horrible to heare,
> Deliver'd strongly through my fixed teeth,
> With full as many signes of deadly hate,
> As leane-fac'd envy in her loathsome cave.
> My tongue should stumble in mine earnest words,
> Mine eyes should sparkle like the beaten Flint,
> Mine haire be fixt an end, as one distract:
> I, every joint should seeme to curse and ban,
> And even now my burthen'd heart would breake
> Should I not curse them. (ll. 1964–75)

What Suffolk describes as he articulates his curses is a transformation of the body. With thickened breath hissing between "fixed teeth," face strained, tongue stumbling, his curses take shape as they pass through joints and "burthen'd heart," an image recalling labor pains. Suffolk, whom Margaret had accused of being a "soft harted wretch" for not joining her tirade against Henry and Warwick, gets effectively gendered feminine as he attempts to voice her curses.

The same happens to York. When he is defeated by the Lancastrians in *3rd Henry VI*, Margaret encourages his "Orizons" after merciless taunting. In response he levels a curse at her, uttered through tears: "There, take the Crowne, and with the Crowne, my Curse, / And in thy need, such comfort come to thee, / As I now reape at thy too cruel hand" (ll. 611–15). The feminine gendering of the old knight is accomplished through his tears, which he describes at some length, and also through the sobbing delivery of the verse, suggested by the concentration of cacophonic *k* sounds(Crowne, Curse, comfort, come, cruel).

The Voice of the Shofar

Shakespeare's rendition of the expansive echoes of Margaret's cursing in the voices of her on-stage auditors matches my discussion in chapter 1 of violent speech in the sermons on the fiery tongue. Clerical writers repeatedly emphasized the overpowering aural assault of feminized violent speech upon the susceptible ears of addressees, audiences, and the soundscape at large. At the same time, they raised the specter of the fiery tongue's capacity to feminize all speakers, destabilizing the binarism of gender.

Critics have devalued Margaret's cursing and its multiple echoes as either prone to male appropriation or inadequate in the face of martial violence.[10] I would suggest instead that the aural terms of her dramatic presentation posit the cursing voice as a worthy challenger to armed violence. When Edward IV claims the throne at the end of *3rd Henry VI*, killing Margaret's son in front of her for what he calls railing, the captive Margaret lashes out with a grievous curse: "But if you ever chance to have a Childe, / Looke in his youth to have him so cut off, / As deathsmen you have rid this sweet yong Prince" (ll. 2918–20), and a bit later, "So come to you, and yours, as to this Prince" (2938). At the end of his coronation speech Edward orders Margaret sent to France and attempts to stifle the aural memory of her curse, calling for the stately sound of "Drums and Trumpets" (3088). But the martial music of state proves inadequate, just as Margaret's exile turns out to be impossible to enforce. At the end of the "scene of mothers" in *Richard III*, the duchess's and Elizabeth's "exclaimes" against Richard, echoing Margaret's aural example, prevail over the trumpet sounds that announce the royal entrance (4.3.138–39). For the first time Richard's march is brought to a halt by the mothers' curses. When coprolalic feminine voices, as a power to be reckoned with, are pitted against the masculine music of state (the sound of the Law), the juxtaposition dramatizes a rupture, an insufficiency in the Logos (in the sense of "what makes sense" historically, legally, politically). It is futile to fight cursing with words, even the words of kings. So it is the *sound* of kings, a disembodied royal "voice" that is marshaled against curses. Yet even this turns out not to be reliably effective.

The momentous pitching of the effusive voices of cursing women against royal fanfare should remind us that there is no Law without voice. In other words, the hierarchically gendered binarism of feminine voice and masculine logos is not a battle of Voice and Word; rather it pits voice against voice. Recall Dolar's analysis of the voice of the shofar, sounded when Moses received the tablets of the Law on Mount Sinai: "The Law itself, in its pure form, before commanding anything specific, is epitomized by the voice, the voice that commands total compliance, although senseless in itself." As Dolar points out, however, even as this "object voice" endows logos with authority, it also brings out its inherent alterity, its intrinsic connection with femininity.[11] Another striking example of the power and feminine alterity of the voice of the Law as represented in the poetry of the divine is the arrival of Beatrice in the griffin-drawn chariot of the church at the end of Dante's *Purgatory*. It is not announced by one of the ravishing hymns characteristic of Mount Purgatory's soundscape but rather by a thunderclap. Beatrice is nothing less than Divine *sapienzia* and justice, the one true Word, and yet the sound that announces her arrival has nothing to do with Logos.

In spite of royal decree, Margaret's curses prove impossible to purge from the soundstage of history. The play text of *Richard III* ends with a royal prayer in the name of "Richmond and Elizabeth" for the peaceful succession of the new Tudor line. But the prayer also asks that "Traitors" "not live to taste this Lands increase"—a curse if there ever was one (5.2.468). In productions of the play that eliminate Margaret or severely cut her part, such an ending unambiguously glorifies the triumph of masculine historic Logos (the Law of History) over the voices of alterity. Other productions, however, from Jane Howell's BBC televised version (1982) to Sulayman Al-Bassam's adaptation *Richard III: An Arab Tragedy* (performed at the Royal Shakespeare Company's Swan Theatre in Stratford-upon-Avon in 2007 and in 2009 at the Kennedy Center in Washington DC), are more attentive to the voice of alterity in the play. Howell had Margaret appear with the dead Richard in her arms on top of a pile of corpses and break out in triumphant, demoniac (and certainly nonverbal) laughter. In Al-Bassam's production, as soon as Richmond, an American general in the Middle East, pronounces the "Amen" in a prayer spoken in English in a performance that is otherwise in Arabic, the audience hears a group of insurgents in the background crying, "Allah-u akbar!"—a powerful and threatening sound, though not semantically comprehensible to most British and American audiences.[12] With a lot of creative license, yet quite appropriately, these directors chose to underscore visually what Margaret challenges her on-stage and off-stage audiences to hear: the radical alterity in the Logos of the victor and the defiant echoes of female speech violence, which the Logos emulates and perpetuates in the soundscapes of history.

NOTES

Introduction

1. The editorial attribution of the speech to Prospero dates back to Dryden and Davenant's radical adaptation of the play in 1667, published in 1670. See Shakespeare, *The Tempest* (1999), 135, 76. The long tradition of directors who have reassigned the speech to Prospero in production starts with Garrick (1757) and Kemble (1789, 1806) and continues as late as Brook (1957) and Purcărete (1995). See Shakespeare, *The Tempest* (2000), 164. Subsequent quotations from *The Tempest* are from the Norton Critical Edition, edited by Hulme and Sherman.
2. Brown and Kushner, "Eruptive Voices," 538.
3. Danner, "Speaking Daggers," 41–43, 47–58.
4. On the late medieval feminization of deviant speech, building on two millennia of misogynistic stereotyping, see Bardsley, *Venomous Tongues*.
5. Bardsley, *Venomous Tongues*, 82, dates the earliest known legal prosecution of scolding to a Colchester case in 1311 and maintains that "scolding was not widely prosecuted until the second half of the fourteenth century and the beginning of the fifteenth century." For scolding as a crime in the early modern era, see Martin Ingram, "'Scolding Women Cucked or Washed': A Crisis in Gender Relations in Early Modern England," in Kermode and Walker, *Women, Crime and the Courts*, 51–52; Sheppard, *A Grand Abridgment of the Common and Statute Law of England*, III, 266. The Acts Against Conjurations, Enchantments and Witchcrafts (5 Eliz. I c. 16) and Against Fond and Fantastical Prophecies (5 Eliz. I c. 15) were approved by Queen Elizabeth at the April 10, 1566, session of Parliament. See Great Britain, *The Parliamentary History of England*, 703. On *scandalum magnatum* (abusive speech against one's social superiors), treasonous speech, and antimonarchical speech, see Cressy, *Dangerous Talk*. Cressy, 266, comments that the loosely phrased Restoration treason statute penalizing "malicious and advised speaking" against the monarch (13 Charles II c. 1, 1661) was interpreted more narrowly as treason only in the case of "words of persuasion to kill the king."
6. Blaugdone, *An Account of the Travels, Sufferings & Persecutions*, 28.
7. Roberts, *A Treatise of Witchcraft*, G3^{r-v}.
8. Walford, "Camden Town and Kentish Town."
9. Hubberthorn, *A Collection of the Several Books and Writings*, 42.

10. On the cucking of scolds, see Brushfield, "On Obsolete Punishments." The "swimming" of witches, followed by an examination for the witch's mark, was the recommended method of witch discovery in a catalogue of such methods listed in the section "The Trial of a Witch" in a revised edition of *The Wonderful Discoverie of the Witchcrafts of Margaret and Phillip Flower*.
11. Cressy, in *Dangerous Talk*, 264, asserts that the anxiety of moralists, councilors, governors, and magistrates about malicious and seditious talk was overblown, as it failed to "erode the bonds of authority." I disagree, as violent speech went a long way in shaping authority and gender relations. In fact Cressy, 271, himself concludes that "the demotic political voice was impossible to suppress."
12. Gowing, *Domestic Dangers*, 200; Thomas, *Religion and the Decline of Magic*, 508; Stirredge, *Strength in Weakness*, 47.
13. Turner, "Symbolic Studies," 149, 150, 154.
14. Butler, *Excitable Speech*, 155, 157–58; Bourdieu, *The Logic of Practice*, 56.
15. Roberts, *Demetrius: On Style*, 431–37.
16. Puttenham, *Art of English Poesy*, 3.10.244. On classical and early modern notions of enargeia, with an emphasis on Shakespeare, see Plett, *Enargeia in Classical Antiquity and the Early Modern Age*.
17. Galyon, "Puttenham's 'Enargeia' and 'Energeia,'" 37.
18. Puttenham, *Art of English Poesy*, 3.19.281.
19. Stephen Greenblatt discusses enargeia in its Aristotelian articulation as visible language, breaking down the boundary between the literal and the metaphoric to describe the "bleeding" of the theatrical demonic into the corporeal world of secular truth ("Shakespeare Bewitched," 121).
20. R. Murray Schafer, the founder of soundscape studies, develops the argument for the sophisticated "sonological competence" of premodern societies and its rapid decline with the industrial and electric revolutions in *The Soundscape*, 71–99, 154. On the significance of the sense of sound for the way early modern Americans in particular made sense of the world, see Rath, *How Early America Sounded*.
21. Taylor, "Remapping Genre through Performance," 1417.
22. Gowing, *Domestic Dangers*; Stretton, *Women Waging Law*; Gibson, *Reading Witchcraft*; Capp, *When Gossips Meet*; Walker, *Crime, Gender and Social Order*.
23. Harvey, *Ventriloquized Voices*; Mazzio, "Sins of the Tongue"; Clarke and Clarke, *This Double Voice*; Bloom, *Voice in Motion*.
24. Clarke and Clarke, *This Double Voice*, 5.
25. Bloom, *Voice in Motion*, 183.
26. Butler, *Undoing Gender*, 43. The impermeability of the male/female binary opposition in the early modern era is challenged in Patricia Phillippy, "The Mat(t)er of Death: The Defense of Eve and the Female *Ars Moriendi*"; Naomi J. Miller, "'Hens should be served first': Prioritizing Maternal Production in the Early Modern Pamphlet Debate"; and Rachel Trubowitz, "Cross-Dressed Women and Natural Mothers: 'Boundary Panic' in *Hic Mulier*." All three analyses of representations of the feminine subjectivity and authority in the early modern era are part of the impor-

tant essay collection, Malcolmson and Suzuki, *Debating Gender in Early Modern England*, 141–208.

1. Contentious Speech and Religious Imagination

1. James 3:6, 8–9, 3–4, 14, King James Bible.
2. Craun, *Lies, Slander, and Obscenity*.
3. Bardsley, *Venomous Tongues*, especially chapter 1, "'Sins of the Tongue' and Social Change," 26–44.
4. Bond, *Certain Sermons or Homilies*, 58.
5. Bond, *Certain Sermons or Homilies*, 9.
6. Thomas Adams, "The Taming of the Tongue," sermon 5 in *The Sacrifice of Thankefulnesse*; John Abernethy, "The poysonous Tongue," in *A Christian and Heavenly Treatise*, 463–85; Perkins, *A Direction for the Government of the Tongue*; Webbe, *The Araignement of an Unruly Tongue*.
7. The impulse to gender violent speech as feminine may have been influenced by the propensity in humanistic discourse to gender generally excessive speech, including the verbal mastery of the orator, as feminine. See Parker, "On the Tongue." On the perceived need to provide instruction and exert vocal control over women in the era, see Henderson and McManus, *Half Humankind*.
8. Henry Goodcole, *The wonderfull discoverie of Elizabeth Sawyer, a Witch* (London, 1621), in Gibson, *Early Modern Witches*, 304, 308, 315.
9. Scot, *The Discoverie of Witchcraft*, 34.
10. The case of Poole versus Parry is described in Suggett, "An Analysis and Calendar of Early Modern Welsh Defamation Suits," 20–21.
11. Goodcole, *The wonderfull discoverie of Elizabeth Sawyer*, 308. Goodcole counted on his readers' apprehensiveness about unruly and inflammatory speech when he attempted in the preface to his work to exonerate himself from dealing with a subject as controversial as witchcraft in a short topical pamphlet. As Gibson points out in *Early Modern Witches*, 302, it took twenty-two years for the next witchcraft pamphlet after *The wonderfull discoverie* to be published in England, a fact suggesting that Goodcole's misgivings expressed in "The Authors Apologie to the Christian Readers" about approaching the controversial topic of witchcraft in a cheap pamphlet may have been well founded.
12. Ingram, "'Scolding Women,'" 51; *Oxford English Dictionary*, online edition, s.v. "scold, n. 1b."
13. "An Homelie against Contencion and Braulinge," in Bond, *Certain Sermons or Homilies*, 194, 200.
14. "An Homelie against Contencion and Braulinge," 191.
15. Perkins, *Direction for the Government of the Tongue*, A8^r–B1^v.
16. On the gendered dichotomy of voice and logos, see Dolar, "The Object Voice."
17. "An Homelie against Contencion and Braulinge," 197, 192.
18. Perkins, *Direction for the Government of the Tongue*, B8^r.
19. "Homelie against Contencion," 195; Adams, "Taming of the Tongue," 43.

20. Webbe, *Araignement of an Unruly Tongue*, 50.
21. Abernethy, "The poysonous Tongue," 469, Adams, "Taming of the Tongue," 42–43. Adams references Zechariah 5:4 and Jeremiah 1:10 in the italicized sections.
22. This description of Pierre Schaeffer's acoustic system is based on its summary in Schafer, *The Soundscape*, 129–30.
23. Adams, "Taming of the Tongue," 39.
24. Abernethy, "The poysonous Tongue," 472, 471.
25. Webbe, *Araignement of an Unruly Tongue*, 26–27.
26. Abernethy, "The poysonous Tongue," 464. The biblical quotations italicized in the original, as was the printing convention of the era, are from, respectively, James 3:8, 6, Psalms 140:3, Romans 3:13, and Job 20.16.
27. Adams, "Taming of the Tongue," 42. "Stella" is likely the great English preacher Launcelot Andrewes (1555–1626), known to his contemporaries as *stella praedicantium*, or "star of preaching."
28. Perkins, *Direction for the Government of the Tongue*, A2ᵛ; Webbe, *Araignement of an Unruly Tongue*, 2–3; Abernethy, "The poysonous Tongue," 470; Adams, "Taming of the Tongue," 25, 27.
29. Webbe, *Araignement of an Unruly Tongue*, 74–75.
30. Adams, "Taming of the Tongue," 36; Webbe, *Araignement of an Unruly Tongue*, 8.
31. Webbe, *Araignement of an Unruly Tongue*, 29.
32. "An Homelie against Contencion and Braulinge," 195, 198.
33. Perkins, *Direction for the Government of the Tongue*, B8ᵛ; Adams, "Taming of the Tongue," 37.
34. Regarding the unpredictable gendering potential of the unruly tongue, it is instructive to consider how carefully the sermonists avoided discussion of the fiery Pentecostal speech of the Apostles.
35. In *Voice in Motion*, Bloom discusses the distinction between the agency of speech and that of the speaker in the context of unmanageable vocal production: the squeaky pubescent voices of boy actors, the aerial detachability of breath and its unpredictable action as delayed echo, the aural obstruction to voice by willfully closed or inattentive ears. My discussion of this distinction concerns gender backformation: the implications of the uncontrollable generation of feminine-gendered contentious speech for the gendering of its producer.
36. Adams, "Taming of the Tongue," 36.
37. Adams, "Taming of the Tongue," 36.
38. On blood as "the humour that makes men men" and the difficulties in controlling it, see Smith, *Shakespeare and Masculinity*, 20–21.

2. Scolding in the Church Courts

1. Sharpe, *Crime in Early Modern England*, 38; Sharpe, *Defamation and Sexual Slander*, 4.
2. Haigh, "Slander and the Church Courts," 2; Gowing, *Domestic Dangers*, 32–33, table 1; Ingram, "'Scolding Women,'" 55–56.
3. Underdown, "The Taming of the Scold," 120.

4. The statistics for Oxfordshire are based on the calendars in Howard-Drake, *Oxford Church Courts: Depositions 1603–1606, Oxford Church Courts: Depositions 1609–1616, Oxford Church Courts: Depositions 1616–1622*. For Hertfordshire, see Wiener, "Sex Roles and Crime in Late Elizabethan Hertfordshire," 57n49; for Salisbury, see Ingram, *Church Courts, Sex and Marriage*, 304.
5. Perkins, *Direction for the Governement of the Tongue*, A2.
6. For instance, Linda Lees's examination of the documentation of the archdeaconry court in Nottinghamshire for 1603–42 yields that thirty-four women and only one man appeared in court on charges of being scolds or common scolds ("'Lewd and Dissolute Women,'" 114).
7. While the relevant documentation of legally prosecuted contentious speech is dispersed among county archives across Britain, representative parts are available in selections compiled by antiquarians and legal historians and, more recently, in critical historical studies of the church courts and their relation to popular morality. My analysis takes into account excerpts from church court libels and depositions included in Hale, *A Series of Precedents and Proceedings*; Raine, *Depositions and Other Ecclesiastical Proceedings*; Court, Church of England, *The Archdeacon's Court*; Court, Church of England, *Norwich Consistory Court Depositions*; Addy, *Sin and Society*; Cox, *Hatred Pursued beyond the Grave*; Quaife, *Wanton Wenches and Wayward Wives*; Thompson, *Wives, Widows, Witches and Bitches*; Ingram, *Church Courts, Sex and Marriage*; Capp, *When Gossips Meet*; Gowing, *Domestic Dangers*. In addition to the legal cases cited in these secondary sources, I have analyzed church courts' representations of contested speech in the surviving records of the bishop's courts of Oxford, indexed by the local historian Jack Howard-Drake, *Oxford Church Courts: Depositions*, vols. 1–8 (1542–1622) and transcribed by him and Joan Howard-Drake.
8. Gowing, *Domestic Dangers*, 41–42.
9. Useful explanations of the complex mediation of the speech of historical scolds in the church court records can be found in Gowing, *Domestic Dangers*, 41–48; Mendelson, "'To shift for a cloak,'" 5–6; Capp, *When Gossips Meet*, 186.
10. For accusations of female sexual misconduct as the heart of defamation causes, see Lees, "'Lewd and Dissolute Women,'" 111, 115; Thompson, *Wives, Widows, Witches and Bitches*, 84–85; Ingram, *Church Courts, Sex and Marriage*, 300; Gowing, *Domestic Dangers*, 59–60.
11. Capp, *When Gossips Meet*, 189.
12. Giese, *London Consistory Court Depositions*, xix; Raine, *Depositions and Other Ecclesiastical Proceedings*, 89; Howard-Drake, Working Papers, 1: 123.
13. Gowing, *Domestic Dangers*, 59; Howard-Drake, Working Papers, 3: 37; Ingram, "'Scolding Women,'" 69; Capp, *When Gossips Meet*, 195; Ingram, *Church Courts, Sex and Marriage*, 313; Howard-Drake, Working Papers, 7: 5, 67.
14. For defamation cases brought to the London consistory courts between 1572 and 1640, Gowing (*Domestic Dangers*, 63, fig. 6) estimates than almost seven times more women than men sued over a direct insult of their sexuality.
15. Gowing, *Domestic Dangers*, 62–64; Capp, *When Gossips Meet*, 252–63.

16. Raine, *Depositions and Other Ecclesiastical Proceedings*, 83, 84, 91, 84; Suggett, "Analysis and Calendar of Early Modern Welsh Defamation Suits," n.p.
17. Raine, *Depositions and Other Ecclesiastical Proceedings*, 70–71; Capp, *When Gossips Meet*, 196, 195; Suggett, "Analysis and Calendar of Early Modern Welsh Defamation Suits," n.p.
18. Thompson, *Wives, Widows, Witches and Bitches*, 87.
19. *Office v. Catherine Barnaby* (1637), London Metropolitan Archives DL/AL/C/012/MS09057/001, 114^v–65^v, 170–75^v. The case is discussed in detail in Ingram, "'Scolding Women,'" 69–70, as well as in Gowing, *Domestic Dangers*, 122–23; Cox, *Hatred Pursued beyond the Grave*, 56.
20. Ingram, "'Scolding Women,'" 69.
21. Addy, *Sin and Society*, 119; Howard-Drake, Working Papers, 6: 44; Capp, *When Gossips Meet*, 191, 258.
22. Lees, "'Lewd and Dissolute Women,'" 116.
23. Gowing, "Gender and the Language of Insult," 5.
24. Cox, *Hatred Pursued beyond the Grave*, 52.
25. Thompson, *Wives, Widows, Witches and Bitches*, 92; Raine, *Depositions and Other Ecclesiastical Proceedings*, 313.
26. Capp, *When Gossips Meet*, 190.
27. Haigh, "Slander and the Church Courts," 3; Suggett, "Analysis and Calendar of Early Modern Welsh Defamation Suits," n.p.; Gowing, "Gender and the Language of Insult," 1.
28. Raine, *Depositions and Other Ecclesiastical Proceedings*, 81, 89; Howard-Drake, Working Papers, 2: 33; Helmholz, *Select Cases on Defamation*, 25; Addy, *Sin and Society*, 116; Suggett, "Analysis and Calendar of Early Modern Welsh Defamation Suits," n.p.; Capp, *When Gossips Meet*, 190.
29. Ingram, *Church Courts, Sex and Marriage*, 315; Cox, *Hatred Pursued beyond the Grave*, 51; Capp, *When Gossips Meet*, 192.
30. Capp, *When Gossips Meet*, 95; Sharpe, *Crime in Early Modern England*, 121; Court, Church of England, *Norwich Consistory Court Depositions*, entry 144; Addy, *Sin and Society*, 118; 1 Kings 21:23.
31. Capp, *When Gossips Meet*, 97; Gowing, *Domestic Dangers*, 103.
32. Gowing, *Domestic Dangers*, 103; London Metropolitan Archives, DL/AL/C/012/MS09057/001, fol. 174^v.
33. Parrot, *Cures for the Itch*, 284. The genre of character epigrams was tremendously popular in the first half of the seventeenth century.
34. Žižek, "'I Hear You with My Eyes,'" 106.
35. Ingram, "'Scolding Women,'" 69.
36. Howard-Drake, *Oxford Church Courts Depositions 1609–1616*, 67.
37. Howard-Drake, Working Papers, 1: 123–24; Howard-Drake, *Oxford Church Court Depositions 1609–1616*, 17; Copeland, "Extracts from the Old Court Books at Bridewell Hospital," 77.
38. Wiener, "Sex-Roles and Crime in Late Elizabethan Hertfordshire," 47; Capp, *When Gossips Meet*, 197.

39. London Archdeaconry Depositions 1566–7, 4ᵛ, quoted in Mendelson and Crawford, *Women in Early Modern England*, 214.
40. Capp, *When Gossips Meet*, 209.
41. Ingram, *Church Courts, Sex and Marriage*, 313; Bloom, *Voice in Motion*, 135. See more generally chapter 3, "Fortress of the Ear: Shakespeare's Late Plays, Protestant Sermons, and Audience," 111–59.
42. Ingram, *Church Courts, Sex and Marriage*, 311; Capp, *When Gossips Meet*, 191; Court, Church of England, *The Archdeacon's Court*, 1: 29, 122.
43. Manchester Court Leet, *The Court Leet Records*, 31.
44. Giese, *London Consistory Court Depositions*, xx; Helmholz, *Select Cases on Defamation to 1600*, 18; Ingram, *Church Courts, Sex and Marriage*, 312.
45. Haigh, "Slander and the Church Courts," 5; Ingram, *Church Courts, Sex and Marriage*, 306–8; Quaife, *Wanton Wenches and Wayward Wives*, 191–92.
46. Ingram, *Church Courts, Sex and Marriage*, 309, 311; Giese, *London Consistory Court Depositions*, xx.
47. Ingram, *Church Courts, Sex and Marriage*, 309; Helmholz, *Select Cases on Defamation to 1600*, 38.
48. Ingram, *Church Courts, Sex and Marriage*, 304.
49. Capp, *When Gossips Meet*, 187.
50. Court, Church of England, *The Archdeacon's Court*, 2: 171.
51. Capp, *When Gossips Meet*, 192–93; Hale, *Series of Precedents and Proceedings*, 245.
52. Butler, *Undoing Gender*, 42–43.
53. Howard-Drake, Working Papers, 4: 7–8.
54. Butler, *Undoing Gender*, 1.
55. Capp, *When Gossips Meet*, 197; Raine, *Depositions and Other Ecclesiastical Proceedings*, 322.
56. Schafer, *The Soundscape*, 10.
57. Schafer, *The Soundscape*, 174, 177.
58. Dolar, "Object Voice," 26. See also Exodus 19.16, 20.18.
59. Schafer, *The Soundscape*, 10.
60. *An Account of a Great & Famous Scolding-match*, 2. The description of "tatterdemalion," so evocative of the rapid discharge of scolding voices, is one used by the aptly named Bess Pierce against her opponent, the Widow Webb, who gets called "Mrs. Spit-Venom" in the same sentence.
61. Gowing, *Domestic Dangers*, 76; Capp, *When Gossips Meet*, 203.
62. Raine, *Depositions and Other Ecclesiastical Proceedings*, 89; Capp, *When Gossips Meet*, 202.
63. Howard-Drake, Working Papers, 7: 4.
64. Raine, *Depositions and Other Ecclesiastical Proceedings*, 88.
65. Gowing, *Domestic Dangers*, 103. Gowing makes the statement regarding the predictable restriction of public discussion of male adultery to the marital sphere in relation to a similar case in which the scold placed the blame on the "other woman" (93).

66. Howard-Drake, Working Papers, 5: 31.
67. Raine, *Depositions and Other Ecclesiastical Proceedings*, 83.
68. Howard-Drake, Working Papers, 4: 8.
69. Suggett, "Analysis and Calendar of Early Modern Welsh Defamation Suits," n.p.
70. Hale, *Series of Precedents and Proceedings*, 231.

3. Unquiet Women on the Early Modern Stage

1. The size and prominence of parts like Petruchio's and Ferando's in the *Shrew* plays would have called for casting the troupes' lead actors. Arguing for a consideration of the professional theater context of the era, David Mann points out that Petruchio's part in Shakespeare's play, at nearly three times the size of Katharine's, makes it unlikely that "*an all-male* company would favour a sympathetic feminist heroine" (*Shakespeare's Women*, 11). I disagree that breaking or calling into question the stereotype of Katharina's character would diminish the audience's interest in Petruchio's part. As for the challenge to a character performed by a "star" actor, theater companies would have had an interest in promoting not only their leads but also their most promising up- and-coming actors, cast in significant female parts, such as Kate's.
2. Butler, *Gender Trouble*, 179.
3. Arthur Halliarg, "The Cruel l Shrow: or, The Patient Mans Woe (London, ca. 1600–1650), reprinted in Shakespeare, *The Taming of the Shrew: Texts and Contexts*, 247–53; "The Scolding Wife" (London, ca. 1675), in *Roxburghe Ballads* 2.407 (London, British Library); "The new German Doctor; or, an infallible cure for a scolding wife" (London, ca. 1670), in *Roxburghe Ballads* 2.382 (London, British Library); "My wife will be my master; or, The Married-Mans Complaint against his Unruly Wife" (London, ca. 1690), in *Roxburghe Ballads* 2.576 (London, British Library); "A Pleasant new Ballad you here may behold, How the Devill, though subtle, was guld by a scold" (London, ca. 1625?), in *Roxburghe Ballads* 1.340–41 (London, British Library); "A Merry Jest of a Shrewd and Curst Wife Lapped in Morel's Skin, for Her Good Behavior" (London, ca. 1550), in Shakespeare, *Taming of the Shrew: Texts and Contexts*, 254–88; "The Scolding Wives Vindication: or, An Answer to the Cuckold's Complaint" (London, ca. 1692), in *Roxburghe Ballads* 2.410 (London, British Library).
4. Heywood, and Anonymous, *Two Tudor Shrew Plays*. For the printing and production history of *Taming of the Shrew*, *Taming of a Shrew*, and *The Tamer Tamed*, see Shakespeare: *The Taming of the Shrew* (2002), 1–6. The theater tradition of domestic scolding was sustained through the adaptations of *Shrew* during the Restoration and the eighteenth century: John Lacy's *Sauny the Scot, or The Taming of the Shrew* (1667), Charles Johnson's *The Cobbler of Preston* (1716) and its competing adaptation of the Christopher Sly story by Christopher Bullock, also called *The Cobbler of Preston* (1716), James Worsdale's adaptation of Lacy's adaptation, *A Cure for a Scold* (1735), and David Garrick's long-lived and widely performed farce *Catharine and Petruchio* (1754). For a discussion of these adaptations, see Haring-Smith, *From*

Farce to Metadrama, 10–22. Subsequent quotations are from Shakespeare's *Taming of the Shrew: Texts and Contexts*; from the anonymous *Taming of a Shrew; Being the Original of Shakespeare's "Taming of the Shrew"*; from Fletcher, *The Tamer Tamed*.
5. Heywood, and Anonymous, *Two Tudor Shrew Plays*, 48.
6. Heywood, and Anonymous, *Two Tudor Shrew Plays*, 58.
7. H[ayman], *Quodlibets*.
8. In her inspiring study of jest and gender in early modern England, Pamela Allen Brown points to the motivation for the improvisatory endurance of scolds and shrews: "In this game of cat and mouse, the mouse is better prepared, more resourceful, and more mobile. She also has more to lose" (*Better a Shrew than a Sheep*, 143).
9. See note 3 this chapter and "A Caution for Scolds: or, a True way of taming a shrew" (London, ca. 1685), in *Roxburghe Ballads* 2.51 (London, British Library).
10. Butler, *Bodies That Matter*, 231.
11. Mann, *Shakespeare's Women*, 122–23.
12. Mann, *Shakespeare's Women*, 41.
13. *Oxford English Dictionary*, "match, v." 3a.
14. For the punning on *court* and *cart*, see Helge Kokeritz, *Shakespeare's Pronunciation*, cited in Schneider, "The Public, the Private, and the Shaming of the Shrew," 243, n34.
15. See my discussion of the defamation case against Elizabeth Hawle from Chipping Norton in chapter 2, as well as Karen Newman's chapter "Renaissance Family Politics and Shakespeare's *Taming of the Shrew*," in *Fashioning Femininity and English Renaissance Drama*, 33–50.
16. As Gowing contends, "few cases reached the point of final sentence" in church court defamation litigation because the mode of operation of these courts was mitigation, not punishment. The public penance for the few defamation cases that ran their course demanded a public apology, typically a public confession at Sunday service or wearing a paper that declared the offender's crime (*Domestic Dangers*, 34, 40).
17. Schneider, "The Public, the Private, and the Shaming of the Shrew," 241–43; Sloan, "'Caparisoned like the horse.'".
18. On Kate's domestication and eventual conversion to a domestic commodity, see Korda, *Shakespeare's Domestic Economies*, 52–75. Brown, *Better a Shrew than a Sheep*, 213–14, brings out the dramatized conflict between such patriarchal domestic values and community values.
19. "An Homelie against Contencion and Braulinge," in Bond, *Certain Sermons or Homilies*, 194; Sheppard, *A Grand Abridgment of the Common and Statute Law of England*, III, 267, quoted in Spargo, *Juridical Folklore*, 121.
20. On the prominent place of litigation, especially slander litigation, in early modern England, see Gowing, *Domestic Dangers*, chapter 2, "Women in Court." Gowing usefully points out, "The phrase 'going to Pauls' was a part of London vernacular," although "the church courts held in St. Paul's Cathedral . . . were one familiar jurisdiction among many others" (30).

21. Boose, "Scolding Brides and Bridling Scolds," 179; Brown, *Better a Shrew than a Sheep*, 213; Detmer, "Civilizing Subordination," 289; Schneider, "The Public, the Private, and the Shaming of the Shrew" 251; Mann, *Shakespeare's Women*, 124.
22. "A declaracion to be made by Elizabeth Tuttie of Mattersey," Nottingham University Library AN/PN356/29 (archdeaconry court of Nottingham), quoted in Postles, "Women's Words."
23. The convicted adulteress Alice Bette of Sturton was sentenced to appear at morning prayer for three consecutive Sundays "havinge a white sheete aboute her & a white rodde in her hande bare headed bare legged & bare footed shall kneele in the sighte of the congregacion till the Gospell be read & a sermon or homilie againste fornicacion & adulterie & then standinge on somme forme or deske before the pulpitte shalle saye with an audible voice" the text of her prescribed penance (Nottingham University Library AN/PN356/31, quoted in Postles, "Women's Words"). On Charles Shawe, see Raine, *Depositions and Other Ecclesiastical Proceedings*, 107. The instruction about delivering the confession loudly appears to have been a staple for the Consistory Court of Ely and is cited in Hall, "Some Elizabethan Penances," 272–73.
24. Raine, *Depositions and Other Ecclesiastical Proceedings*, 107.
25. "An Homelie against Contencion and Braulinge," in Bond, *Certain Sermons or Homilies*, 201.
26. Hall, "Some Elizabethan Penances," 272, 274.
27. Raine, *Depositions and Other Ecclesiastical Proceedings*, 107.
28. Ingram, *Church Courts, Sex and Marriage*, 52–53.
29. Thanks to John Watkins and Carole Levin for suggesting the consideration of Eleanor Cobnam's penance.
30. Chamberlain, *The Letters*, 334.
31. Little, "The Persuasion of 'These poor informal women,'" 94–95.
32. Little, "The Persuasion of 'These poor informal women,'" 97.
33. *Oxford English Dictionary*, "vail, v.¹" 2a.
34. There is, of course, a third option, popular among contemporary directors, and that is to turn the comedy into a tragedy. This was the choice of Charles Marowitz in a 1973 production in which Kate delivered her final speech in chains after having been raped by her husband, and of a 1989 Turkish production in which at the end of the final speech she is revealed to have slit her wrists. See Kemp, *Women in the Age of Shakespeare*, 148. Powerful as such creative choices may be for modern audiences, they throw little light on early modern notions of women's contentious speech.
35. Mann, *Shakespeare's Women*, 117.
36. See Haring-Smith, *From Farce to Metadrama*, chapter 7, "A Play about Plays: John Barton's Influence," 150–67.
37. Haring-Smith, *From Farce to Metadrama*, 118–19.
38. Haring-Smith, *From Farce to Metadrama*, 120.
39. On Renaissance tales of the low-born sleeper treated to a night of aristocratic entertainment, and their derivation from the *Arabian Nights*, see Boas's introduction to *The Taming of a Shrew*, xiv–xvii.

4. Witch-Speak in Elizabethan Docufiction

1. England's cultural obsession with witchcraft in the early modern era is discussed in Kittredge, "English Witchcraft and James the First," 46; Macfarlane, *Witchcraft in Tudor and Stuart England*, 205–6; Thomas, *Religion and the Decline of Magic*, 45; Clark, *Thinking with Demons*; Bostridge, *Witchcraft and Its Transformations*.
2. For both England and Scotland, the end of the sixteenth century was marked by peaks in witch persecution. See Ewen, *Witch Hunting and Witch Trials*, 31; Haining, *The Witchcraft Papers*, 14. For the disproportion between the intensity of the persecutions and their discursive representations, see Macfarlane, "Witchcraft in Tudor and Stuart Essex," 77–78.
3. Clark, *Thinking with Demons*, 133, and more generally "Part I: Language," 1–147. Clark first developed the argument about the ideological use of witchcraft in the inversionary mind-set of the early modern period in "Inversion, Misrule and the Meaning of Witchcraft." He was building on Christina Larner's discussion of the Scottish witch hunts as a process, instrumental for the development of the repressive and ideological institutions of the early modern state. See Larner, *Enemies of God*, 192–203.
4. Daneau, *A Dialogue of Witches*, K1^v.
5. Clark, *Thinking with Demons*, 134–47.
6. Larner, *Enemies of God*, 89–102; Hester, *Lewd Women and Wicked Witches*, 200; Barstow, *Witchcraze*. See also Purkiss, "Desire and Its Deformities." The thesis has its roots in the writings of feminist activists like Barbara Ehrenreich and Deirdre English, *Witches, Midwives, and Nurses*, 6, 8; and Mary Daly, *Gyn/Ecology*. Other important works that discuss the witch hunts in the context of male-female power relations include E. William Monter's study of the witchcraze in the Swiss-French borderlands, *Witchcraft in France and Switzerland*; Robert Muchembled's *La sorcière au village* and *Le roi et la sorcière*; and two studies on the New England persecutions: Karlsen, *The Devil in the Shape of a Woman*; Demos, *Entertaining Satan*.
7. The view of the witch as a powerless victim of historical change is a corollary of the "functionalist" understanding of the witch hunts as a mechanism for controlling social anxieties about population increase, inflation, religious controversies, and growing poverty. This functionalist approach is notably represented by Thomas, *Religion and the Decline of Magic*; Macfarlane, *Witchcraft in Tudor and Stuart England*; Stephens, "Witches Who Steal Penises." Diane Purkiss has critiqued this position in *The Witch in History*, 63–67.
8. As the anthropologist Jeanne Favret-Saada has pointed out in her study of witchcraft and performativity in the Bocage of western France, the subject position of the witch is never freely claimed, however malevolent the witch's intent may be. Rather it is ascribed to a person of perceived superpotency, one who is abnormally avid to increase his or her domain or vital space. From the point of view of the "victims," the only desirable resolution of the witch's encroachment on their domains is to counter the force of the witch with the force of an unwitcher—a tactic that could

entail the defeat or even death of the weaker antagonist and that eventually leads to the proliferation of witchcraft. See Favret-Saada, *Deadly Words*, 69–71, 194–216.

9. Dubisch, *Gender and Power in Rural Greece*, 13, 25.
10. Sharpe, *Witchcraft in Seventeenth-Century Yorkshire*, 14–15.
11. For the involvement of women in the legal process see Sharpe, "Women, Witchcraft and the Legal Process"; Holmes, "Women: Witnesses and Witches." I should note that male conjurers and sorcerers, like John Walsh, Dr. Fian, and Dr. Lamb, also appeared in the literature of the street, usually as the demonized hirelings of a political and religious enemy. However, the culture of early modern England never turned the demonic into a gender trait of masculinity.
12. Marion Gibson, in a perceptive discussion of the change of emphasis in the witchcraft pamphlet genre from the legal-documentary subgenre dominant in the Elizabethan era to the narrative-persuasive Jacobean subgenre, points to the different rhetorical purposes driving the two. While authors of documentary pamphlets sifted through the available information in the interest of moral reform, as was publicly declared in their prefaces (and a host of other implied rhetorical purposes), the later authors of narrative witchcraft pamphlets substituted factual responsibility with catering to the entertainment of their readers and the writerly joys of engaging in scientific and political controversy while spinning a good tale. See her *Reading Witchcraft*, 128–39, 159–71, 145–53, 171–85. Elizabethan pamphlets featuring witches with a keen sense of humor, impressive rhetorical skills, or appealing feistiness therefore are especially useful as sources for the witches' "fighting words." Such deviations from generic form are unlikely to be the imaginative constructs of the pamphlets' authors.
13. Sharpe, *Instruments of Darkness*, 173–86.
14. Bernard, *A Guide to Grand-jury Men*, 172–73.
15. Austin, *How to Do Things with Words*, 98–101. See also his "Performative Utterances," in *Philosophical Papers*, 249–50.
16. Butler, *Excitable Speech*, 49.
17. Galis, *A brief treatise*, 70, 67. The original Roman font used in the blackletter pamphlet to render a quote has been rendered as italics here. As Gibson notes, Galis describes his extreme and bizarre responses to visions and physical suffering he credits to the witches, thus undermining his reliability as a reporter (50).
18. Thomas Andrew Green provides a helpful discussion of the pragmatics of gathering evidence in early modern criminal trials in *Verdict According to Conscience*. Katharine Eisaman Maus has discussed the ways in which the early modern crimes of witchcraft and treason, conceived as inward crimes occurring in the mind alone prior to any external manifestations, were especially baffling for juries searching for publicly available incriminating evidence (*Inwardness and Theater in the English Renaissance*, 104–18).
19. Gaule, *Select Cases of Conscience*, 194.
20. Quoted in Gowing, *Domestic Dangers*, 197, emphasis added. For a complete account, and a strong reading of this case as an assertion of female sexuality and power, see 196–98.
21. Hothersall, "Matrimonial Problems in West Sussex."

22. *The most strange and admirable discoverie of the three witches of Warboys*, 256. For an insightful analysis of the complex authorship of the pamphlet, and specifically for Henry Pickering's authorial contribution, see Gibson, *Reading Witchcraft*, 123.
23. Butler, *Excitable Speech*, 141–47. Butler's argument about the role of the body in the kind of insurrectionary speech acts that can upset legitimate relations of power builds on and critiques Bourdieu's understanding of ordinary language as recording and preserving social structure.
24. See note 21 in the introduction.
25. *A Detection of Damnable Driftes*, 44 (emphasis added).
26. *A Detection of Damnable Driftes*, 46; Salgado, *The Elizabethan Underworld*, 91.
27. Rushton, "Women, Witchcraft, and Slander," 128; Addy, *Sin and Society*, 124–25; Great Britain, *Depositions from the Castle of York*, 29.
28. *A Detection of Damnable Driftes*, 43.
29. Hale, *Series of Precedents and Proceedings*, 213; Sharpe, *Crime in Early Modern England*, 88; Suggett, "An Analysis and Calendar of Early Modern Welsh Defamation Suits," 18; Thomas, *Religion and the Decline of Magic*, 508 (for a larger discussion of the practice of formal cursing, see 502–12).
30. On the use of words as vehicles of female power in early modern England, see Wiener, "Sex Roles and Crime in Late Elizabethan Hertfordshire," 46–49; Sharpe, *Defamation and Sexual Slander*; Underdown, "The Taming of the Scold," 116–35; Gaskill, "Witchcraft and Power"; Gowing, *Domestic Dangers*.
31. *Detection of Damnable Driftes*, 46, 44; W. W., *A True and Just Recorde*, 111.
32. *The most strange and admirable discoverie of the three witches of Warboys*, 294, 280.
33. Gibson, *Reading Witchcraft*, 113–17.
34. *The Most Cruell and Bloody Murther*, 155–56. Gibson, 151, suggests that the story of the Harrisons was based on observation and casual overhearing at the Herford assizes in 1606, where two witches were condemned to death, although they were not the Harrisons, but Alice and Christian Stokes.
35. Scot, *The Discoverie of Witchcraft*, 1, 4 (emphasis added). See also Gifford, *A Discourse*, 21, 44.
36. Butler, *Excitable Speech*, 3.
37. As Larner argues in *Witchcraft and Religion*, 18, during James's reign the number of the actual prosecutions declined, while the variety and number of their popular representations multiplied. On the spectacularly "muddled" representations of witchcraft in the pamphlets and the drama of the period and their usefulness for understanding the early modern construction of witchcraft, see Purkiss, *The Witch in History*, 181–275; Gibson, *Reading Witchcraft*, especially Part II, "Pamphlets," 113–85.
38. The single Elizabethan witchcraft ballad I have been able to identify is the anonymous "A newe ballad of the life and deaths of three witches arrayned and executed at Chelmsford" (London, 1589). Another ballad on the Warboys witches was registered in 1593 but is no longer extant. See Haining, *Witchcraft Papers*, 73. Unlike other "last farewells," the ballad on the Chelmsford case is cast in the third-person perspective, thus denying the witches a voice. The same is true of the two surviving

Jacobean witchcraft ballads, "Damnable Practises Of three Lincolne-shire Witches, Joane Flower, and her two daughters, Margret and Phillip Flower" (London, 1619) and "The Tragedy of Doctor Lambe, The great supposed Coniurer, who was wounded to death by Saylers and other Lads, on Fryday the 14. of Iune, 1628" (London, 1628).

39. Purkiss conjectures that the lost play *Mother Redcap* may have been about a cunning woman, or else about the case of Alice Gooderidge and Elizabeth Wright, who were tried in 1597, when the play was entered in Henslowe's diary. Another nonextant play possibly based on a real-life case is *The Witch of Islington* dating from the same year. Finally, there was the lost *Black Joan*, a possible influence on Shakespeare's Pucelle in *1 Henry VI* (Purkiss, *The Witch in History*, 189, 197).

40. For Francis Dorington's credentials and his relation to the Throckmorton family, see Gibson, *Reading Witchcraft* 214n39.

41. *The most strange and admirable discoverie of the three witches of Warboys*, 275–78.

42. An excellent discussion of the multiple authorship of the *Most strange and admirable discoverie* can be found in Gibson, *Reading Witchcraft*, 120–26.

43. Willis, *Malevolent Nurture*, 86–87.

44. For a verse exhortation "to all faithfull men" to "contemne those godless actes," see John Phillips's preface to *The Examination and Confession of Certaine Wytches at Chensforde*, 15. The equation between "Sorcerie and Witchcraft," on the one hand, and "the fruites of Papistes and papistrye, and their yll exercises of their ydle lives" is drawn in *The Examination of John Walsh*, 26. For a description of witchcraft as God's scourge for "the manifest unpietie and carelesse contempt of his woorde," see the epistle to the reader opening *A Rehearsall Both Straung and True*, 34. The "impietie" and "villainie" of the witches' acts are described in the preface to *A Detection of Damnable Driftes*, 42. W. W.'s call for rigorous punishment of witches so as "to appease the wrath of God ... and to reforme all the detestable abuses" features in his address to Thomas Darcy which begins *A True and Just Recorde*, 75. The call "to with-drawe our filthy affections and naughty dispositions, from the use of such detestable dealinges" occurs in the address to the reader opening *The Apprehension and Confession of Three Notorious Witches*, 130.

45. Gibson, *Reading Witchcraft*, 159.

46. *The Examination and Confession of Certaine Wytches at Chensforde*, 12, 16.

47. W. W., *True and Just Recorde*, 75, emphasis added.

48. W. W., *True and Just Recorde*, 77.

49. *The Examination and Confession of Certaine Wytches at Chensforde*, 19.

50. W. W., *True and just Recorde*, 124.

51. *A Detection of Damnable Driftes*, 42.

52. *Newes from Scotland*, 197, 194.

53. *The Apprehension and Confession of Three Notorious Witches*, 135–36.

54. *The most strange and admirable discoverie of the three witches of Warboys*, 296–97.

55. Lake, "Deeds against Nature," 262.

56. Clark, *The Elizabethan Pamphleteers*, 108.

57. T. I., *A memoriall of certaine most notorious witches*, 147.
58. T. I., *A memoriall of certaine most notorious witches*, 146.
59. *The Examination and Confession of Certaine Wytches at Chensforde*, 17.
60. *A Rehearsall Both Straung and True*, 38; Galis, *A brief treatise*, 63, 70.
61. *The most strange and admirable discoverie of the three witches of Warboys*, 280–81.
62. Gibson, *Reading Witchcraft*, 26.
63. *The Examination and Confession of Certaine Wytches at Chensforde*, 17–20, 22.
64. *The most strange and admirable discoverie of the three witches of Warboys*, 280, 272.
65. Purkiss, *The Witch in History*, 137–38.
66. It is possible that Mother White-coate's daughter may have added, "Yea and that a s[t]inger," punning on the stinging quality of the bee and her own behavior as a provocative stinger. Thanks to Michael Cornett and Sarah Beckwith for suggesting this reading of "s[t]inging."
67. T. I., *A memoriall of certaine most notorious witches*, 149.
68. T. I., *A memoriall of certaine most notorious witches*, 147–48.
69. *Newes from Scotland*, 199–200.
70. Gifford, *A Dialogue Concerning Witches and Witchcrafts*, 135; Rowley et al., *The Witch of Edmonton*, 186.
71. Copley, *Wits Fittes and Fancies*, 158–59.
72. Clark, "Protestant Demonology," 55, 57.
73. Daneau, *Dialogue of Witches*, K1^v.
74. Gifford, *Dialogue Concerning Witches and Witchcrafts*, 138.
75. Willis, *Malevolent Nurture*, 102.
76. Foucault, *Discipline and Punish*, 26, 30.
77. The concept of "neighborly nurture" (good neighboring that intersected with good mothering) is developed by Willis, *Malevolent Nurture*, 14–15, 41–65. Willis argues that in the village-level discourse the witch was a dominating bad mother, a malevolent nurturer, a portrayal that was refigured in gentry-level and aristocratic texts in terms of a perverse but patriarchal Satanic family. See also Briggs, *Witches and Neighbors*, 93–95, 115–21, 137–68.

5. Courtly Witch-Speak on the Jacobean Stage

1. On the distinctions and overlap between the legal-documentary subgenre of the witchcraft pamphlet dominant in the Elizabethan era and the narrative-persuasive Jacobean subgenre, see note 12 in chapter 4.
2. Gibson, *Reading Witchcraft*, 150.
3. *Witches Apprehended, Examined and Executed*, B1^{k-v}.
4. See Potts, *The Wonderfull Discoverie of Witches in the Countie of Lancaster*, C. In *Reading Witchcraft*, 181, Gibson views this prefacer's meticulous documentation of his demonological readings as an indication that "the discussion of witchcraft has become a science with an approved bibliography."
5. "Historical witchcraft," of course, remains a conjectural product of historical research, taking into account the fact that early modern records of witch-speak are

the products of multiple authors—accused witches, witnesses, accusers, magistrates, court clerks, pamphleteers—catering to the expectations of a variety of audiences. This idea is fully developed by Gibson in *Reading Witchcraft*.

6. Kenneth Gross discusses cursing, a subtype of witch-speak, as exemplary of the bond of "mutual need" that transforms both speaker and addressee in all forms of ill-speaking (*Shakespeare's Noise*, 3).
7. Willis, *Malevolent Nurture*, 77, comments that "it is striking how much the witch had in common with her female accuser," especially in verbal violence and their belief in maternal omnipotence. Gibson, *Reading Witchcraft*, 105–8, notes numerous instances in the pamphlets of the interchangeability of witch and victim.
8. *A Detection of Damnable Driftes*, 98.
9. *The Most Cruell and Bloody Murther*, extract in Rosen, *Witchcraft in England*, 325.
10. Psalm 137, King James Version. I am grateful to Alan Nagel for suggesting this intertextual connection.
11. *The Wonderful Discoverie of the Witchcrafts of Margaret and Philip Flower*, extract in Rosen, *Witchcraft in England*, 371.
12. See the stage directions following 4.1.100, 198, and the opening of 5.1 in the edition of Marston's *Tragedy of Sophonisba* included in Corbin and Sedge, *Three Jacobean Witchcraft Plays*.
13. Traub, *Desire and Anxiety*, 44.
14. *Oxford English Dictionary*, "limber, *adj*." 1c.
15. Eggert, *Showing Like a Queen*, 162.
16. Schalkyk, "'A Lady's "Verily,"'" 247; Eggert, *Showing Like a Queen*, 162.
17. *The most strange and admirable discoverie of the three witches of Warboys*, 245; Gifford, *A Dialogue Concerning Witches and Witchcrafts*, G1.
18. Gibson, *Reading Witchcraft*, 175.
19. Neely, "*The Winter's Tale*," 252–53.
20. The discussion of the collective subject of witch-speak in this and the previous chapter (as distinct from its speaking subject) builds on Butler's theorizing of the "subject-effect" in injurious speech as citational and iterable in *Excitable Speech*, 49–52.
21. For the opposite view, of women's words and worth as repressed and appropriated by patriarchal power, see, for instance, Traub, *Desire and Anxiety*, 46–49; Schalkyk, "'A Lady's "Verily,"'" 264–72.
22. Wolf, "'Like an Old Tale Still.'"
23. In their introduction to Marston, *The Tragedy of Sophonisba* in *Three Jacobean Witchcraft Plays*, 6, Corbin and Sedge refute critical claims that Marston "out-Lucans Lucan," providing in the notes to the play Graves's translations of source passages from Lucan.
24. Quoted in Gibson, *Reading Witchcraft*, 22.
25. Citations from *The Witch* follow Corbin and Sedge's edition in *Three Jacobean Witchcraft Plays*.
26. Lancashire, "*The Witch*," 173.
27. Purkiss, *The Witch in History*, 217.

28. Bald, "The Chronology of Middleton's Plays"; Roberts, "A Re-examination of the Magical Material in Middleton's *The Witch*"; Bromham, "The Date of *The Witch* and the Essex Divorce Case"; Lancashire, "*The Witch*," 169–72; Lindley, *The Trials of Frances Howard*, 97–99.
29. Purkiss, *The Witch in History*, 216–17.
30. Marcus, *Politics of Mirth*, 103.
31. On the affinities between Sycorax and Prospero, see Bate, *Shakespeare and Ovid*, 254. The extended debate on the blackness or whiteness of Prospero's magic has been summarized in Corfield, "Why Does Prospero Abjure his 'Rough Magic'?," 32–33.
32. Danner, "Speaking Daggers," 32.
33. Lamb, "Engendering the Narrative Act," 542, 545.
34. The relationship between Shakespeare's and Golding's translation of Medea's Ovidian speech was first detailed in Baldwin, *William Shakspere's Small Latine & Lesse Greeke*, 2: 443–53. More recently Lamb, "Engendering the Narrative Act," 546–47, has pressed the analogy between Prospero's speech and Medea's incantation to show how early modern demonological discourse would have interpreted both as authored by the Devil.
35. A[rmin], *The Valiant Welshman*, Sig. E4ᵛ. Published a year before Armin's death and enacted by the Prince of Wales's Men, this play appears to have been written for the public playhouse.
36. Graves, *The Greek Myths*, 557–58. Graves claims that Medea's murder of her two sons is the creation of the dramatist Euripides, bribed with fifteen talents of silver by the Corinthians to absolve them of guilt.
37. The "frozen magic" embodied by the architecture of the Banqueting House is described in Hart, *Art and Magic in the Court of the Stuarts*, 136–54.
38. Quoted in Cox and Norman, "The Banqueting House."
39. Orrell, "The Theaters," 96, describes the double spectacle at Jacobean court performances, as does Cook, "Audiences." Parry, "Entertainments at Court," 200–205, comments on the symbolic and political functions of the annual tradition of Twelfth Night royal masques. James's ability to tell between rightfully and wrongly accused witches is celebrated in Thomas Cooper's *Mystery of Witchcraft*, 287. For Prospero's acknowledgment of his failing magical powers, see Shakespeare, *The Tempest*, Epilogue, 1.
40. Jonson, *Ben Jonson*, 6: 509.
41. Gibson, *Reading Witchcraft* 80.

6. Gender and Politics in Quaker Women's "Cries"

1. Mack, "The Prophet and Her Audience," 150n.
2. Howgill, *A Remarkable Letter*, 2–4. The first Quakers to deliver the divine message to Cromwell were John Camm and Francis Howgill, who visited the Lord Protector in his chamber "for the most part of an hour" in the spring of 1654 but were dismissed after Cromwell got tired trying to convince them of the wisdom of "keeping favour with all" religious persuasions. Camm and Howgill were followed by William Pearson in July and then again in November of the same year.

In the spring of 1655 Pearson "cleared his conscience" to the Protector and tore the linen cap he wore on his head as a sign of how Cromwell's counsels would be rent into pieces. Pearson, along with Gervase Benson and Thomas Aldam, petitioned the release of imprisoned Friends later that spring. George Fox clearly impressed Cromwell during their first meeting, in March 1655, when he brought tears to the Protector's eyes and succeeded in clearing Friends from the rumors about their alleged plots against Cromwell's life. Braithwaite, *The Beginnings of Quakerism*, 435, 156, 436–37, 180.

3. Carlyle, *Thomas Carlyle's Works*, 139.
4. Howgill, *Remarkable Letter*, 2.
5. Žižek, "'I Hear You with My Eyes,'" 106. See also chapter 2, this volume.
6. Butler, *Excitable Speech*, 4.
7. The definition of rhetoric as style *and* delivery follows the prioritization of the elocution stage in the aftermath of the influential reforms in the field of rhetoric instigated by the French Renaissance philosopher and rhetorician Peter Ramus. Ramus called for a clear differentiation between the arts of logic and rhetoric. The former included the *inventio* of arguments and their arrangement (*dispositio* or *iudicium*), the latter style (the use of tropes and figures) and delivery (which received little attention by Ramus and his followers). See Ong, *Rhetoric, Romance and Technologies*, 83.
8. Bourdieu, *The Logic of Practice*, 56.
9. In her influential monograph on seventeenth-century ecstatic prophecy, *Visionary Women*, Mack discusses the experience of testifying by Quaker ministers, male and female, as involving a kind of ungendering, a disengagement of "their individual gendered selves from their personae as prophets" (175). I disagree. While female ministers certainly made use of the dynamic gendering of their own speech acts and those of others, including the symbolic use of womanhood to signify inability to preach or disassociation with the divine, the embodiment of speaking inevitably reinstalled gender to rhetorical function. As a result the speaker's gender came into rhetorical relief even as she shifted the normative descriptors of gender. The effect, to my mind, is not ungendering but rather enhancing the performative variability of gender. See also Hobby, *Virtue of Necessity*, 38, 48.
10. Smith, *The Acoustic World of Early Modern England*, 51.
11. Howgill, *Remarkable Letter*, 3–4.
12. Fox, *The Journal*, 263.
13. The popular idea of the musical harmony of the human body and soul derives from Boethius's concept of *Musica humana*, the inaudible harmony of human bodies and souls, of the rational and the irrational. Musica humana is one of the three categories of music he elaborates in his treatise *De Institutione Musica*, which was highly influential during the early modern era. The other two are *Musica mundane*, the harmony of the spheres, and *Musica instrumentalis*, vocal and instrumental music. Godwin, *The Harmony of the Spheres*, 86.
14. The seventeenth-century Quaker writer Robert Barclay renders the physical experience of the divine Word dwelling within the believer: "The Word is nigh, in thy

Mouth and in thy Heart; that is the Word of Faith, which we preach" (*Truth Triumphant*, 128). As Barclay and others have contended, attending to God's voice within was a major doctrinal difference between Quakers and other Christians in the mid-seventeenth century. For the latter, the Word of God was recorded in the Scriptures and further revelations were no longer possible. While Quakers certainly knew their Scriptures and venerated them as an account of God's messages to earlier believers, they in no way believed that the Word of God could be restricted to any one physical written text. See also Bauman, *Let Your Words Be Few*, 25–26.

15. W[hite], *A Diligent Search*, 1.
16. Matthew 13:4–23; Mark 4:3–29; Luke 8:5–21.
17. Folkerth, *The Sound of Shakespeare*, 46–47.
18. Stirredge, *Strength in Weakness*, 162, emphasis added.
19. Stirredge, *Strength in Weakness*, 162–63, emphasis added.
20. Luke 1:42–45.
21. Moore, *The Light in Their Consciences*, 6.
22. "A Word of Wisdom and Counsel to the Officers and Souldiers of the Army in England, &c." in Hubberthorn, *A Collection of the Several Books and Writings*, 239.
23. Stirredge, *Strength in Weakness*, 47, 114.
24. The notion of prophetic Quaker "cries" as not fully under the control of their speakers concurs with Gina Bloom's argument that in the early modern era breath was conceptualized as "inherently disjointed from the bodies that produce it," generating meaning that "exceeds the more limited significations of . . . verbal language" (*Voice in Motion*, 108–9).
25. Martindell, *A Relation of the Labour, Travail and Suffering*, n.p.
26. Fox, *"No More but My Love,"*, letters 35, 17. Curiously the Minute Book of Meetings for Sufferings in Banbury, Oxfordshire, records an excerpt from a different letter from George Fox, dated "the 2 of the 11th mo. 1673." It reads, with no reservations whatsoever, "Women are to prophesie, and prophecy is not to be quenched" (Oxfordshire History Centre, NQ1/1/A6/1).
27. Fox, *Journal*, 12; Farnworth, *The Spirit of God Speaking in the Temple of God*, 14.
28. On Hooton, see Muggleton and Reeve, *A Volume of Spiritual Epistles*, 227. On Waugh, see Parnell, *The Lambs Defence Against Lyes*, 29–30. Regarding the persecution of Quaker women in New England, Mack estimates that between 1656 and 1664 New England theocrats leveled half of all witchcraft accusations against Quaker women (*Visionary Women*, 259).
29. Cope, "Seventeenth-Century Quaker Style." The similarities between witch-speak and early Quaker style may appear less puzzling when we consider the fact that the Quaker movement originated in those northern counties known in the seventeenth century for the highest number of witchcraft persecutions.
30. Such warnings include a nationwide petition against tithes, *These Several Papers*, presented to the Rump Parliament with a preface by Mary Forster and signed by seven thousand Quaker women; a petition *For the King and Both Houses of Parliament* against the persecution of Friends by Ann Whitehead, Rebecca Travers, Mary

Elson, Susanna Yokely, Priscilla Eccleston, Prudence Wapshott, and thirty other women; and an epistle, also addressed *To the King and both Houses of Parliament*, from the Nottinghamshire Quakers Anne Ingall and ninety-seven other women and Thomas Ingall and 118 other men.

31. Weiser, "Access and Petitioning during the Reign of Charles II," 205–6, 203.
32. Stirredge, *Strength in Weakness*, 37–38.
33. Gilman, *An Epistle to Friends*, 6, 8.
34. Pepys, *The Diary*, 5: 12. Foxton, *"Hear the Word of the Lord,"* 70, suggests that the "pretty Quaker" was Margaret Fell's sixteen-year-old daughter, Mary, whose discursive challenge to the king would have been occasioned by George Fox's imprisonment four days earlier, on January 7, 1664.
35. My reading of the young Quaker woman's silence as a vehicle for political resistance parallels Mihoko Suzuki's perceptive analysis of the political intervention of Shakespeare's Isabella in *Measure for Measure*. Shakespeare's choice to have the rhetorically powerful Isabella respond to the duke's proposal with silence, Suzuki argues, may well suggest her resistance to being domesticated as a wife and subject (*Subordinate Subjects*, 93).
36. Marshall, *The Journal*, 89. See also Bauman, *Let Your Words Be Few*, 21–24.
37. On the location of the Whitehall landing used by the public, see Pepys, *The Diary*, 10: 484. Simon Thurley, *Whitehall Palace*, 101, also identifies the Whitehall stairs from the Thames landing as a public slipway in a caption to Wenceslaus Hollar's 1647 engraving *Whitehall from the Thames*. Whitehall's sprawling ground plan made it widely accessible from both the river and St. James's Park, but a public encounter with the king was more likely during his fast-paced strolls through the palace grounds rather than when he was hunting in the park. For formal architectural plans, see Thurley, *The Whitehall Palace Plan of 1670*. For Charles's exercising habits, see Jesse, *Memoirs of the Court of England*, 469–70.
38. Hooton's age in 1661 and the events in New England are described in her self-narrative (1661), Library of the Religious Society of Friends, London (LSF), MS. PORT. 3/27, transcribed in Manners, *Elizabeth Hooton*, 30–33; the conditions of the passage to England are referred to in LSF MS. PORT. 3/34, transcribed in Manners, *Elizabeth Hooton*, 36.
39. In a later letter to Charles II (undated) in LSF MS. PORT. 3/50, Hooton writes, "It has cost me abundance of Labour besides charges in roming up to thee this 6 or 7 times an hundred mile a Time" (the distance to London from her home in Leicestershire). Hooton's visits to the court may have been in obedience to a divine call, as she asserts in her letter of October 17, 1662, but she was also determined to be recompensed for losses incurred by the confiscation from her son of a team of horses belonging to her, when he refused to swear an oath. This is evident from her letter "To the King and the Lord Chamberlaine" (undated), LSF MS. PORT. 3/7.
40. Smith recalls that in the sixteenth and early seventeenth centuries Whitehall's inner court was known as the "Sermon Court" or the "Preaching Court." The space for outdoor preaching and declamation, it was complete with a pulpit and a sounding

board above it. See his *Acoustic World*, 89 for the acoustics of the inner court, and 58 for the prominence of human conversation on the streets of preindustrial London.

41. Jesse, *Memoirs of the Court of England*, 472.
42. Schafer, *The Soundscape*, 177–75. See also the discussion of the functions of bell ringing and fanfare in chapter 2, this volume.
43. Hooton, LSF MS. PORT. 3/34, transcribed in Manners, *Elizabeth Hooton*, 36.
44. Hooton, LSF MS. PORT. 3/34, transcribed in Manners, 37.
45. Hooton, LSF MS. PORT. 3/34, transcribed in Manners, 37; Revelation 11:3–13.
46. Hooton, LSF MS. PORT. 3/9, 3/50, 3/70.
47. Mack, "The Prophet and Her Audience," 146.

Epilogue

1. Citations and references are from the Applause First Folio Editions of the plays in Shakespeare's first tetralogy, prepared and annotated by Neil Freeman: *The First Part of Henry the Sixt* [sic]; *The Second Part of Henry the Sixt*; *The Third Part of Henry the Sixt*; *The Tragedie of Richard III*.
2. Stapleton, "'I of Old Contemptes Complayne,'" 125–26.
3. Rackin, "Engendering the Tragic Audience," 52–54; Rackin and Howard, *Engendering a Nation*, 105; Smith, "Martial Maids and Murdering Mothers," 155–56.
4. Brown and Kushner, "Eruptive Voices," 539.
5. Modern editors routinely interpret this part of the line as addressed to Suffolk, who has just urged Margaret to cease cursing and has declared that he is ready for his exile. The First Folio, however, places a significant comma in the line, suggesting a shift of addressee in Margaret's response to her own curse: "Fye Coward Woman, and Softhearted Wretch / Hast thou not spirit to curse thine enemy?" (ll. 2021–2).
6. Weimann, *Shakespeare and the Popular Tradition*, 73–85.
7. The designation "the scene of mothers" belongs to Nicole Loraux, *Mothers in Mourning*, quoted in Liebler and Shea, "Shakespeare's Queen Margaret," 93. For the Senecan overtones of the mourning scene of mothers, see Stapleton, "'I of Old Contemptes Complayne,'" 104. The Easter liturgy connection has been argued by Mason, "'Foul Wrinkled Witch,'" 32. Elizabeth mourns her "tender babes" and calls them to "hover" about her "with airy wings"; the three women—Elizabeth, Anne, and the Duchess of York—are met by a strange figure, Margaret's, by the site where the princes have been entombed, not unlike Christ's appearance after his death to his disciples.
8. Hirsh, *Shakespeare and the History of Soliloquies*, 125–61.
9. Puttenham, *Art of English Poesy*, 3.22.345–46. He associates this "Figure of Sense Uncertain" with cozening by false prophets and political sedition.
10. Rackin, "Engendering the Tragic Audience," 52–54; Smith, "Martial Maids and Murdering Mothers," 153, 156.
11. Dolar, "Object Voice," 25–26, 28.
12. Stapleton, "'I of Old Contemptes Complayne,'" 125; Holderness, "From Summit to Tragedy," 133.

BIBLIOGRAPHY

Unpublished Primary Sources

General Examination and Deposition Book, 1632–38. London Metropolitan Archives, City of London. DL/AL/C/012/MS09057/001.

Hooton, Elizabeth. Letters. Library of the Religious Society of Friends in Britain, London (LSF) MS. PORT. 3/7, 3/9, 3/34, 3/50, 3/70.

———. Self-narrative. LSF MS. PORT. 3/27.

Howard-Drake, Jack. Working Papers on Diocesan Court Books, vol. 1 (1542–50), 1991; vol. 2 (1570–74); vol. 3 (1581–86); vol. 4 (1589–93); vol. 5 (1592–96); vol. 6 (1603–6); vol. 7 (1609–16). Oxfordshire History Centre, Cowley, Oxford (OHC).

Minute Book of Meetings for Sufferings in Banbury, Oxfordshire, 1700–1722. OHC NQ1/1/A6/1.

Published Primary Sources

Abernethy, John. *A Christian and Heavenly Treatise Containing Physicke for the Soule . . . Newly Corrected and Inlarged by the Author, M. I. Abernathy, Now B. of Cathnes.* London, 1622.

An Account of a Great & Famous Scolding-match Between Four Remarkable Scolding Fish-women of Rosemary-lane, and the Like Number of Basket-women of Golden-lane, Near Cripplegate, on Monday Last, Upon a Wager for Five Guinea's. London, 1699.

Adams, Thomas. *The Sacrifice of Thankefulnesse A Sermon Preached at Pauls Crosse, the Third of December, Being the First Adventuall Sunday, Anno 1615. By Tho. Adams.* London, 1616.

The Apprehension and Confession of Three Notorious Witches. Arreigned and by Justice Condemned and Executed at Chelmes-forde, in the Countye of Essex, the 5. Day of Julye, Last Past. 1589 With the Manner of Their Divelish Practices and Keeping of Thier Spirits, Whose Fourmes Are Heerein Truelye Proportioned. London, 1589. In Gibson, *Early Modern Witches*, 129–37.

A[rmin], R[obert]. *The Valiant Welshman, or The True Chronicle History of the Life and Valiant Deedes of Caradoc the Great, King of Cambria, Now Called Wales As It Hath Beene Sundry Times Acted by the Prince of Wales His Seruants.* London, 1615.

Barclay, Robert. *Truth Triumphant through the Spiritual Warfare, Christian Labours, and Writings of That Able and Faithful Servant of Jesus Christ, Robert Barclay, Who Deceased at His Own House at Urie in the Kingdom of Scotland, the 3 Day of the 8 Month 1690*. London, 1692.

Bernard, Richard. *A Guide to Grand-jury Men Divided into Two Books*. London, 1630.

Blaugdone, Barbara. *An Account of the Travels, Sufferings and Persecutions of Barbara Blaugdone. Given Forth as a Testimony to the Lord's Power, and for the Encouragement of Friends*. London, 1691.

Bond, Roland, ed. *Certain Sermons or Homilies (1547); And, A Homily Against Disobedience and Wilful Rebellion (1570): A Critical Edition*. Toronto: University of Toronto Press, 1987.

Carlyle, Thomas. *Thomas Carlyle's Works: Oliver Cromwell's Letters and Speeches: with Elucidations*. Vol. 3. London: Chapman and Hall, 1886.

Chamberlain, John. *The Letters of John Chamberlain*, edited by Norman Egbert McClure. Memoirs of the American Philosophical Society . . . Vol. 12. Pt. 1–2. Philadelphia: American Philosophical Society, 1939.

Cooper, Thomas. *Mystery of Witchcraft: discovering the Truth, Nature, Occasions, Growth and Power thereof: together with the Detection and Punishment of the same*. London, 1617.

Copeland, Alfred James. "Extracts from the Old Court Books at Bridewell Hospital from 1559–1634." *Under the Dome: The Quarterly Magazine of Bethlem Royal Hospital*, no. 11 (1902).

Copley, Anthony. *Wits Fittes and Fancies Fronted and Entermedled with Presidentes of Honour and Wisdome*. London, 1596.

Corbin, Peter, and Douglas Sedge, eds. *Three Jacobean Witchcraft Plays*. Manchester, UK: Manchester University Press, 1986.

Court, Church of England, Archdeaconry of Oxford. *The Archdeacon's Court: Liber Actorum, 1584*. Reprinted by Oxfordshire Record Society, 1942.

Court, Church of England, Diocese of Norwich Consistory. *Norwich Consistory Court Depositions, 1499–1512 and 1518–1530*. Calendared by E. D. Stone. Revised and arranged by B. Cozens-Hardy. Reprinted by Norfolk Record Society, 1938.

"Damnable Practises Of three Lincolne-shire Witches, Joane Flower, and her two daughters, Margret and Phillip Flower." London, 1619.

Daneau, Lambert. *A Dialogue of Witches, in Foretime Named Lot-tellers, and Now Commonly Called Sorcerers Wherein Is Declared Breefely and Effectually, What Souever May Be Required, Touching That Argument. Written in Latin by Lambertus Danæus. And Now Translated into English*. London, 1575.

A Detection of damnable driftes, practized by three Witches arraigned at Chelmisforde in Essex, at the laste Assises there holden, whiche were executed in Aprill. 1579 Set forthe to discouer the Ambushementes of Sathan, whereby he would surprise us lulled in securitie, and hardened with contempte of Gods vengeance threatened for our offences. London, 1579. In Gibson, *Early Modern Witches*, 41–49.

Ewen, C. L'Estrange, ed. *Witch Hunting and Witch Trials. The Indictments for Witchcraft from the Records of 1373 Assizes Held for the Home Circuit A.D. 1559–1736*. London: Kegan Paul, 1929.

The Examination and Confession of Certaine Wytches at Chensforde in the Countie of Essex: Before the Quenes Maiesties Judges, the Xxvi Daye of July, Anno 1566, at the Assise Holden There as Then, and One of Them Put to Death for the Same Offence, as Their Examination Declareth More at Large. London, 1566. In Gibson, *Early Modern Witches*, 10–24.

The Examination of John Walsh before Maister Thomas Williams..., Upon Certayne Interrogatories Touchyng Wytchcrafte and Sorcerye... London, 1566. In Gibson, *Early Modern Witches*, 25–32.

Farnworth, Richard. *The Spirit of God Speaking in the Temple of God, or, Gods Spiritual Teachings in His People Puts Flesh to Silence That the Spirit of Christ May Speak in the Church &c.* London, 1663.

Fletcher, John. *The Tamer Tamed: Or, The Woman's Prize*, edited by Celia R Daileader and Gary Taylor. Manchester, UK: Manchester University Press, 2006.

Forster, Mary, et al. *These Several Papers Was Sent to the Parliament the Twentieth Day of the Fifth Moneth, 1659. Being Above Seven Thousand of the Names of the Hand-maids and Daughters of the Lord, and Such as Feels the Oppression of Tithes, in the Names of Many More of the Said Handmaids and Daughters of the Lord, Who Witness Against the Oppression of Tithes and Other Things as Followeth*. London, 1659.

Fox, George. *The Journal of George Fox*, edited by John L. Nicholls. 2nd revised edition. Cambridge: Cambridge University Press, 1975.

———. *No More but My Love: Letters of George Fox, 1624–91*. London: Quaker Home Service, 1980.

Galis, Richard *A brief treatise conteyning the most strange and horrible crueltye of Elizabeth Stile alias Bockingham & hir confederates executed at Abington upon Richard Galis*. London, 1579. In Gibson, *Early Modern Witches*, 50–71.

Gaule, John. *Select Cases of Conscience Touching Witches and Witchcrafts*. London, 1646.

Gibson, Marion, ed. *Early Modern Witches: Witchcraft Cases in Contemporary Writing*. London: Routledge, 2000.

Giese, Loreen, ed. *London Consistory Court Depositions, 1586–1611: List and Indexes*. Publications of the London Record Society. Vol. 32. London: London Record Society, 1995.

Gifford, George. *A Dialogue Concerning Witches and Witchcrafts*. London, 1593. In Haining, *Witchcraft Papers*, 76–139.

———. *A Discourse of the Subtill Practises of Devilles by Witches and Sorcerers By Which Men Are and Have Bin Greatly Deluded: The Antiquitie of Them: Their Divers Sorts and Names*. London, 1587.

Gilman, Anne. *An Epistle to Friends Being a Tender Salutation to the Faithful in God Everywhere: Also a Letter to Charles, King of England &c.* London, 1662.

Goodcole, Henry. *The wonderfull discoverie of Elizabeth Sawyer, a Witch*. London, 1621. In Gibson, *Early Modern Witches*, 299–315.

Great Britain. *Depositions from the Castle of York, Relating to Offenses Committed in the Northern Counties in the Seventeenth Century*. Publications of the Surtees Society, Vol. 40. Durham, UK: Frances Andrews, 1861.

Haining, Peter, ed. *The Witchcraft Papers: Contemporary Records of the Witchcraft Hysteria in Essex 1560–1700*. Secaucus NJ: University Books, 1974.

Hale, William. *A Series of Precedents and Proceedings in Criminal Causes from 1475 to 1640*. London: Francis and John Rivington, 1847.

H[ayman], R[obert]. *Quodlibets, Lately Come over from New Britaniola, Old Newfoundland. Epigrams and other small parcels, both Morall and Divine*. London, 1628.

Helmholz, R. H., ed. *Select Cases on Defamation to 1600*. Publications of the Selden Society, 101. London: Selden Society, 1985.

Heywood, John, and Anonymous. *Two Tudor Shrew Plays: John John the Husband, Tib His Wife, and Sir John the Priest; Tom Tiler and His Wife (1908)*. Museum Dramatists, no. 4. London: Gibbings, 1908.

Howard-Drake, Jack. *Oxford Church Courts: Depositions 1542–1550*. Oxford: Oxfordshire County Council, 1991.

———. *Oxford Church Courts Depositions, 1570–1574*. Oxford: Oxfordshire County Council, 1993.

———. *Oxford Church Courts: Depositions 1581–1586*. Oxford: Oxfordshire County Council, 1994.

———. *Oxford Church Courts: Depositions 1589–1593*. Oxford: Oxfordshire County Council, 1997.

———. *Oxford Church Courts: Depositions 1592–1596*. Oxford: Oxfordshire County Council, 1998.

———. *Oxford Church Courts: Depositions 1603–1606*. Oxford: Oxfordshire County Council, 1999.

———. *Oxford Church Courts: Depositions 1609–1616*. Oxford: Oxfordshire County Council, 2003.

———. *Oxford Church Courts: Depositions 1616–1622*. Oxford: Oxfordshire County Council, 2005.

Howgill, Mary. *A Remarkable Letter of Mary Howgill to Oliver Cromwell, Called Protector a Copy Whereof Was Delivered by Her Self to His Own Hands Some Moneths Ago, with Whom She Had Face to Face a Large Discourse Thereupon: Unto Which Is Annexed a Paper of Hers to the Inhabitants of the Town of Dover*. London, 1657.

Hubberthorn, Richard. *A Collection of the Several Books and Writings of That Faithful Servant of God, Richard Hubberthorn Who Finished His Testimony (being a Prisoner in Newgate for the Truths Sake) the 17th of the 6th Month, 1662*. London, 1663.

T. I. *A memoriall of certaine most notorious witches, and of their dealings*. London, 1595. In Gibson *Early Modern Witches*, 146–50.

Ingall, Anne, Thomas Ingall, et al. *To the King and both Houses of Parliament*. London, 1671.

Jesse, John Heneage. *Memoirs of the Court of England during the Reign of the Stuarts, Including the Protectorate*. Vol. 2. London: George Bell, 1889.

Jonson, Ben. *Ben Jonson*, edited by C. H. Herford, Percy Simpson, and Evelyn Simpson. 11 vols. Oxford: Clarendon Press, 1925–52.

Manchester Court Leet. *The Court Leet Records of the Manor of Manchester, from the Year 1552 to the Year 1686, and from the Year 1731 to the Year 1846*. Vol. 3 (1618–41). Manchester, UK: Henry Blacklock, 1886.

Marshall, Charles. *The Journal of Charles Marshall*. London, 1884.

Marston, John. *The Wonder of Women or The Tragedy of Sophonisba*. In Corbin and Sedge, *Three Jacobean Witchcraft Plays*, 33–84.

Martindell, Anne. *A Relation of the Labour, Travail and Suffering of That Faithful Servant of the Lord Alice Curwen Who Departed This Life the 7th Day of the 6th Moneth, 1679. and Resteth in Peace with the Lord*. London, 1680.

Middleton, Thomas. *The Witch*. In Corbin and Sedge, *Three Jacobean Witchcraft Plays*, 85–142.

Moore, Rosemary Anne. *The Light in Their Consciences: Early Quakers in Britain, 1646–1666*. University Park: Pennsylvania State University Press, 2000.

Morley, Henry, ed. *Character Writings of the Seventeenth Century*. London: Routledge, 1891.

The Most Cruell and Bloody Murther Committed by an Inkeepers Wife, Called Annis Dell, and Her Sonne George Dell . . . With the Seuerall Witch-crafts, and Most Damnable Practises of One Johane Harrison and Her Daughter Upon Severall Persons, Men and Women at Royston, Who Were All Executed at Hartford the 4 of August Last Past. 1606. London, 1606. In Gibson, *Early Modern Witches*, 151–57.

The most strange and admirable discoverie of the three witches of Warboys arraigned, convicted, and executed at the last assises at Huntington, for the bewitching of the five daughters of Robert Throckmorton esquire, and diuers other persons, with sundrie divellish and grievous torments: and also for the witching to death of the Lady Crumwell, the like hath not been heard of in this age. London, 1593. Excerpt in Rosen, *Witchcraft in England*, 239–97.

Muggleton, Lodowick, and John Reeve. *A Volume of Spiritual Epistles: Being the Copies of Several Letters Written . . .* London, (1755) 1820.

"A newe ballad of the life and deaths of three witches arrayned and executed at Chelmsford." London, 1589.

Newes from Scotland, Declaring the Damnable Life and Death of Doctor Fian a Notable Sorcerer, Who Was Burned at Edenbrough in Ianuary Last. 1591. Which Doctor Was Regester to the Divell That Sundry Times Preached at North Barrick Kirke, to a Number of Notorious Witches . . . Published According to the Scottish Coppie. London, 1592 [?]. Excerpt in Rosen, *Witchcraft in England*, 190–203.

Parnell, James. *The Lambs Defence Against Lyes. And a True Testimony Given Concerning the Sufferings and Death of James Parnell. And the Ground Thereof*. London, 1656.

Parrot, Henry. *Cures for the Itch. Characters. Epigrams. Epitaphs*. London, 1626. In Morley, *Character Writings*, 284.

Pepys, Samuel. *The Diary of Samuel Pepys*, edited by Robert Latham and William Matthews. Vol. 5. 1664–. Vol. 10. Companion. Berkeley: University of California Press, 1971.

Perkins, William. *A Direction for the Governement of the Tongue According to Gods Word*. Edinburgh, 1634.

Postles, D. A. "Women's Words: Sources: Courts." Centre for English Local History, University of Leicester. http://www.le.ac.uk/elh/pot/esh/women1.html (accessed June 9, 2005).

Potts, Thomas. *The Wonderfull Discoverie of Witches in the Countie of Lancaster With the Arraignement and Triall of Nineteene Notorious Witches, at the Assizes and Generall Gaole Deliuerie, Holden at the Castle of Lancaster, Upon Munday, the Seuenteenth of August Last, 1612 . . . Together with the Arraignement and Triall of Jennet Preston, at the Assizes Holden at the Castle of Yorke, the Seven and Twentieth Day of Julie Last Past, with Her Execution for the Murther of Master Lister by Witchcraft*. London, 1613.

Puttenham, George. *The Art of English Poesy by George Puttenham: A Critical Edition*, edited by Frank Whigham and Wayne A. Rebhorn. Ithaca NY: Cornell University Press, 2007.

Raine, James, ed. *Depositions and Other Ecclesiastical Proceedings from the Courts of Durham, Extending from 1311 to the Reign of Elizabeth*. Publications of the Surtees Society . . . [Vol. 21]. London: J. B. Nichols and Son, 1845.

A Rehearsall Both Straung and True, of Hainous and Horrible Actes Committed by Elizabeth Stile Alias Rockingham, Mother Dutten, Mother Deuell, Mother Margaret, Fower Notorious Witches . . . London, 1579. In Gibson, *Early Modern Witches*, 33–40.

Roberts, Alexander. *A Treatise of Witchcraft Wherein Sundry Propositions Are Laid Downe, Plainely Discovering the Wickednesse of That Damnable Art . . . With a True Narration of the Witchcrafts Which Mary Smith, Wife of Henry Smith Glover, Did Practise: Of Her Contract Vocally Made Between the Devill and Her, in Solemne Termes, by Whose Meanes She Hurt Sundry Persons Whom She Enuied* . . . London, 1616.

Roberts, W. Rhys, trans. *Aristotle: The Poetics; "Longinus": On the Sublime; Demetrius: On Style*. London: W. Heinemann, 1927.

Rosen, Barbara, ed. *Witchcraft in England, 1558–1618*. Amherst: University of Massachusetts Press, 1991.

Rowley, William, Thomas Dekker, John Ford, et al. *The Witch of Edmonton*. In Corbin and Sedge, *Three Jacobean Witchcraft Plays*, 143–209.

The Roxburghe Ballads, edited by W. Chapell and J. Ebsworth. 9 vols. Hertford, UK: Austin, 1866–99.

Scot, Reginald. *The Discoverie of Witchcraft Wherein the Lewde Dealing of Witches and Witchmongers Is Notablie Detected, the Knaverie of Conjurors, the Impietie of Inchantors, the Follie of Soothsaiers, the Impudent Falshood of Cousenors, the Infidelitie of Atheists, the Pestilent Practises of Pythonists, the Curiositie of Figurecasters, the Vanitie of Dreamers, the Beggerlie Art of Alcumystrie, the Abhomination of Idolatrie, the Horrible Art of Poisoning, the Vertue and Power of Naturall Magike, and All the Conveiances of Legierdemaine and Juggling Are Deciphered* . . . London, 1584.

Shakespeare, William. *The First Part of Henry the Sixt*, edited by Neil Freeman. Applause Shakespeare Library. New York: Applause, 2000.

———. *Hamlet*, edited by Ann Thompson and Neil Taylor. Arden Shakespeare, 3rd series. London: Thomson Learning, 2006.

———. *The Second Part of Henry the Sixt: With the Death of the Good Duke Humfrey*, edited by Neil Freeman. Applause Shakespeare Library. New York: Applause, 2000.

———. *The Taming of the Shrew*, edited by Elizabeth Schafer. Shakespeare in Production. Cambridge: Cambridge University Press, 2002.

———. *The Taming of the Shrew: Texts and Contexts*, edited by Frances E. Dolan. Boston: Bedford Books of St. Martin's Press, 1996.

———. *The Tempest*, edited by Christine Dymkowski. Cambridge: Cambridge University Press, 2000.

———. *The Tempest*, edited by Virginia Mason Vaughan and Alden T. Vaughan. Arden Shakespeare, 3rd series. London: Thomson Learning, 1999.

———. *The Tempest: Sources and Contexts, Criticism, Rewritings and Appropriations*, edited by Peter Hulme and William H. Sherman. New York: Norton, 2004.

———. *The Third Part of Henry the Sixt: With the Death of the Duke of Yorke*, edited by Neil Freeman. Applause Shakespeare Library. New York: Applause, 2000.

———. *The Tragedy of Richard the Third: With the Landing of Earle Richmond, and the Battle at Bosworth Field*, edited by Neil Freeman. New York: Applause, 2000.

Sheppard, William. *A Grand Abridgment of the Common and Statute Law of England Alphabetically Digested Under Proper Heads and Titles Very Usefull and Beneficiall for All Persons Whatsoever That Desire to Have Any Knowledge in the Said Laws: In Four Parts*. London, 1675.

Spargo, John. *Juridical Folklore in England Illustrated by the Cucking-Stool*. Durham NC: Duke University Press, 1944.

Stirredge, Elizabeth. *Strength in Weakness Manifest in the Life, Trials and Christian Testimony of That Faithful Servant and Handmaid of the Lord, Elizabeth Stirredge, Who Departed This Life, at Her House at Hempsted in Hertford-shire, in the 72d Year of Her Age*. Philadelphia, 1726.

The Taming of a Shrew; Being the Original of Shakespeare's "Taming of the Shrew," edited by F. S. Boas. Shakespeare Library. Vol. 8. New York: Duffield, 1908.

"The Tragedy of Doctor Lambe, The great supposed Conjurer, who was wounded to death by Saylers and other Lads, on Fryday the 14. of Iune, 1628." London, 1628.

W. W. *A True and Just Recorde, of the Information, Examination and Confession of All the Witches, Taken at S. Oses in the Countie of Essex Whereof Some Were Executed, and Other Some Entreated According to the Determination of Lawe*. London, 1582. In Gibson, *Early Modern Witches*, 72–124.

Webbe, George. *The Araignement of an Unruly Tongue Wherein the Faults of an Evill Tongue Are Opened, the Danger Discovered, the Remedies Prescribed, for the Taming of a Bad Tongue, the Right Ordering of the Tongue, and the Pacifying of a Troubled Minde Against the Wrongs of an Evill Tongue*. London, 1619.

W[hite], D[orothy]. *A Diligent Search Amongst Rulers, Priests, Professors, and People and a Warning to All Sorts High and Low, That Are Out of the Doctrine of Christ, and Fear Not God. Put Forth by Dorothy White Living in Waymouth*. London, 1659.

Whitehead, Ann, et al. *For the King and Both Houses of Parliament*. London, 1670.
Witches Apprehended, Examined and Executed, for Notable Villanies by Them Committed Both by Land and Water With a Strange and Most True Triall How to Know Whether a Woman Be a Witch or Not. London, 1613.
Wither, George. *A Collection of Emblemes, Ancient and Moderne*. London, 1635.
The Wonderful Discoverie of the Witchcrafts of Margaret and Phillip Flower, Daughters of Joan Flower Neere Bever Castle: Executed at Lincolne, March 11. 1618 . . . Together with the Severall Examinations and Confessions of Anne Baker, Joan Willimot, and Ellen Greene, Witches in Leicestershire. London, 1619.

Published Secondary Sources

Addy, John. *Sin and Society in the Seventeenth Century*. London: Routledge, 1989.
Austin, J. L. *How to Do Things with Words*. Cambridge MA: Harvard University Press, 1962.
———. *Philosophical Papers*, edited by J. O. Urmston and G. J. Warnock. 3rd ed. Oxford: Oxford University Press, 1979.
Bald, R. C. "The Chronology of Middleton's Plays." MLR 32 (1937): 33–43.
Baldwin, T. W. *William Shakspere's Small Latine & Lesse Greeke*. Urbana: University of Illinois Press, 1944.
Bardsley, Sandy. *Venomous Tongues: Speech and Gender in Late Medieval England*. Philadelphia: University of Pennsylvania Press, 2006.
Barstow, Anne Llewellyn. *Witchcraze: A New History of the European Witch Hunts*. San Francisco: Pandora, 1994.
Bate, Jonathan. *Shakespeare and Ovid*. Oxford: Clarendon Press, 1994.
Bauman, Richard. *Let Your Words Be Few: Symbolism of Speaking and Silence among Seventeenth-Century Quakers*. Cambridge Studies in Oral and Literate Culture, no. 8. Cambridge: Cambridge University Press, 1983.
Bloom, Gina. *Voice in Motion: Staging Gender, Shaping Sound in Early Modern England*. Philadelphia: University of Pennsylvania Press, 2007.
Boas, F. S. Introduction to *The Taming of the Shrew*, by William Shakespeare, ix–xl. New York: Duffield, 1908.
Boose, Linda. "Scolding Brides and Bridling Scolds: Taming the Woman's Unruly Member." *Shakespeare Quarterly* 42, no. 2 (1991): 179–213.
Bostridge, Ian. *Witchcraft and Its Transformations, c. 1650–c. 1750*. Oxford Historical Monographs. Oxford: Clarendon Press, 1997.
Bourdieu, Pierre. *The Logic of Practice*, translated by Richard Nice. Cambridge, UK: Polity, 1980.
Braithwaite, William. *The Beginnings of Quakerism*. 2nd edition. Cambridge: Cambridge University Press, 1961.
Briggs, Robin. *Witches and Neighbors: The Social and Cultural Context of European Witchcraft*. New York: Viking, 1996.
Bromham, A. A. "The Date of *The Witch* and the Essex Divorce Case." *Notes and Queries* 225 (1980): 149–52.

Brown, Kate E., and Howard I. Kushner. "Eruptive Voices: Coprolalia, Malediction, and the Poetics of Cursing." *New Literary History* 32, no. 3 (2001): 537–62.

Brown, Pamela Allen. *Better a Shrew than a Sheep: Women, Drama, and the Culture of Jest in Early Modern England*. Ithaca NY: Cornell University Press, 2003.

Brushfield, T. N. "On Obsolete Punishments, with Particular Reference to Those of Cheshire. Part II: The Cucking Stool and Allied Punishments." *Journal of the Architectural, Archaeological and Historic Society, for the County, City and Neighbourhood of Chester*, 1st series, no. 2 (1864): 203–34.

Butler, Judith. *Bodies That Matter: On the Discursive Limits of "Sex."* London: Routledge, 1993.

———. *Excitable Speech: A Politics of the Performative*. London: Routledge, 1997.

———. *Gender Trouble: Feminism and the Subversion of Identity*. London: Routledge, 1990.

———. *Undoing Gender*. London: Routledge, 2004.

Capp, Bernard S. *When Gossips Meet: Women, Family, and Neighbourhood in Early Modern England*. Oxford Studies in Social History. Oxford: Oxford University Press, 2003.

Clark, Sandra. *The Elizabethan Pamphleteers: Popular Moralistic Pamphlets, 1580–1640*. Rutherford NJ: Fairleigh Dickinson University Press, 1983.

Clark, Stuart. "Inversion, Misrule and the Meaning of Witchcraft." *Past and Present* 87 (1980): 98–127.

———. "Protestant Demonology: Sin, Superstition, and Society (c. 1520–c. 1630)." In *Early Modern European Witchcraft: Centres and Peripheries*, edited by Bengt Ankarloo and Gustav Henningsen, 45–81. Oxford: Clarendon Press, 1990.

———. *Thinking with Demons: The Idea of Witchcraft in Early Modern Europe*. Oxford: Clarendon Press, 1997.

Clarke, Danielle, and Elizabeth Clarke. *This Double Voice: Gendered Writing in Early Modern England*. New York: St. Martin's Press, 2000.

Cook, Ann Jennalie. "Audiences: Investigation, Interpretation, Invention." In Cox and Kastan, *A New History of Early English Drama*, 305–20.

Cope, Jackson I. "Seventeenth-Century Quaker Style." *PMLA* 71 (1956): 725–54.

Corfield, Cosmo. "Why Does Prospero Abjure His 'Rough Magic'?" *Shakespeare Quarterly* 36 (1985): 31–48.

Cox, Jane. *Hatred Pursued beyond the Grave: Tales of Our Ancestors from the London Church Courts*. London: HMSO, 1993.

Cox, Jeffrey N., and Larry J. Reynolds. *New Historical Literary Study: Essays on Reproducing Texts, Representing History*. Princeton NJ: Princeton University Press, 1993.

Cox, John D., and David Scott Kastan, eds. *A New History of Early English Drama*. New York: Columbia University Press, 1997.

Cox, Montagu H., and Philip Norman, eds. "The Banqueting House." In *Survey of London: Volume 13: St Margaret, Westminster, part II: Whitehall I* (1930), 116–39. British History Online. http://www.british-history.ac.uk/report.aspx?compid=67777&strquery=banqueting+house (accessed May 10, 2009).

Craun, Edwin D. *Lies, Slander, and Obscenity in Medieval English Literature: Pastoral Rhetoric and the Deviant Speaker*. Cambridge Studies in Medieval Literature, 31. Cambridge: Cambridge University Press, 1997.

Cressy, David. *Dangerous Talk: Scandalous, Seditious, and Treasonable Speech in Premodern England*. Oxford: Oxford University Press, 2010.

Daly, Mary. *Gyn/ecology, the Metaethics of Radical Feminism*. Boston: Beacon Press, 1978.

Danner, Bruce. "Speaking Daggers." *Shakespeare Quarterly* 54, no. 1 (2003): 29–62.

Demos, John. *Entertaining Satan: Witchcraft and the Culture of Early New England*. New York: Oxford University Press, 1982.

Detmer, Emily. "Civilizing Subordination: Domestic Violence and *The Taming of the Shrew*." *Shakespeare Quarterly* 48, no. 3 (1997): 273–94.

Dolar, Mladen. "The Object Voice." In Salecl and Žižek, *Gaze and Voice as Love Objects*, 7–31.

Dubisch, Jill, ed. *Gender and Power in Rural Greece*. Princeton NJ: Princeton University Press, 1986.

Eggert, Katherine. *Showing Like a Queen: Female Authority and Literary Experiment in Spenser, Shakespeare, and Milton*. Philadelphia: University of Pennsylvania Press, 2000.

Ehrenreich, Barbara, and Deirdre English. *Witches, Midwives, and Nurses: A History of Women Healers*. New York: Feminist Press, 1973.

Favret-Saada, Jeanne. *Deadly Words: Witchcraft in the Bocage*. Cambridge: Cambridge University Press, 1980.

Folkerth, Wes. *The Sound of Shakespeare*. Accents on Shakespeare. London: Routledge, 2002.

Foucault, Michel. *Discipline and Punish: The Birth of the Prison*, translated by Alan Sheridan. New York: Vintage Books, 1977.

Foxton, Rosemary. *"Hear the Word of the Lord": A Critical and Bibliographical Study of Quaker Women's Writing, 1650–1700*. Melbourne: Bibliographical Society of Australia and New Zealand, 1997.

Galyon, Linda. "Puttenham's 'Enargeia' and 'Energeia': New Twists for Old Terms." *Philological Quarterly* 60, no. 1 (1981): 29–40.

Gaskill, Malcolm. "Witchcraft and Power in Early Modern England: The Case of Margaret Moore." In Kermode and Walker, *Women, Crime and the Courts*, 125–45.

Gibson, Marion. *Reading Witchcraft: Stories of Early English Witches*. London: Routledge, 1999.

Godwin, Joselyn, ed. *The Harmony of the Spheres: A Sourcebook of the Pythagorean Tradition in Music*. Rochester VT: Inner Traditions International, 1993.

Gowing, Laura. *Domestic Dangers: Women, Words, and Sex in Early Modern London*. Oxford Studies in Social History. Oxford: Clarendon Press, 1996.

———. "Gender and the Language of Insult in Early Modern London." *History Workshop* 35, no. 1 (1993): 1–21.

Graves, Robert. *The Greek Myths*. London: Folio Society, 1996.

Great Britain. *The Parliamentary History of England from the Earliest Period to the Year 1803.* Vol. 1 (1066–1625). London: Longman, 1806.

Green, Thomas Andrew. *Verdict According to Conscience: Perspectives on the English Criminal Trial Jury, 1200–1800.* Chicago: University of Chicago Press, 1985.

Greenblatt, Stephen. "Shakespeare Bewitched." In *New Historical Literary Study: Essays on Reproducing Texts, Representing History*, edited by Jeffrey N. Cox and Larry J. Reynolds, 108–35. Princeton NJ: Princeton University Press, 1993.

Gross, Kenneth. *Shakespeare's Noise.* Chicago: University of Chicago Press, 2001.

Haigh, C. A. "Slander and the Church Courts in the Sixteenth Century." *Transactions of the Lancashire and Cheshire Antiquarian Society* 78 (1975): 1–13.

Hall, Hubert. "Some Elizabethan Penances in the Diocese of Ely." *Transactions of the Royal Historical Society*, 3rd series, 1 (1907): 263–77.

Haring-Smith, Tori. *From Farce to Metadrama: A Stage History of* The Taming of the Shrew, *1594–1983.* Contributions in Drama and Theatre Studies, no. 16. Westport CT: Greenwood Press, 1985.

Hart, Vaughan. *Art and Magic in the Court of the Stuarts.* New York: Routledge, 1994.

Harvey, Elizabeth D. *Ventriloquized Voices: Feminist Theory and English Renaissance Texts.* London: Routledge, 1992.

Henderson, Katherine Usher, and Barbara F. McManus. *Half Humankind: Contexts and Texts of the Controversy about Women in England, 1540–1640.* Urbana: University of Illinois Press, 1985.

Hester, Marianne. *Lewd Women and Wicked Witches: A Study of the Dynamics of Male Domination.* London: Routledge, 1992.

Hillman, David, and Carla Mazzio. *The Body in Parts: Fantasies of Corporeality in Early Modern Europe.* London: Routledge, 2013.

Hirsh, James E. *Shakespeare and the History of Soliloquies.* Madison NJ: Fairleigh Dickinson University Press, 2003.

Hobby, Elaine. *Virtue of Necessity: English Women's Writing, 1646–1688.* London: Virago, 1988.

Holderness, Graham. "From Summit to Tragedy: Sulayman Al-Bassam's *Richard III* and Political Theatre." *Critical Survey* 19, no. 3 (2007): 124–43.

Holmes, Clive. "Women: Witnesses and Witches." *Past and Present* 140 (1993): 45–78.

Hothersall, George. "Matrimonial Problems in West Sussex 1556–1603." *West Sussex History* 4 (1990): 6–11.

Howard, Jean E. *Engendering a Nation: A Feminist Account of Shakespeare's English Histories.* Feminist Readings of Shakespeare. London: Routledge, 1997.

Ingram, Martin. *Church Courts, Sex, and Marriage in England, 1570–1640.* Past and Present Publications. Cambridge: Cambridge University Press, 1987.

Karlsen, Carol. *The Devil in the Shape of a Woman: Witchcraft in Colonial New England.* New York: Norton, 1987.

Kemp, Theresa D. *Women in the Age of Shakespeare.* Santa Barbara CA: Greenwood Press, 2010.

Kermode, Jennifer, and Garthine Walker, eds. *Women, Crime and the Courts in Early Modern England*. Chapel Hill: University of North Carolina Press, 1994.

Kittredge, George Lyman. "English Witchcraft and James the First." In *Studies in the History of Religion Presented to Crawford Howell Joy by Pupils, Colleagues, and Friends*, edited by David Lyon and George Moore, 1–65. New York: Macmillan, 1912.

Korda, Natasha. *Shakespeare's Domestic Economies: Gender and Property in Early Modern England*. Philadelphia: University of Pennsylvania Press, 2002.

Lake, Peter. "Deeds against Nature: Cheap Print, Protestantism and Murder in Early Seventeenth-Century England." In *Culture and Politics in Early Stuart England*, edited by Kevin Sharpe and Peter Lake, 257–84. Stanford: Stanford University Press, 1993.

Lamb, Mary Ellen. "Engendering the Narrative Act: Old Wives' Tales in *The Winter's Tale*, *Macbeth*, and *The Tempest*." *Criticism* 40, no. 4 (1998): 529–53.

Lancashire, Anne. "*The Witch*: Stage Flop or Political Mistake?" In *"Accompaninge the players": Essays Celebrating Thomas Middleton, 1580–1980*, edited by Kenneth Friedenreich, 161–81. New York: AMS Press, 1983.

Laqueur, Thomas. *Making Sex: Body and Gender from the Greeks to Freud*. Cambridge MA: Harvard University Press, 1992.

Larner, Christina. *Enemies of God: The Witch-Hunt in Scotland*. Baltimore: Johns Hopkins University Press, 1981.

———. *Witchcraft and Religion: The Politics of Popular Belief*. New York: Blackwell, 1984.

Lees, Linda. "'Lewd and Dissolute Women': Women and Crime in Seventeenth Century Nottinghamshire." *Transactions of the Thoroton Society Nottinghamshire* 105 (2001): 111–21.

Liebler, Naomi C., and Lisa Scancella Shea. "Shakespeare's Queen Margaret: Unruly or Unruled?" In Pendleton, *Henry VI*, 79–96.

Lindley, David. *The Trials of Frances Howard: Fact and Fiction at the Court of King James*. London: Routledge, 1993.

Little, Megan. "The Persuasion of 'These poor informal women.'" *Explorations in Renaissance Culture* 33, no. 1 (2007): 83–108.

Loraux, Nicole. *Mothers in Mourning: With the Essay of Amnesty and Its Opposite*. Myth and Poetics. Ithaca NY: Cornell University Press, 1998.

Macfarlane, Alan. *Witchcraft in Tudor and Stuart England: A Regional and Comparative Study*. London: Routledge, 1970.

———. "Witchcraft in Tudor and Stuart Essex." In *Crime in England 1550–1800*, edited by J. C. Cockburn, 72–89. Princeton NJ: Princeton University Press, 1977.

Mack, Phyllis. "The Prophet and Her Audience: Gender and Knowledge in the World Turned Upside Down." In *Reviving the English Revolution: Reflections and Elaborations on the Work of Christopher Hill*, edited by Geoff Eley and William Hunt, 139–52. London: Verso, 1988.

———. *Visionary Women: Ecstatic Prophecy in Seventeenth-Century England*. Berkeley: University of California Press, 1992.

Malcolmson, Cristina, and Mihoko Suzuki. *Debating Gender in Early Modern England, 1500–1700*. New York: Palgrave Macmillan, 2002.

Mann, David. *Shakespeare's Women: Performance and Conception*. Cambridge: Cambridge University Press, 2008.

Manners, Emily. *Elizabeth Hooton: First Quaker Woman Preacher (1600–1672)*. London: Headley Brothers, 1914.

Marcus, Leah S. *The Politics of Mirth: Jonson, Herrick, Milton, Marvell, and the Defense of Old Holiday Pastimes*. Chicago: University of Chicago Press, 1986.

Mason, S. Carr. "'Foul Wrinkled Witch': Superstition, Skepticism, and Margaret of Anjou in Shakespeare's *Richard III*." *Cahiers Élisabéthains* 52 (1997): 25–37.

Maus, Katharine Eisaman. *Inwardness and Theater in the English Renaissance*. Chicago: University of Chicago Press, 1995.

Mazzio, Carla. "Sins of the Tongue." In Hillman and Mazzio, *The Body in Parts*, 53–79.

Mendelson, Sara Heller. "'To shift for a cloak': Disorderly Women in the Church Courts." In *Women and History: Voices from Early Modern England*, edited by Valerie Frith, 3–18. Toronto: Coach House Press, 1995.

Mendelson, Sara Heller, and Patricia Crawford. *Women in Early Modern England, 1550–1720*. Oxford: Clarendon Press, 1998.

Monter, E. William. *Witchcraft in France and Switzerland: The Borderlands during the Reformation*. Ithaca NY: Cornell University Press, 1976.

Morley, Henry. *Character Writings of the Seventeenth Century*. London: Routledge, 1891.

Muchembled, Robert. *Le roi et la sorcière: L'Europe de bûchers (XVe–XVIIIe siècle)*. Paris: Desclée, 1993.

———. *La sorcière au village: XVe–XVIIe siècle*. Paris: Éditions Juillard-Gallimard, 1979.

Neely, Carol Thomas. "*The Winter's Tale*: The Triumph of Speech." In *The Winter's Tale: Critical Essays*, edited by Maurice Hunt, 243–57. New York: Garland, 1995.

Newman, Karen. *Fashioning Femininity and English Renaissance Drama*. Women in Culture and Society. Chicago: University of Chicago Press, 1991.

Ong, Walter J. *Rhetoric, Romance, and Technology; Studies in the Interaction of Expression and Culture*. Ithaca NY: Cornell University Press, 1971.

Orrell, John. "The Theaters." In Cox and Kastan, *A New History of Early English Drama*, 93–112.

Parker, Patricia. "On the Tongue: Cross Gendering, Effeminacy, and the Art of Words." *Style* 23 (1989): 445–65.

Parry, Graham. "Entertainments at Court." In Cox and Kastan, *A New History of Early English Drama*, 195–212.

Paster, Gail Kern. *The Body Embarrassed: Drama and the Disciplines of Shame in Early Modern England*. Ithaca NY: Cornell University Press, 1993.

Pendleton, Thomas A., ed. *Henry VI: Critical Essays*. Shakespeare Criticism. London: Routledge, 2001.

Plett, Heinrich F. *Enargeia in Classical Antiquity and the Early Modern Age: The Aesthetics of Evidence*. International Studies in the History of Rhetoric, vol. 4. Leiden: Brill, 2012.

Purkiss, Diane. "Desire and Its Deformities: Fantasies of Witchcraft in the English Civil War." *Journal of Medieval and Early Modern Studies* 27 (1997): 103–32.
———. *The Witch in History: Early Modern and Twentieth-Century Representations*. London: Routledge, 1996.
Quaife, G. R. *Wanton Wenches and Wayward Wives: Peasants and Illicit Sex in Early Seventeenth Century England*. New Brunswick NJ: Rutgers University Press, 1979.
Rackin, Phyllis. "Engendering the Tragic Audience: The Case of *Richard III*." *Studies in the Literary Imagination* 26, no. 1 (1993): 47–65.
Rackin, Phyllis, and Jean Howard. *Engendering a Nation: A Feminist Account of Shakespeare's English Histories*. London: Routledge, 1997.
Rath, Richard Cullen. *How Early America Sounded*. Ithaca NY: Cornell University Press, 2003.
Roberts, Gareth. "A Re-examination of the Magical Material in Middleton's *The Witch*." *Notes and Queries* 221, new series 23 (1976): 218–19.
Rushton, Peter. "Women, Witchcraft, and Slander in Early Modern England: Cases from the Church Courts of Durham, 1560–1675." *Northern History* 18 (1982): 116–32.
Salecl, Renata, and Slavoj Žižek, eds. *Gaze and Voice as Love Objects*. Durham NC: Duke University Press, 1996.
Salgado, Gamini. *The Elizabethan Underworld*. London: J. M. Dent, 1977.
Schafer, R. Murray. *The Soundscape: Our Sonic Environment and the Tuning of the World*. Rochester VT: Destiny Books, 1994.
Schalkyk, David. "'A Lady's "Verily" Is as Potent as a Lord's': Women, Word and Witchcraft in *The Winter's Tale*." *English Literary Renaissance* 22, no. 2 (1992): 242–72.
Schneider, Gary. "The Public, the Private, and the Shaming of the Shrew." *Studies in English Literature, 1500–1900* 42 (2002): 235–59.
Sharpe, J. A. *Crime in Early Modern England, 1550–1750*. 2nd ed. Themes in British Social History. London: Longman, 1999.
———. *Defamation and Sexual Slander in Early Modern England: The Church Courts at York*. Borthwick Papers, no. 58. York, UK: Borthwick Institute of Historical Research, 1980.
———. *Instruments of Darkness: Witchcraft in Early Modern England*. Philadelphia: University of Pennsylvania Press, 1997.
———. *Witchcraft in Seventeenth Century Yorkshire: Accusations and Counter Measures*. Borthwick Paper, no. 81. York, UK: Borthwick Institute of Historical Research, University of York, 1992.
———. "Women, Witchcraft and the Legal Process." In Kermode and Walker, *Women, Crime and the Courts*, 106–24.
Sloan, LaRue Love. "'Caparisoned like the horse': Tongue and Tail in Shakespeare's *The Taming of the Shrew*." *Early Modern Literary Studies* 10, no. 2 (2004): 1.1–24. http://extra.shu.ac.uk/emls/10-2/sloacapa.htm.
Smith, Bruce R. *The Acoustic World of Early Modern England: Attending to the O-factor*. Chicago: University of Chicago Press, 1999.

―――. *Shakespeare and Masculinity*. Oxford Shakespeare Topics. Oxford: Oxford University Press, 2000.

Smith, Kristin M. "Martial Maids and Murdering Mothers: Women, Witchcraft and Motherly Transgression in *Henry VI* and *Richard III*." *Shakespeare* 3 (2007): 143–60.

Stapleton, M. L. "'I of Old Contemptes Complayne': Margaret of Anjou and English Seneca." *Comparative Literature Studies* 43 (2006): 100–133.

Stephens, Walter. "Witches Who Steal Penises: Impotence and Illusion in *Malleus maleficarum*." *Journal of Medieval and Early Modern Studies* 28 (1998): 495–529.

Stretton, Tim. *Women Waging Law in Elizabethan England*. Cambridge Studies in Early Modern British History. Cambridge: Cambridge University Press, 1998.

Suggett, Richard. "An Analysis and Calendar of Early Modern Welsh Defamation Suits." End of grant report. London: Social Science Research Council, 1981. British Library.

Suzuki, Mihoko. *Subordinate Subjects: Gender, the Political Nation, and Literary Form in England, 1588–1688*. Women and Gender in the Early Modern World. Aldershot, UK: Ashgate, 2003.

Taylor, Diana. "Remapping Genre through Performance: From 'American' to 'Hemispheric' Studies." *PMLA* 122, no. 5 (2007): 1416–30.

Thomas, Keith. *Religion and the Decline of Magic*. New York: Charles Scribner's Sons, 1971.

Thompson, Janet A. *Wives, Widows, Witches and Bitches: Women in Seventeenth-Century Devon*. American University Studies, vol. 106. New York: Peter Lang, 1993.

Thurley, Simon. *Whitehall Palace: An Architectural History of the Royal Apartments, 1240–1698*. London: Yale University Press, 1999.

―――. *The Whitehall Palace Plan of 1670*. London: London Topographical Society, 1998.

Traub, Valerie. *Desire and Anxiety: Circulations of Sexuality in Shakespearean Drama*. Gender, Culture, Difference. London: Routledge, 1992.

Turner, Victor. "Symbolic Studies." *Annual Review of Anthropology* 4 (1975): 145–61.

Underdown, D. E. "The Taming of the Scold: The Enforcement of Patriarchal Authority in Early Modern England." In *Order and Disorder in Early Modern England*, edited by Anthony Fletcher and John Stevenson, 116–36. Cambridge: Cambridge University Press, 1985.

Walford, Edward. "Camden Town and Kentish Town." *Old and New London: Volume 5* (1878), 309–24. British History Online. http://www.british-history.ac.uk/report.aspx?compid=45239 (accessed January 7, 2013).

Walker, Garthine. *Crime, Gender, and Social Order in Early Modern England*. Cambridge Studies in Early Modern British History. Cambridge: Cambridge University Press, 2003.

Weimann, Robert. *Shakespeare and the Popular Tradition in the Theater: Studies in the Social Dimension of Dramatic Form and Function*. Baltimore: Johns Hopkins University Press, 1978.

Weiser, Brian. "Access and Petitioning during the Reign of Charles II." In *The Stuart Courts*, edited by Eveline Cruickshanks, 203–13. Phoenix Mill, UK: Sutton, 2000.

Wiener, Carol Z. "Sex Roles and Crime in Late Elizabethan Hertfordshire." *Journal of Social History* 8, no. 4 (1975): 38–60.

Willis, Deborah. *Malevolent Nurture: Witch-Hunting and Maternal Power in Early Modern England*. Ithaca NY: Cornell University Press, 1995.

Wolf, Janet S. "'Like an Old Tale Still': Paulina, 'Triple Hecate,' and the Persephone Myth in *The Winter's Tale*." In *Images of Persephone: Feminist Readings in Western Literature*, edited by Elizabeth T. Hayes, 32–44. Gainesville: University Press of Florida, 1994.

Žižek, Slavoj. "'I Hear You with My Eyes'; or, The Invisible Master." In Salecl and Žižek, *Gaze and Voice as Love Objects*, 90–128.

INDEX

Abernethy, John, 3, 8, 9, 10, 11, 12
An Account of a Great & Famous Scolding-Match, 39
Act against Conjuration, Witchcraft and Dealing with Evil and Wicked Spirits (1604), 119
Adams, Thomas, 3, 8, 9, 11, 12, 13, 14, 15, 160n27
Amends for Ladies (Field), 60
The Araignement of an Unruly Tongue (Webbe), 3, 12, 13
Armestrong, Janet, 42, 43
assize court, xvii, xxii, 41, 71, 73, 78, 79, 101, 169n34
Austin, J. L., 75, 115

ballads, xv, xxiv, 2, 46–48, 84, 169–70n38
Barnaby, Catherine, 23, 28–29, 39. *See also* scold: sociopathic
barratry, xv, 2. *See also* scolding
Bernard, Richard, 74
Blaugdone, Barbara, xv
Bloom, Gina, xxiii, 31, 160n35, 175n24
Bourdieu, Pierre, xviii, 131, 169n23
Bradshew, Mary, 41, 43
bridling, 18, 37, 51, 137. *See also* scolding: punishment for
The Broken Heart (Ford), 105–6, 109, 110; *enargeia* in, 106; music in, 111; overspeaking in, 109
Butler, Judith, 83, 169n23; and embodied speech, xviii; and gender, xiii, xxiv, 36, 37, 38, 45, 48, 158n26; and injurious speech, 75, 77, 131, 172n20; and sexuality, 69

Caliban, xiii–xiv, 122, 123, 124, 125. *See also The Tempest* (Shakespeare); witch-speak
Capp, Bernard, xxiii, 20, 21, 28, 30, 31
carting, 37, 50, 54. *See also* scolding: punishment for
Challoner, Margaret, 43, 44. *See also* scold: sociopathic
Chamberlain, John, 60
character epigram, 28, 162n33
Charles I, King, xxii, 3, 127
Charles II, King, 129, 138, 142
church courts, xvii, xxii, 17, 21, 32, 33, 35, 50, 52, 57, 78, 161n7, 165n16, 165n20; depositions of, xxi, 18, 20, 44, 45, 51; documents and records of, 19, 22, 29, 44, 55, 161n9; hearings, 40; ritual, 54. *See also* defamation; slander, sexual
Clark, Sandra, 93
Clark, Stuart, 71, 72, 99, 167n3
conjurations, xv, 79. *See also* witch; witch-speak
Cope, Jackson, 137, 175n29
coprolalia, 148–50, 153. *See also* speech, contentious; Margaret, Queen
Cromwell, Francis (bishop of Lincoln), 94
Cromwell, Oliver, xxii, 129, 130, 132, 139, 173–74n2

"cry," prophetic, 129, 132, 133, 135–36, 142, 154. *See also* prophesy: ecstatic

cucking. *See* ducking (cucking)

curse, xxii, 13, 55, 73, 74, 97, 101, 105, 147, 148, 149, 150, 153, 177n5; as cause for legal action, 2; and connection to scolding or witchcraft, xv, 3–4, 27, 18, 43, 136, 137, 172n6; and control of history, 147, 149, 150–52, 154; and control of nature, 8–9, 147, 150–52; and contaminating effect on auditors, 97, 148, 152; formal, 79–80, 115; and power, xiv, 73; and regendering, 13, 147, 152; ritual, xvii, 27, 79–80, 105, 110, 120, 147; in *The Tempest*, xiii–xiv, 123. *See also* prophesy; witch-speak

Curwen, Alice, 136

Cymbeline (Shakespeare), 105, 108–9, 110; eroticism in, 106, 109; shaming in, 108

Dalton, Janet, 41, 42, 43

defamation, xxi, 20, 26, 28, 29, 34, 37, 51, 76, 147; case verdicts, 53; and defamer as victim of, 10; and gender, 18; legal action against, 17, 19, 26, 27, 165n16; and relationship to scolding, xv, 17, 50; and sexual reputation, 22, 23, 161n14; targets of, 31, 33, 34. *See also* church courts; scolding; slander, sexual

demonology, 84, 126, 171n4, 173n34; and pastor-demologists, 72, 100, 102; theory of, xv; treatises on, 71, 104

A Detection of damnable driftes, 79, 169nn25–26, 169n28, 169n31, 170n44, 170n51, 172n8. *See also* Mother Staunton; Smithe, Elleine

A Dialogue Concerning Witches and Witchcrafts (Gifford), 98, 100

A Direction for the Government of the Tongue (Perkins), 3

docufiction, xv, xxiii, xxiv, 71–102, 106, 109, 122

Dolar, Mladen, 39, 154

ducking (cucking), xvii, 18, 22, 37, 50. *See also* scolding: punishment for

Eaton, Elizabeth, 25, 26, 39

Echo, figure of, xxiii

enargeia, xix, 77, 111, 120, 122, 123, 149, 158n19; and aural effect, xix, 136; and injurious speech, 43, 123; and poetic language, xix, 113, 137; and vividness, xix; violent, xix

encomium, paradoxical, 62, 65, 66

energeia, xix, xx, 113, 151

Epistle of James, xx, 1, 2, 10, 12, 56, 57

The Examination and Confession of Certaine Wytches at Chensforde (pamphlet), 86, 88, 94, 170n44. *See also* Mother Waterhouse

excommunication, 37, 53, 58. *See also* scolding: punishment for

Favret-Saada, Jeanne, 167n8

femininity, xiv, 15, 36, 108, 140, 144, 154; hyper-, 37, 44, 49; negative, 15, 46, 51; and political sphere, xxii, 114; and spirituality, 134, 135, 145; and violent speech, xv, 147, 159n7

Field, Nathan, 60

fighting words, 77, 105; scolding as, xxi; of witches, xxii, 73, 74, 102, 168n12; women's, xviii, xx, xxiii, 73, 85. *See also* speech, contentious; words, injurious

First Publishers of the Truth, 134, 137

Fletcher, Elizabeth, xvii

Fletcher, John, xxi, 46, 47, 68, 69

Folkerth, Wes, 133, 134

Ford, John, xxii, 104, 105, 109, 111

Frith, Mary (Moll Cutpurse), 60

gender, xx, xxi, xxii, xxiii, 2, 16, 20, 36, 44, 66, 131, 132–37, 160nn34–35, 168n11, 174n9; as compulsory practice, 48; of contentious speaker, 15, 18; fluidity, xiii, xxi, 45; identity, formation of, xiv, 38, 45, 131; as improvisational process, 37; instability of, xv, 38, 45, 63; norms, xvii, 36, 44, 48, 49; parodic assignment of, 140; politics, xiv; and regendering through speech, xiv, xxiv, 15, 152; restrictions, 38; roles, 63, 68, 131; and social hierarchy, xvii, xx, 37, 106, 143; and spiritual hierarchy, xx, 53, 135, 137, 144; and transgendering through speech, xiv, xxiv, 15, 19, 37, 44, 69, 135; and violent or contentious speech, xv, 8, 11, 13, 15, 158n11, 159n7; and vocal agency, 13–16, 36–44

gender binarism or binary, xiii, 13, 15, 36, 45, 52, 55, 58, 69, 154, 158n26; blurring, destabilizing, or undoing of, xxii, 44, 102, 153; doubts regarding, xx, 14; reinforced, 52, 53; subverting, 37, 63

gender hierarchy, xvii, xxi, 72, 106, 131

Gibson, Marion, xxiii, 93, 95, 103, 116, 172n5, 172n7; and witchcraft, 81, 86, 104, 127, 159n11, 168n12, 171n4

Gifford, George, 82, 98, 100, 101

Gilman, Anne, 139

Goodcole, Henry, 3, 4, 159n11

Gowing, Laura, xxiii, 19, 21, 28, 42, 163n65, 165n16, 165n20

Greenblatt, Stephen, xix, 158n19

Gross, Kenneth, 105, 172n6

Guide to Grand-Jury Men (Bernard), 74

Haring-Smith, Tori, 66, 67

Harrison, Johane, 81. See also *The most cruell and bloody murther committed by an Innkeepers Wife*

Higges, Jane, 43

"Homelie against Contencion and Braulynge" (Latimer), 7, 14, 56

honesty, sexual, 20, 21, 30, 33. See also reputation, sexual

Hooper, Ann, 25, 26, 39. See also Eaton, Elizabeth; Willey, Elizabeth

Hooton, Elizabeth, 136, 141–44, 176nn38–39

Howgill, Mary, 129–31, 132, 133, 139, 173n2

Ingram, Martin, 5, 23, 29, 33, 34, 35, 58

Ingram, Richard, 33

John John the Husband, Tyb His Wife, and Sir John the Priest, xxi, 46

Jones, Margaret, 43–44. See also scold: sociopathic

Katharina/Kate (fictional character), 49, 50, 51, 52, 53, 54, 58–66, 67, 68, 69, 164n1, 166n34. See also penance; scold; *The Taming of the Shrew* (Shakespeare)

Lake, Peter, 92

Lamb, Mary Ellen, 124

Lancashire, Anne, 121

Laqueur, Thomas, 15

Larner, Christina, 73, 167n3, 169n37

Leavens, Elizabeth, xvii

letters, xv, xvii, 60, 130, 139, 141, 142

Little, Megan, 62, 64

Macbeth (Shakespeare), 103, 105, 109, 110, 113; eroticism in, 107, 108; and Hecate, 112; music in, 111–12, 113, 120; overspeaking in, 106, 107, 108; witch-speak in, 106, 108, 112, 113, 119

Mack, Phyllis, 145, 174n9, 175n28

magic, xxii, 98, 99, 111, 112, 124, 125, 126; and architecture, 125, 173n37; love, 109, 119, 120, 121; Neoplatonic, 122

Mann, David, 48, 49, 55, 66, 164n1

Margaret, Queen (fictional character), xxii, 147–55. See also coprolalia; *The Second Part of King Henry VI* (Shakespeare); *Richard III* (Shakespeare); *The Third Part of King Henry VI* (Shakespeare)

Marston, John, xxii, 103, 111, 118, 119, 172n23

Index 197

Mazzio, Carla, xxiii
Metamorphoses (Ovid), xxiii, 67, 124
Middleton, Thomas, xxii, 60, 103, 104, 111, 118, 120, 121, 122, 125
ministers, traveling Quaker, xix, 129. See also First Publishers of the Truth
Miranda, xiii–xiv, 123, 125. See also *The Tempest* (Shakespeare)
Moll Cutpurse. See Frith, Mary
monarchy, 73, 101
monarchy, marvelous, xxii, 105, 125
The most cruell and bloody murther committed by an Innkeepers Wife, 169n34. See also Mother Nokes
The most strange and admirable discoverie of the three witches of Warboys, 77, 116, 169n22, 170n42; eroticism in, 92; jest in, 81. See also Mother (Alice) Samuel; Warboys witches
Mother (Alice) Samuel, 77, 81, 85, 94–95, 96. See also *The most strange and admirable discoverie of the three witches of Warboys*; Warboys witches
Mother Damnable (Mother Red Cap), xvii
Mother Nokes, 106–7
Mother Red Cap. See Mother Damnable
Mother Staunton, 78, 79, 80. See also *A Detection of damnable driftes*
Mother Waterhouse, 87, 95. See also *The Examination and Confession of Certaine Wytches at Chensforde*
Mother White-coate, 93, 96, 97, 171n66. See also *A World of Wonders* (T. I.)

narrative protocols, xxii, 20, 53; in legal discourse, 19; of witchcraft pamphlets, xxii
Newes from Scotland, 89

Overbury trial, 121–22
Ovid, xxiii, 67, 124, 125

pamphlets, xv, xxi, 3, 12, 73, 74, 76, 78, 83, 89, 90, 95, 96, 97, 98, 100, 103, 106, 116, 122, 168n17, 169n37; on demoniac possession, 77; documentary, xvii, 81, 92, 94, 168n12; news, 71; popular, 101; prefatory materials of, 86, 87, 93, 159n11; readers, 72, 102; rhetorical goals of, 86, 92, 93; witch-speak in, 4, 75, 79, 84, 85, 87, 104. See also witchcraft: pamphlets
penance, 54, 55, 57, 68; performance of, 53, 56, 61, 64, 67; public, as punishment for scolding, 37, 43, 50, 53, 54, 55, 57, 59, 62, 165n16; ritual of, xxi, 54, 55–58, 61; script of, 54, 56, 61, 64, 65, 166n23; subversive, 58–66. See also scolding: punishment for
Pepys, Samuel, 139, 140
Perkins, William, 3, 7, 12, 14
pew disputes, 35. See also scold; scolding
plays, xv, xxii, 2, 110, 116, 147, 150, 154, 170n39, 173n35; court performances of, 126; performances of magic and witchcraft in, 111; and play-within-the-play, 49, 66, 67; scolding in, 46; shrew, xxi, 45–49, 50–55, 59, 62, 63, 65, 66, 68, 164n1; witches in, 98, 120, 121, 122, 125; witch-speak in, 105, 106, 118
poetry, xix, 1, 111, 154
Powel, Joanna, xviii, 80
"The Poysonous Tongue" (Abernethy), 3, 160n26
prophesy, 13, 59, 60, 115, 132, 133, 136, 137, 138, 143, 144, 147; aural qualities of, 132, 133; as cause for legal action, 2; ecstatic, xv, 133, 137, 174n9; efficacy, 131; and Old Testament symbolism, 27, 130, 131; performative strategy of, 131, 137, 139, 140, 145, 174n9
prophetic "cry," 129, 132, 133, 135–36, 142, 154, 174n14. See also prophesy: ecstatic
prophets, xvii, xix, xxiii, 129, 132, 135, 138, 143, 144, 174n9; biblical, 28; as distinct from witch or scold, xv; in Old Testament, 27; Quaker women, xxii, 131, 136,

137, 145; violent speech of female, xx; voice of, 133
Purkiss, Diane, 73, 96, 121, 167n7, 169n37, 170n39
Puttenham, George, xix, 151

Quakers, xvii, xviii, 27, 130, 131, 132, 133, 136, 137, 138, 144, 173–74n2, 174n9, 175n24; discourse of, 134, 135; and God's speech, 140, 174–75n14; and silence, 140; and speech, 139, 140, 175n29. *See also* Society of Friends
Quaker women, xvii, 129, 130, 133, 136, 138, 139, 140, 144, 175–76n30, 176nn34–35; injurious words of, 132; ministers, xv, 132, 137, 174n9; persecution of, 175n28; prophets, xxii, 131, 136, 137, 145. *See also* Blaugdone, Barbara; Howgill, Mary; Society of Friends

A Remarkable Letter of Mary Howgill to Oliver Cromwell, 130, 132, 133, 173n2. *See also* Cromwell, Oliver; Howgill, Mary
reputation, 22, 30, 34, 49, 51, 52, 58, 61, 138; and defamation, 17, 31, 33; destruction of or damage to, 32, 36, 58, 118; restoring, 115; threats to or jeopardization of, 37, 40; of witches, 76, 98. *See also* reputation, moral; reputation, sexual
reputation, moral, 19, 40. *See also* reputation; reputation, sexual
reputation, sexual, 20, 22, 23, 30, 31, 34, 35, 36. *See also* honesty, sexual
Richard III (Shakespeare), 147, 149, 150, 153, 154
The Roaring Girl (Middleton), 60
royalty, theatrical portrayal of, xxii, 103, 105, 127

Samuel, Alice, 92, 94, 96. *See also* Mother (Alice) Samuel; Warboys witches
Schaeffer, Pierre, 9

Schafer, R. Murray, 38, 39, 142, 158n20
scold, xvii, xxiii, 11, 14, 18, 19, 21, 24, 28, 29, 32, 35, 40–41, 43, 47, 49, 50–52, 58, 84, 104, 147; acoustic dominance of, 38–39; and enhanced livability, 19, 38; equated with witches, xv, 4, 136, 137; gender of, 13, 18, 36, 161n6; as hyperwomen, 37; identity of, 46, 48; legal connotations of the term, 5; and noise, 30, 47; as patrolling the status quo, 35; and penance, 61, 62, 65, 66, 69; rhetorical goals of, 24; role of, 18, 31; sociopathic, 43–44; stage representations of, xxi, 44, 46, 49, 54; stereotype of, 49; use of hyperbole by, 25, 26. *See also* scolding; shrew
scolding, xix, 5, 13, 20, 24, 27, 36, 46, 50, 57, 78; aural qualities of, 29, 68; as cause for legal action, 2, 33; and church courts, 17–44; connection to witchcraft, xv, 4, 77, 137; and defamation, 17, 18, 23, 50, 53; and economic consequences, 23, 32, 34–35, 42, 57; effects of, 31, 34, 37; equated with whoredom, 20, 21, 22, 25, 36; and gendering, 3, 13, 18, 19, 36–37, 38, 49; punishment for, xvii, 18, 37, 43, 50, 157n5; sexualized vocabulary of, 22; and social hierarchy, xx, 41, 131; social role of, 18, 40; and spiritual trauma, 32; stylistic features of, 26; targets of, 24, 32, 40; and vocal authority, xxi, 20; wife, 47, 48, 68; witnesses to, xxi, 29, 30, 41. *See also* bridling; carting; ducking (cucking); excommunication; speech, contentious; speech acts: malicious
Scot, Reginald, 4, 82, 83
The Second Part of King Henry VI (Shakespeare), 59, 148, 150, 152
sermons, xv, 2–3, 5, 8, 16, 17, 18, 29, 31, 32, 53; as part of penance ritual, 55, 58, 63, 66, 68, 166n23; and Quakers, 133, 134; and scolding, 32, 37; on the tongue, xx, 2, 3, 9, 15, 45, 153

Index 199

Shakespeare, William, xiii, xxi, 46, 50, 51, 55, 58, 62, 63, 65, 105, 153, 157n1, 164n1, 170n39, 173n34, 176n35, 177n7; critics, 48; and demonic rhetoric, 103; first tetralogy of, xxii, 147; and injurious performatives, 104; and penance, 54, 59; and shrews, 5, 49, 52, 53, 64, 66, 67, 68, 69; and witchcraft, 111, 116, 122; and witch-speak, xxii, 118. *See also individual plays*

shaming, 51, 52, 53, 64, 99, 106, 108; integrated in witch-speak, 114; as public declaration of scolds, 51, 52

Sharpe, J. A., 17, 74

Shawe, Charles, 56, 57

shrew, xix, 5, 45, 46, 47, 67, 68; ballads, 46–48; clues for the performance of the character of, 55, 69; and gender, xxi, 165n8; management, 49–55; plays, 46, 66, 164n1; shaming, 52, 53; and shrew tamers, xxi, 45, 53; taming, xxi, 46, 48, 52, 53, 62, 64, 65, 66, 68, 69; theater stereotype of, xxi, 45, 48, 49

silence, 31, 42, 47, 117, 132, 133, 135, 140, 143, 151, 176n35

slander, sexual, 21, 22, 27, 33. *See also* church courts; defamation

Smith, Bruce, 132, 141, 176–77n40

Smithe, Elleine, 78, 80. See also *A Detection of damnable driftes*

Society of Friends, xix, xxii, 129. *See also* Quakers; Quaker women

soundmark, xx, 16, 39, 40, 78

soundscape, 16, 38, 132, 141, 142, 143, 151, 154, 155, 158n20; imagined, xxiv; qualities of, 9; and violent speech, xxii, xiv, 153

speech, xiv, xv, xviii, xix; embodiment of, xviii, xx, 19, 30, 131, 142, 174n9; and individual agency, xv, xxiii, 10, 14, 36–44, 83, 150, 160n35; regendering, xxiv, 13, 15; and regulation of body humors, 7, 8, 14, 15, 16, 29, 45; as sound object, xx, 9

speech, contentious, xx, xxiii, 2–5, 11, 13, 15, 37, 50, 52, 53, 62, 161n7; aural effect of, 8, 9; and authority, xxi, 20, 31, 36–44, 53; and effect on marriage, 32, 33–34; and gender, 13, 15, 160n35; and humor, 15, 16, 45; and pragmatics, 9, 20, 36; and semantics, xxi, 5, 7, 9, 20–22, 29, 30, 50, 72, 136, 139, 151; and stylistic strategies, xxi, 15, 20, 22–29, 71. *See also* coprolalia; scolding

speech acts, xvii, xviii, 3, 16, 76, 93, 138, 169n23, 174n9; animative, xx, 28; effects of, 9–13, 18, 30–36; malicious, 20, 87; performative, xx, 44, 58, 131

speech-speaker ties, xxiii

Stirredge, Elizabeth, xviii, 134, 135, 138, 139

Sycorax, xiv, 122, 123, 124, 125, 173n31. See also *The Tempest* (Shakespeare); witch

The Taming of a Shrew, 46, 49, 68, 69, 164n4

The Taming of the Shrew (Shakespeare), xxi, 46, 49, 50, 55, 59, 66; adaptations of, 164n4; contemporary productions of, 66–67, 166n34

"Taming of the Tongue" (Adams), 3, 160n21, 160n27

Tarlton, Richard, 99

Taylor, Diana, xx, 78

The Tempest (Shakespeare), xiii–xiv, 111, 118, 125, 126–27, 157n1, 173n39; *enargeia* in, 122, 123, 124; injurious speech in, xiii, 123, 124; and Medea, 124–25; Neoplatonic magic in, 122; overspeaking in, 123; performed at the Blackfriars Theater, 122, 126; performed at Whitehall Palace, 125

theater, xviii, xxi, xxiii, 126, 164n1, 164n4, 173n39; audiences, xxii; illusionism, 67; monarchs, 118; and stereotypes, 48, 49; and theater-goers, 45, 124; and witch-speak, 103, 104, 127, 129; women's speech in, xx

The Third Part of King Henry VI (Shakespeare), 147, 152, 153

Thomas, Keith, 79
Throckmorton, Robert, 77, 96; family, 85, 94, 96, 116. *See also* Warboys witches
Tom Tyler and His Wife, 46, 47
tongue, xvii, 1, 5, 8, 12, 13, 14, 37, 44, 50, 51, 53, 57, 76, 114, 160n34; control of, 53; cutting the, as "treatment" of scold, 48; emblem of unruly, 6; iconography, xx, 16; injurious impact of, 9–11, 12; and penance, 54, 60; sins of, 1–2, 3, 4, 18; as woman's weapon, 15. *See also* sermons: on the tongue; tongue, fiery
tongue, fiery, 3, 4, 29, 31, 37, 43, 44, 50, 54, 56, 153; feminine, 53, 68; and gender, 2, 14, 16; impact of, xx, 9, 32; as soundmark, 16; taming of, 68. *See also* sermons: on the tongue; tongue
Turner, Victor, xviii
Tuttie, Elizabeth, 55–58, 62

Underdown, David, 17

violence, xv, xxiii, 30, 40, 44, 48, 52, 73, 74, 104, 108, 109, 116, 153; domestic, 42; and *enargeia*, xix, 113; political, 113; sexual, 73; speech, xiv, xx, 18, 148, 155; and voice, xxiii, xxiv, 44. *See also* violence, verbal or rhetorical
violence, verbal or rhetorical, xxi, 37, 44, 52, 58, 80, 113, 147, 172n7; feminine, xvii, 49; in place of physical, xiv, 123. *See also* violence
voice, xiv, xxiii, xxiv, 7–9, 20, 21, 41, 44, 77, 84, 109, 137, 142, 147, 149, 150, 151, 175n14; and accompaniment, 29–30, 38; and agency, xxiii, 13–16, 36–44, 74, 160n35; and authority, xxi, 20, 53; of biblical prophet, 27, 28; echoic, xxiii; of the Law, xxi, xxiii, 39, 40, 43, 44, 148; prophetic, 133, 138; of the shofar, 153–55; and speaking subject, xxiii; unreliability of, 53

Walker, Garthine, xxiii
Warboys witches, 92, 94, 96, 116, 169n38
Webbe, George, 3, 10, 12, 13, 14
Weimann, Robert, 149
White, Dorothy, 133
Whitehall Palace, xxii, 129, 130, 132, 138, 142, 144, 145, 176n37; and Banqueting House, 125; and performances of witchcraft, 103; and prophesies, 140; soundscape of, 141, 143, 176–77n40
Willey, Elizabeth, 25, 26, 39. *See also* Eaton, Elizabeth; Hooper, Ann
Willis, Deborah, 85, 101, 171n77, 172n7
Wilson, Susanna, 76
The Winter's Tale (Shakespeare), 113–15, 116–17, 118; eroticism in, 114; Persephone myth in, 117; shaming in, 114
witch, 3, 22, 25, 28, 71, 72, 75, 77–82, 88–90, *91*, 93, 97, 98, 101, 107, 127, 170n44, 171n77; and agency, 74, 82; as authority figure, 72, 102; in ballad, 84; as clear and present danger, xxii, 101; discovery, 158n10; and *enargeia*, xix, 77; and familiars, 88, 95, 96; historical, xxii, xxiii, 84, 104, 106; and humor, 98, 168n12; hunts, 73, 167n3, 167nn6–7; as outsider, 86, 100, 102; and power, 73, 74, 83, 84, 86, 100; as product of pamphlet, 83, 84, 85, 87, 94, 95; Prospero as, xiv; and resistance to violence, 74; and scold, xv, xvii, 4, 136, 137; and shame or shaming, 99; subject position of, 167n8; testimony of, 94; in theater, xxiii, 103, 104, 105; and wit, 98, 99; words as weapon of, 74. *See also* scold; scolding; Warboys witches; witchcraft; witch-speak
The Witch (Middleton), 111, 118, 120, 122, 125; and Hecate, 120, 121, 125; love magic in, 121
witchcraft, xv, 13, 21, 33, 74, 75, 81–83, 94, 96, 98, 99, 100, 115, 116, 168n18, 169n37, 170n44; in assize court records, xxii, 71, 73, 78, 79, 101; ballads, 169–70n38;

Index 201

witchcraft (*cont.*)
and connection to humor, 81, 97; and connection to scolding, xv, 4; docufiction, 109; as gendered crime, 71, 74, 137, 175n28; as heresy, 77, 114; legal narratives of, 127; and morbid sexuality, 89; pamphlets, xxi, 74, 79, 81, 83–87, 89, 92–94, 102–4, 106, 159n11, 168n12, 171n1; persecution, 73, 82, 167n2; shaping public knowledge of, 71, 74, 76; in the theater, 103, 105, 111, 118, 126. *See also* scolding; speech, contentious; witch-speak

The Witch of Edmonton, 98

witch-speak, xv, xxi–xxii, 3, 4, 27, 71, 79, 80; aestheticized, xxii, 104; allure of, xxii, 93–101, 127; aristocratic, xxii, 104, 127, 129; collective subject of, 83, 172n20; documentary, 79, 81, 84, 87, 92, 168n12, 171n1; and *enargeia*, 76, 77, 82, 104; and eroticism, 90, 92, 104, 105, 106, 114; formulaic reports of, 74, 85, 87; and jest, 81, 83, 96, 98, 99; makings of, 74–83; mysteriousness of, 72, 75, 76; as overspeaking, 72, 106; performative force of, 72, 82, 104; and political rhetoric, 105–13; and power, 72, 75, 77, 78, 82, 83, 84, 100, 102, 103, 105, 109, 114, 116, 117; resistant, 74, 76, 99, 102, 113; soundmark of, 78; speaking subject of, 82, 83; and theater music, 106, 111, 112, 120; theatrical, 103–5, 105–13, 113–17, 118–27. *See also* witchcraft

Wits Fittes and Fancies (Copley), 99

Wolf, Janet S., 117

The Woman's Prize or the Tamer Tamed (Fletcher), xxi, 46

The Wonder of Women or the Tragedy of Sophonisba (Marston), 111, 118; artistic witchcraft in, 111; *enargeia* in, 120; and Erictho, 103, 111, 119, 120; love magic in, 119, 120; music in, 111, 120; necrophilia in, 111, 119

words, injurious, xv, 132, 140

A World of Wonders (T. I.), 93. *See also* Mother White-coate

Žižek, Slavoj, 28–29, 130

In the Early Modern Cultural Studies series:

At the First Table: Food and Social Identity in Early Modern Spain
By Jodi Campbell

Separation Scenes: Domestic Drama in Early Modern England
By Ann. C. Christensen

Portrait of an Island: The Architecture and Material Culture of Gorée Sénégal, 1758-1837
By Mark Hinchman

Words Like Daggers: Violent Female Speech in Early Modern England
By Kirilka Stavreva

My First Booke of My Life
By Alice Thornton
Edited and with an introduction by Raymond A. Anselment

The Other Exchange: Women, Servants, and the Urban Underclass in Early Modern English Literature
By Denys Van Renen

To order or obtain more information on these or other University of Nebraska Press titles, visit nebraskapress.unl.edu.

www.ingramcontent.com/pod-product-compliance
Lightning Source LLC
Chambersburg PA
CBHW022058160426
43198CB00008B/276